Endorsements

"I endorse and recommend a great book: *Korean Dream: A Vision for a Unified Korea*, written by Dr. Hyun Jin P. Moon, Founder and Chairman of Global Peace Foundation. As Dr. Moon wrote in his book: 'After my father met with Kim Il-sung a door into North Korea was opened. But at this time there was no clear national vision or shared purpose and strategy for developing that opening.' The good news is that right now in his book, Dr. Moon has written this vision and strategy for a United Korea. A world peace leader is giving us a peace plan for Northeast Asia, providing more than a political or economic integration and based on universal principles and moral values."

Óscar Álvarez Araya, PhD, Professor,
National University of Costa Rica

"Dr. Hyun Jin Moon is a person of peace, who values that we are one family under God. This book is an inspiration, this is well worth reading, offering hope through his peace principles, based on his vision and powerful dream of a unified Korea, with a reminder to us of the value and importance of pursuing the historic Korean philosophy of Hongik Ingan, or 'living and working for the benefit of all humankind.' I appreciate his dedication and leadership to build a global movement for peace so we can all live in harmony, as we are one family under God."

H.E. Vinicio Marco Cerezo, Former President,
Republic of Guatemala, Founder and President,
Esquipulas Foundation for Central American Integration

"Dr. Hyun Jin Moon is a credible moral force for peace, security, and reconciliation in Northeast Asia and the world. In this book, he shares his vision to bring about re-unification in the Korean Peninsula and actually, he mobilizes units of civil society in Track II diplomacy to reduce conflict, strengthen families and communities, and in small but appreciable ways, contribute to mankind's economic and social development."

Jose De Venecia, Former five-time Speaker, Philippine House of Representatives; Founding Chairman of the International Conference of Asian Political Parties. Founder-President, Centrist Asia Pacific Democrats International

"Today, one of the hotspots in the world is the unending unrest between North and South Korea. This book approaches the resolution of the Korean conflict and the challenges they face for the unification of these two countries and one people. It also addresses global crises like Iran's nuclear bomb capabilities that I believe are being tested and upgraded in North Korea. Therefore, I encourage readers to explore *Korean Dream* by Dr. Moon. It gives a cogent path to peace for the Koreas and the world."

Harold E. Doley, Jr., Founder, Doley Securities Group, New York. Former U.S. Ambassador, Cote d' Ivoire. Former Board Member, United Nations Commission on Disarmament Education, Conflict Resolution and Peace

"I would like to congratulate Hyun Jin Moon on the publication of *Korean Dream*. From my experience, I can testify that Dr. Moon's emphasis on unification based on a common dream that is good for all, and sound universal and transcendent principles that emphasize both rights and responsibilities, will be required if the unification of Korea, or any state divided by ethnicity, religion, ideology, or political party, is to be realized."

Sir James R. Mancham, Founding President, Republic of Seychelles

"As a personal friend of Dr. Hyun Jin P. Moon, I can tell you that he has a sincere reverence and love for humankind. In the depth of his soul is a desire to create peace throughout the world. Korea is at the top of his list. His vision for a unified Korea is contagious. His insights and plans need to be implemented. The time is ripe for Korea to experience peace. Success is possible. Believe in the dream. Read the book."

Dr. Robert A. Schuller, Evangelist and Author

"This book takes a wonderful outside-the-box approach to Korean unification. It highlights the author's insights based on thorough knowledge and details of Korean affairs and his vision of a new nation that can unite Korean people all over the world. His insights connect present political challenges and Korean identity to his vision of practical benefits—security and economic growth—that unification could bring. This book is worthy of being a good college textbook."

Dr. Jin Shin, Professor, Department of Political Science and Diplomacy; President, National Strategy Institute, Chungnam National University; and President, Institute for Peace Affairs

Excerpts from book reviews of the Korean edition

"*Korean Dream* is a book that works on unification in a bigger context. Hyun Jin Moon points out the need for the 'start of serious discussions concerning the principles and values that will be the founding principle of the new nation to be born.' In other words, discussion of government, political, and economic systems are secondary matters .... Commenting on the need for a discussion about the appearance of our future nation after unification prior to the discussing the process of unification is indeed an excellent idea."

Geo-il Bok, Novelist

"*Korean Dream* is the future of a united Korea. It will bring peace and prosperity to the Korean peninsula while benefiting the Northeast region and the world as a unified nation. By giving a detailed analysis with regards to it and proposing specific solutions to actualize them, the book has become a precious book that explicitly showed us our goal. Without unification, world peace is unattainable .... By clearly narrating that achieving unification is the first objective in fulfilling the *Korean Dream*, the book has shown us the task of our generation."

Soon Kyung Hong, Chairperson of Committee for Democratization of North Korea; Member of Presidential Committee for National Cohesion

"[Hyun Jin Moon] understands that the unification of the Korean peninsula with Hongik Ingan as its ideology is not only desired by the nation but also linked with the future of the world …. [The] ideology of Hongik Ingan and the Korean peninsula on which it would be manifest would be the ultimate factor in stabilizing the Northeast Asia region and a factor in the actualization of world peace …. Individuals, authorities of unification policies in the government, and researchers of unification challenges in academic circles must read *Korean Dream*."

Kyu-suk Cho, Former Head of the Editorial Department, *Segye Times*. Editorial Writer of the Korea Journalists Club

"*Korean Dream* … speaks about the unification of a Korean nation in the larger context of world history and in the history of civilizations …. By practicing Hongik Ingan, the spiritual symbol and the calling of our nation, we will be able to unite, and thus, the world can become one family. 'Benefiting All Mankind' is the ideal of our nation and I believe that it's [Dr. Moon's] dream to achieve a 'large global family that sings of permanent peace.' And such is the conclusion of *Korean Dream*: A dream dreamed by everyone becomes reality. *Korean Dream* is an invitation to such a dream."

Jin Gon Lee, Professor, Department of Political Science and Diplomacy, KyungHee University

"My dream, your dream, our dream; all become one in *Korean Dream*."

Jiha Kim, Poet

Korean Dream

KOREAN DREAM
A VISION FOR A UNIFIED KOREA

CENTENNIAL EDITION

HYUN JIN PRESTON MOON

NEW YORK

LONDON • NASHVILLE • MELBOURNE • VANCOUVER

KOREAN DREAM

A Vision for a Unified Korea

Published in New York, New York, by Morgan James Publishing. Morgan James is a trademark of Morgan James, LLC. www.MorganJamesPublishing.com

ISBN 9781642799804 case laminate
ISBN 9781642799811 paperback
ISBN 9781642799828 eBook
Library of Congress Control Number: 2020900220

Interior Design by:
Chris Treccani
www.3dogcreative.net

Morgan James is a proud partner of Habitat for Humanity Peninsula and Greater Williamsburg. Partners in building since 2006.

Get involved today! Visit
MorganJamesPublishing.com/giving-back

AWARDS

2014 Book of the Year, Republic of Korea Award for Publication, Culture and the Arts by the Readers News of the Seoul Media Group

U.S. Defense Intelligence Agency, 2018 Director's Reading List

CONTENTS

FOREWORD

Throughout my professional life I have had a deep interest in Korea and a heartfelt connection with its people. I believe that today Korea stands at an important transition point. The peninsula remains divided.

That division remains the primary obstacle to the future economic prosperity of the region as well as a threat to global security. More than ever, scholars and policy experts, faced with the failure of past efforts to improve the situation, see Korean unification as the necessary way forward, even though it will be challenging to achieve.

The question of unification and how it can be achieved is in the air. This makes Dr. Moon's book, *Korean Dream*, most timely. More importantly, his perspectives make a unique contribution to the discussion on Korean unification. Based on Korean history, culture, and social relations, the scope of the book is remarkably wide-ranging as it discusses the likely geopolitical and economic consequences of unification.

However, the most noteworthy and original aspects of *Korean Dream* are its emphasis on the importance of an overarching vision for a united Korea and the principles that should guide that vision; and the need for a vigorous civil society to play a central role in the pursuit of unification.

As an American with a profound respect for the American Founding and its expression in our Declaration of Independence, I find Dr. Moon's emphasis on the importance of fundamental principles for a future unified Korea both significant and inspiring. He views such a Korea from a perspective that steps outside of the current artificial ideological and political division that has existed since World War II.

Rather, he stresses the shared values of history, culture, and ethnicity that have bound the Korean people together for thousands of years. Most important, he highlights certain foundational principles that guided Korean culture and history. He emphasizes the principle of Hongik Ingan, which means "to live for the greater benefit of humanity," a principle that is associated with the very origins of the Korean nation.

This principle has served as an aspirational ideal and a moral touchstone throughout the course of Korean history. *Korean Dream* highlights the need to move the pursuit of unification outside the exclusive sphere of government to engage the support of the Korean people as a whole. He examines in the first instance the people of South Korea, followed by Koreans in the diaspora, particularly in the United States, as well as in Japan and China.

Civil society organizations are the instruments that are central for creating this engagement. As an admirer of the work of Alexis de Tocqueville, I have long been an advocate of the importance of the private voluntary associations that form civil society and that are the expressions of a healthy, vibrant democracy with widespread citizen involvement.

The mobilization of citizen groups around common principles, particularly with the common goal of unification, will have huge significance for the future of Koreans in both parts of the Korean peninsula.

The author describes the beginning of such a process through the establishment of Action for Korea United, a coalition of organizations committed to developing a peaceful, prosperous, and united future for the Korean people. I have twice attended large meetings of this coalition and can attest to the energy and hope generated there as a unifying set of principles that can be translated into practical initiatives. This is truly an example of civil society at its best.

The possibilities for major change on the Korean peninsula are real. And they may become more likely as North Korea can no longer count on the support of China and Russia, its former supporters and allies. We should not underestimate the practical challenges both in moving toward unification and dealing with possible post-unification political scenarios. Yet, it is important not to lose sight of the forest for the trees.

Finally, it is my conviction that the bedrock of a successful civil society is belief in a divine being and that this belief forms the basis for principled human interaction. This is also the view expressed in Dr. Moon's *Korean Dream* as it looks to the foundations for peace in the future, not just on the Korean peninsula but in the wider world as well.

As moments of historic transition call for a broader perspective that necessitates principles as well as practicalities, *Korean Dream* offers a timely view on what should be the guiding principles on the historic movement toward Korean unification.

Edwin J. Feulner, PhD
Founder, The Heritage Foundation

Dr. Edwin J. Feulner is a Founding Trustee, Chairman of the Asian Studies Center, and Chung Ju-yung Fellow at the Heritage Foundation, one of the nation's leading research and public policy institutions located in Washington, D.C.

Dr. Feulner served as Heritage's president from 1977 to 2013 and again in 2017. He has provided essential leadership and policy guidance on the principles of free enterprise, limited government, individual freedom, and civil society engagement to leaders in the U.S. and around the world. He has also led numerous commissions and distinguished boards and served as Chairman of the U.S. Advisory Commission on Public Diplomacy.

Dr. Feulner has a long record of engagement with East Asian affairs, with special expertise on Korean issues. He was awarded the Gwanghwa Medal, Order of Diplomatic Service by the President and National Assembly of Korea, and the Presidential Citizen Award, the second-highest civilian award in the United States, conferred by President Ronald Reagan.

He is the author of several books and a contributor to numerous journals and magazines, and a frequent speaker on public policy issues. In expert forums in the United States and abroad, Dr. Feulner has spoken on issues relating to Korean reunification, notably the "Role of Civil Society and Global Cooperation in Furthering a Unified Korea" in Seoul, Korea and "The Power of Freedom in Addressing the Divided Human Family: Empowering the Voice of North Korean Defectors" at a GPF forum at the U.S.-Korea Institute at the Johns Hopkins School of Advanced International Studies in Washington.

FOREWORDS FROM THE
KOREAN EDITION OF *KOREAN DREAM*

Since President Geun-hye Park described Korean unification as an economic "jackpot" [in her 2014 Dresden Declaration], interest in unification has rapidly increased. South Korean attitudes toward unification have evolved from apathy and wariness to seeing unification as an opportunity and a blessing. In addition, the mindset of experts from neighboring countries has greatly changed. Observers who viewed South Koreans as passive toward unification now are finding a firmer conviction in support of unification among citizens. This is a highly desirable change.

Yet, will these changing attitudes bring about unification or will the Korean peninsula remain permanently divided? The time for our nation to make a major decision has come. The systemic failure of North Korea is increasingly evident as the national power of China rises. Therefore, if we South Koreans take a passive position with regards to unification, there will be a high risk of Sinicization of North Korea—where North Korea could quickly become a vassal state of the Chinese.

At this point, our nation's willingness and readiness for unification are the most important elements. So, what type of unification would our society want? How will this be achieved? What are the benefits of such unification? There are numerous political and economic considerations with regard to unification. However, before engaging in such discussions, we must ask, why should our nation aspire to unification? What is the purpose, the value, and the cause for unification? There is little discussion on the philosophy and idealism of unification in our society. In a sense, we have the how but lack the why in the unification discussion. Despite numerous proposals of methods for unification, the vision for unification is absent.

In this context, *Korean Dream* by Dr. Hyun Jin Moon addresses the philosophy, idealism, and vision of unification.

That is why this book is so significant. The result of deep contemplation and reflection, the book advances a vision for unification based on the ideal of Hongik Ingan (living for the benefit of all humankind), the founding philosophy of Korea, which embraces a "grand magnanimity" toward other religions and nations along with a universal outlook which respects rationalism and reason. These are the spiritual assets and pride of our nation.

We need to achieve unification of the Korean peninsula rooted in this proud philosophy with a great sense of duty and vision; furthermore, we must work to actualize this ideal not only in East Asia but internationally. This is the author's assertion. I agree with it.

Hongik Ingan is not only an ideal of the past but an ideal of a future yet to come. Hongik Ingan can embrace national left wing and right wing ideas, advanced and developing countries, the spirit of East and the civilization of the West. When the unification of our nation is based upon this spirit, this idealism, the unification of the Korean peninsula will not just end as a blessing for the Korean peninsula, but a blessing for East Asia and all nations.

From a political and economic point of view, the unification of the Korean peninsula will certainly be a turning point for peace and prosperity in East Asia. However, if it fails, conflicts between South and North Korea will intensify, with growing confrontation and hostility between US-Japan and China-Russia—in other words, a new Cold War in the Far East. Therefore, numerous experts view peace and prosperity in East Asia as impossible without the unification of the Korean peninsula. It is only through unification that we will see the complementary economies of the North and South begin to emerge and skyrocket, leading to an era of rapid growth for the three provinces of Dongbei of China, the Maritime Province, and the far eastern Siberian region of Russia. Then, as a result of such growth, an East Asian Economic Community, as well as East Asian security agreements, could be formed, promising greater peace and prosperity for East Asia.

In order to begin the era of the East Asian Community, simple congruence of economic and security understanding is not enough. There must be a universal yet advanced idealism and philosophy that is sympathized with, embraced, and supported by all East Asians. I completely concur with the author that the Hongik Ingan philosophy can offer ideals not only for the unification of the Korean peninsula but also for the entire East Asian community, and even of humankind in the twenty-first century.

Until now, we have exerted our efforts to advance the foundations for a modern Korea after liberation through industrialization and democratization, busying ourselves to learn Western ideas while forgetting our own outstanding traditions, thoughts, cultures, and values. Korea today aims to become a leading nation in the world. Beyond simply imitating the West, our nation is at the stage of advancement where we need to creatively blend our own ideals with the civilization of the West. In such a view, I believe the direction of the Korean Dream emphasized by this book is certainly correct.

Moreover, this book stresses the importance of the extended family model as a way for our nation to overcome the catastrophe of selfish individualism as practiced by the West. There is no doubt that the book looks back to past traditions, but I consider that this offers thoughtful insights [about the present and future]. Especially as Korea is becoming an aging society in a major way, such a model should be given serious consideration as a path for social policy. The problem lies in how to concretize and institutionalize the extended family model under the circumstances of the twenty-first century. The biggest challenge will be to establish an economic, social, spiritual, and technological environment where the extended family model can prosper.

The insights in this book that distinguish between the religious leader and spiritual leader are also valuable. In our history, we have an idea of "Sunbi" (a man of virtue); Sunbi, which is a purely Korean word, signifies a political, spiritual, and ethical leader of Korean people. Dangun is the very first Sunbi. However, we have been living in a society where the Sunbi culture is fading. I believe that the concept of a spiritual leader, not simply a leader of a specific religion but one who transcends religion, is similar to the concept of Sunbi. I have often stressed the importance of "Sunbi Democracy" and "Sunbi Capitalism" which greatly values the spirit of Sunbi, and it was fascinating to come across this book which has a very similar claim emphasizing the spiritual leader.

But one aspect distresses me: the issue of who will drive the unification movement rooted in Hongik Ingan idealism. There is a lot of emphasis on the importance of civil society and NGOs in this book, and that is important. However, the awakening of civil society, intellectuals, and religious groups is not enough to start a new history. Political leadership is a decisive factor. It is through political leadership under the flag of a unification movement rooted in Hongik Ingan idealism that history will rewrite itself. However, our political reality cannot possibly actualize this. Who can and will actualize such a unification?

Currently, there is severe confusion in the administration of state affairs, which has raised much concern among citizens. What is the cause of this confusion within the government? Isn't it because we have lost a national vision, the dreams of our citizens, and our national aspirations? These are the reasons why the voices proposing unification as a "jackpot" leading to a new vision for the country, and the voices emphasizing the importance of a reconstruction of the country to actualize such a vision, are getting louder.

Yet, simple arguments and strategies concerning unification are not the main points. What is truly important is the philosophy and ideal for reconstructing the nation in the era of unification. This is the most important problem that we all need to solve.

Addressing this problem, and proposing answers, is an important focus of this book. With its publication, I sincerely hope that more discussion on a unification philosophy and vision within our nation, along with research and discussion about the nation's ideals and the national spirit, will be invigorated. Until now, we have busied ourselves receiving and adopting Western ideas for industrialization and democratization. Now, I hope we will start a new chapter with new ideas for the entire world. I earnestly hope our nation will inaugurate an era of Korea as the "Lamp of the East," enlightening the current world in chaos. I would like to salute the publication of this book and suggest to those who love our nation, our country, and those who wish for the peace and prosperity of humankind to read it.

Dr. Se-il Park
Professor Emeritus, Seoul National University
Standing Advisor, Hansun Foundation
(1948-2017)

Often referred to as the father of Korean conservatism, the late Dr. Se-Il Park was a staunch advocate of peaceful reunification. Dr. Park supported the launching and growth of Action for Korea United (AKU), a grassroots movement of civil society organizations working toward a unified Korea based on the strategic framework outlined in this book.

Dr. Park was a member of the Presidential Committee for Unification Preparation for the Republic of Korea. He was founder and president of the Hansun Foundation, a bi-partisan, nonprofit, private think tank in Korea that researches and promotes public policies for Korea's advancement and the peaceful integration of the Korean peninsula based on the foundational principles and values of democracy, human rights, the free market economy, and rule of law.

Dr. Park identified globalization as a significant challenge to Korea and recommended what he coined as "segyehwe" policies and reforms which included limited state intervention in financial markets but state expansion in the areas of education and welfare. In 1995 he was appointed as President Kim Young Sam's Senior Secretary for Policy Development and Social Welfare, and received a special award from the President, the Order of Service Merit with Yellow Stripes, in 1997.

Dr. Park was a law professor at the Graduate School of International Studies at Seoul National University for over twenty years and served as a visiting scholar to Stanford University, Columbia Law School, Brookings Institution, and the Heritage Foundation. His research interests included labor and industrial relations, economic development, education reform, and strategies for globalization with publications such as Unification Strategy for Advanced Korea *(2013),* Korea's Creative Globalization Strategy *(2010),* Korea's Grand National Strategy *(2009),* Communitarian Liberalism *(co-authored) (2008),* Korea's Strategy for National Advancement *(2006), and* Law and Economics *(2000).*

D r. Hyun Jin Moon, the author of *Korean Dream*, is an ardent activist for Korean unification. He is also a historian, thinker, activist for world peace, spiritual leader, as well as a dynamic speaker. I am honored to write an endorsement for his book and its comprehensive and forward-looking vision for the future. I hope my message will help readers in understanding this book.

I first became aware of Dr. Moon at an international conference on the unification of the Korean peninsula hosted by the Global Peace Foundation (GPF). At this event, I was impressed by his keynote speech and began to take an interest in the global peace theory he espoused. I was deeply moved and impressed by Dr. Moon's vision for the peaceful unification of North and South Korea.

Since then, I've ardently supported the mission of the Global Peace Foundation. At that time, he was advocating the "Korean Dream" introduced in this book. He impressed all the participants in the conference with his passion and dynamism, as well as his historical perspective of the vision for the Korean peninsula.

As an international relations scholar and former President of Korea Institute for National Unification, the think tank of the Korean government, I've spent my entire life researching ways to solve the problems of the Korean peninsula. I've grieved when the relationship between the two Koreas deteriorated and I felt sorrow when discussions about unification between the conservative and progressive parties became yet another cause of division within our nation.

So how will we solve the problems of the Korean peninsula and achieve a peaceful unification in the future? Dr. Moon proposes the "Korean Dream" as advocated in this book. He emphasizes the need to first work towards a futuristic vision of what a united Korea will be as a country and then build a nationwide consensus on such a vision.

As a scholar who has been researching solutions to realize the unification of the Korean peninsula, the futuristic vision and proposal for unification laid out by the author has impressed me with its originality and innovative ideas. The vision that Dr. Moon laid out has been eye-opening.

The author was not satisfied with merely uniting North and South Korea into one Korea. Rather, he argues that a new country reborn through unification must become the advanced country dreamed of by our ancestors for more than five thousand years. He points out that we have been overlooking a most important historical fact and asks us to remember our history as the Korean nation.

Since the liberation from Japan to the Korean War and through the years of ideological and political rivalry, we, the Han nation, have forgotten the existence of an ideology and the objective yearned for during millennia. We've neglected the fact that we were one, not just in blood relations but also in terms of ideals and objectives; and yet we still talk of unification.

Dr. Moon reminds us that the true objective of unification is to recall our original identity. He emphasizes that it is undesirable to plan on procedures with the objective of unification without building such an agreement. The unification of the Korean peninsula is not just about removing a border and then composing a unified government. Rather, the most important step to achieve unification is for our nation to become one in identity.

Currently there is conflict in South Korea, with Conservatives and Progressives constantly unable to reach consensus. Under such circumstances, if the unification of the peninsula were to occur, how would we as a nation be united and how would harmony and prosperity be achieved? It is for these important reasons that the author emphasizes the need to discover a common identity the entire nation can resonate with and that this understanding must then be the foundation for unification.

Our nation was founded on the principle of Hongik Ingan. This ideology has been with us throughout history and was the foundation for establishing an ideal political system and national community. It has been present in the very lives of our people and has led to the formation of a unique nationalism.

The author boldly proclaims that the country yearned for by our people is a nation that considers the value and dignity of humanity as the most important factors—where everyone lives as one family under God. I agree with him. Furthermore, he states that founding a new nation will lead the world into peace and prosperity, resolving the conflicts between different ideas, cultures, and civilizations while blending the strengths of both Eastern and Western civilization in his "Korean Dream."

The author believes that unification is only achievable if the national dream is noble and large enough to overcome the division of North and South Korea. It is only through this great dream that we can awaken the hearts of all citizens in the Koreas to establish a new unified country. I firmly believe that this book will be the guide to such a dream.

Without a doubt the author is working to realize this dream through the international humanitarian endeavors and the activities of the Global Peace Foundation. These are the personal goals of Dr. Moon and he has been silently and dynamically exerting his efforts not just in East Asia but throughout North and South America, Africa, and Southeast Asia. I sincerely and proudly salute his emergence as a Korean world peace activist and I thank him for his efforts and dedication to global peace.

Moreover, the author encourages us to prepare for unification rather than to fret over and analyze fundamental changes in a tumultuous international system while viewing the domestic circumstance of North Korea and unification as far distant problems. He asks us to awaken to the idea that we—not a foreign power and not the government—are responsible to take charge of such a destiny. He outlines the differing yet critical roles that civil society—NGOs, religious leaders, and overseas Koreans—can play in this work and in the future of North and South Korea relations.

The author proposes moral and ethical standards that pursue both individual and group well-being through explorations of Korean and world history, modern Western philosophies, national ideology, and universal principles and values. In so doing, he proposes a global solution for identity-based conflicts between religions and civilizations that are the causes war and terrorism. He also speaks of the mission of our nation and for the world from an international perspective while speaking of the "Korean Dream." He does not fall into chauvinism, which makes this book especially valuable.

I expect that many readers will share my views on the comprehensive knowledge, keen and thoughtful analysis, and forward-looking proposals and vision laid out in this book. This book is indeed a rare masterpiece that calls for a national awakening to prepare for the unification of North and South Korea. It as a must-read for Koreans in the homeland as well as Koreans living all over the world. It is also my especial wish for our fellow countrymen, North Koreans and their leaders, to read this book.

Dr. Tae-Hwan Kwak
Former President, Korea Institute for National Unification
Professor Emeritus, Eastern Kentucky University

Dr. Tae-Hwan Kwak is Chair of the Institute for Korean Peninsula Future Strategies, Chair of Korean Peninsula Unification Council through

Neutralization, and Chair-Professor at Kyungnam University. He serves as the Executive Director of the Northeast Asian Community Studies Institute and President of Korean Unification Strategies Research Council located in Los Angeles, California USA.

He served as former President of KINU (Korea Institute for National Unification), a think tank formed by the South Korean government during the Sunshine Policy to coordinate national efforts for peaceful unification and explore appropriate policy options.

Dr. Kwak taught international relations and East Asian politics for over thirty years at Eastern Kentucky University and at Korean universities. He has developed a wealth of knowledge in Northeast Asian affairs, inter-Korean relations and Korean peace and reunification issues with over 250 published scholarly articles and thirty-one books including In Search for Peace and Unification on the Korean Peninsula *(1986)*, North Korea and Security Cooperation in Northeast Asia *(2014), and* One Korea: Visions of Korean Unification *(2017).*

AUTHOR'S PREFACE

The writing of this book and the articulation of the Korean Dream has been the culmination of several converging factors. First, it is part of my family heritage. My father devoted his life to heal the division of the two Koreas. He saw the unification of the peninsula as an essential part of building a global foundation for world peace. He suffered for his convictions in a North Korean labor camp but ultimately pioneered an opening to the North through his 1991 meeting with Kim Il-sung. Further back in time, my great grand-uncle, Moon Yoon-guk, helped to draft the 1919 Korean Declaration of Independence.

In addition to this heritage, I have always been an avid student of history with a particular interest in Korea. At Columbia University, I wrote my honors thesis on the interwar years in Korea between 1945, the end of World War II, and 1950, the beginning of the Korean War. After my studies, with a major in history from Columbia, a Master of Business Administration from Harvard, and then a Master of Religious Education from the Unification Theological Seminary, I worked closely with my father to advance his world peace initiatives and, particularly, his efforts for Korean unification. This eclectic educational background ranging from history to business and religion gave me a unique perspective on the issue of unification and the importance of vision, principles, and tangible outcomes.

To me, the way forward should not be defined by reactive policy decisions without any clarity on what unification should create. Rather, it should start with our identity as the Korean people, defined by our unique historical legacy. That identity, then, should define our destiny and, in turn, clarify the goal of unification and our people's larger role in the world.

Throughout my life, from early childhood to my current work, I have traveled widely around the world, especially to the emerging nations of the global South. I have led a global peace movement and launched numerous service, educational, and business projects in these countries. Through this global foundation, I have gained a unique perspective on international affairs, the developing world, and the role that a united Korea would be poised to play in both.

My heritage, my studies, and my life experiences and accomplishments have all combined to engender the ideas in this book. It is not a book about policy and the process of unification. It is an aspirational treatise about a vision that should precede that process and serve as a compass to guide us through it, a vision of Korean history, identity, and destiny.

This book was written originally for a Korean audience. I believe the vision that I articulate has the power to transcend the current political division and unite the Korean people. I call on Koreans to reassess their current values and priorities and to live up to the highest ideals embodied in their history, particularly the principle of Hongik Ingan—"living to broadly benefit all humanity." This means focusing less on the past and more on the future. It means creating a nation based on universal principles and values that will benefit the Northeast Asia region with greater peace, security, and prosperity.

Since the pursuit of a principled unification of Korea will have such a wide impact throughout the Northeast Asia region, the initial 2014 Korean language publication of *Korean Dream* was closely followed by the Japanese language edition in 2015.

Of course, the future of the Korean peninsula has implications that reach far beyond the boundaries of Northeast Asia. It will affect peace and prosperity globally—for better or for worse. The United States, in particular, has strong geopolitical, security, and economic interests in the region. More important, it has intimate ties with Korea that run deep. Americans spilled their blood together with their Korean brothers to preserve the freedom of South Korea during the Korean War.

Since then, the ties between the two nations have grown closer so that South Korea has become one of America's strongest allies. South Korea has also grown remarkably so that today it is active as a leader on the global stage and stands as a full partner with the United States and other advanced nations. American interests are closely aligned with South Korea's, not least because both nations stand upon and honor certain fundamental and universal principles and values, the central theme of my book.

With this in mind, I am honored to now present *Korean Dream* to an English-speaking audience, particularly in America. There are many friends of Korea in America who understand that the future of the two countries are tied together. There is also a growing Korean diaspora in America with many second and third generation Koreans who feel a tie to their ancestral land but do not read Korean well.

This English edition is intended for such readers, to show them the great possibilities that will arise from a Korea unified on a foundation of principle, and to engage their support in promoting that dream. A united people that embodies the Korean Dream will not only be a catalyst for peace and prosperity in Asia. It will also offer a powerful model for overcoming many of the conflicts that are tearing apart our world today.

Circumstances today are making peaceful unification an ever more real possibility. Since the year 2014 we have seen the vision of unification shift from being a far distant prospect to now occupying the center of international attention. That is why it is urgent that we prepare and build a strong moral foundation for unification.

In August 2014, Pope Francis visited Korea urging reconciliation between North and South Korea and encouraging the search for new approaches to peace. He called on all Koreans to "shape a culture formed by the noblest traditional values of the Korean people."

In the following pages I articulate a vision for the future of Korea built upon those values and the destiny toward which they point Koreans. I hope that this book will inspire many outside Korea, particularly Koreans in the diaspora and their American friends, to share this vision and work to make it a reality.

Hyun Jin Preston Moon

BUILDING THE KOREAN DREAM
Introduction to the Centennial Edition

In the years since its original publication, *Korean Dream: A Vision for a Unified Korea* has been a catalyst for the vision it put forth, building robust multi-sector civil society support at home and abroad.

Significant steps have been made since 2014 in bringing global awareness to the Korean peninsula and moving the divided Korea closer to becoming one again. The Global Peace Foundation (GPF) and Action for Korea United (AKU) have been working together to advance understanding of and support for the Korean Dream approach internationally but especially among the South Korean public, engaging policy experts, universities, and the general public, particularly youth.

The *Korean Dream* is inspiring a dynamic citizen movement coordinated by the civil society coalition Action for Korea United. AKU has grown rapidly since its inception in 2011 and official launch in 2012, and today includes over 1,000 member organizations that support the Korean Dream. Most recently, AKU has expanded its network to engage diaspora Koreans, who number over 7.4 million people across 194 nations around the world, with especially significant bases in Japan and the United States.

A Korean Dream Unification Academy works to conduct an ongoing series of public forums on the topic. Over 4,000 college students have taken part in seminars, and textbooks have been published in cooperation with the ROK government for middle and high school students.

GPF holds expert policy forums in Korea on the Korean Dream and unification. In Washington, D.C., it co-sponsored a series of five forums on unification with the Center for Strategic and International Studies, a leading U.S. think tank on international affairs. These forums helped to bring Korean unification to the forefront as an issue for policy makers and experts.

Outreach extends beyond experts, schools, and colleges. There has been a strong cultural outreach through the One K Global Campaign. The highlight of the campaign's launch was the collaboration with leading Korean songwriters to produce the New Era Unification Song. The music video featured K-pop artists and politicians from across party lines in a show of solidarity. Over thirty K-pop artists performed at the first One K Concert in Seoul in October 2015 for an audience of 40,000 young people. The song was the culmination of the concert and the entire performance was broadcast nationwide by SBS. Years later, at the historic inter-Korea summit between North and South Korean leaders, this song was selected and played as the theme song.

The campaign has since gone global. World-renowned artists including Peabo Bryson, Dami Im, Edray, Zendee, and Sabrina joined together with K-pop stars including Psy, SHINee, CNBlue, BAP, BtoB, AOA, and B1A4 for the 2017 One K Concert at Manila's Mall of Asia Arena. A new unification song, "Korean Dream," was premiered at the concert which was produced by Grammy Award winners Jimmy Jam and Terry Lewis.

The third One K Concert on March 1, 2019 was a part of the March 1, 1919 Independence Movement Centennial Commemoration where dozens of One K stars performed at the National Assembly Plaza in Seoul to celebrate 100 years since the March First Movement and to envision a future of reunification and peace.

Other initiatives seek to engage a wider public with the unification issue on a practical basis. There are annual Unification projects and Unification essay contests for students. The Power of 1,000 Won campaign encourages younger students to put aside a little money every day to support bakeries that feed orphans in the North. AKU also actively engages with growing numbers of North Koreans living in South Korea, providing practical support to help defectors adapt to modern city life. AKU also works with groups of defectors who want to send information into North Korea to the people they had to leave behind.

This growing support for the Korean Dream has been captured by the Korean media which has followed all the activities quite closely. This work has been featured in all the daily newspapers, major magazines, and television networks. SBS was the broadcast partner of the March 1, 2019 event, which aired live throughout Korea and was rebroadcasted thereafter multiple times. SBS even developed a special program aired throughout its networks in the Asian region. Social media campaigns, including video message drives, have engaged tens of thousands throughout the world on the Korean issue, building awareness and interest in realizing the Korean Dream.

The year 2019 marks 100 years since Koreans rallied around their vision for an ideal nation in the Declaration of Independence proclaimed on March 1, 1919. Based on this important milestone, we have issued this Centennial Edition of Korean Dream. In this edition, we have included exclusive photos to showcase the many exciting moments and activities in the building of the Korean Dream movement.

It is our hope that the publication of the Centennial Edition of this important book will continue to advance the vision of the One Korea of our dreams.

Editorial Team of Korean Dream: The Centennial Edition

CHAPTER 1

The Korean Dream

"If one person has a dream, it is just a dream, but if all people have that dream, it becomes a reality."
– GENGHIS KHAN

The Korean people have always been one, united by a shared five-thousand-year history, a common language, and a common cultural heritage. Yet, since the end of World War II, we have been divided into two nations, arbitrarily separated against our wishes on the cutting block of rising geopolitical tensions between the West and the Soviet bloc. The legacy of this division, like a wound that has not been treated, festers and threatens the very health of the Korean people, the region, and the world to this day.

In the South, the "Miracle on the Han River" has transformed the country from a poor agricultural backwater to a manufacturing, trading, and technological powerhouse—one of the top fifteen economies in the world—in the space of just two generations. However, prosperity has

1

come at a cost. Many of our most cherished cultural traditions and values are being eroded in the pursuit of material comforts, Western progressive ideals, and popular culture. Yet, historically, our unique Korean heritage is what enabled us to endure and transcend a long history of suffering—the DNA that engendered the prosperity that the South enjoys today. Losing this Korean identity as a common people and, at one time, as a whole nation, South Koreans have increasingly turned away from the hopes and moral imperative of unification.

The North, in reality and in our imaginations, has become a black hole. We are all familiar with the satellite photos that show lights blazing throughout this region at night, especially in the major metropolitan centers of Seoul, Busan, Tokyo, Beijing, and the great seaboard cities of China. Yet, north of the 38th parallel up to the Tumen and Yalu Rivers, all we see is an area of unrelieved darkness. To most observers, the darkness that enshrouds the North without a single flickering light of hope is a fitting image for the realities of that regime. The people of North Korea are desperately impoverished and destitute. Their government is incapable of feeding them, and its citizens, denied all semblance of freedoms and human rights, have few opportunities for creativity and enterprise.

Because information about and contact with the North has been so tightly controlled, North Koreans seem increasingly alien to people in the South. Although the Soviet Union has collapsed and the failures of communism have been exposed, the North continues to maintain the ideological, political, military, and economic frameworks of the Cold War era, unable to recognize its obsolescence in our current age of globalization. This reality is deepening the gulf between the two Koreas along social, political, and economic lines, making unification a harder proposition as we move forward.

When we Koreans, in both North and South, look at our common history, the current seventy-year division is but a drop in the ocean of centuries of shared experiences, traditions, and culture.

We must look beyond our current divisions and seek a new united future rooted in a common past.

I am a man who believes in big dreams. I also believe that Korea today is ripe for such a challenge. In this book I want to show that a great and historic opportunity lies within our grasp. I want to lay out a new vision for Korea that can transform the peninsula, the Northeast region, and the world. What will that dream look like?

Before exploring that question, I want to emphasize the power of a big dream in shaping the course of human history. Dreamers frame new possibilities that can transcend the limitations of current reality. When people are inspired to pursue those possibilities, the world is changed, often in remarkable and unforeseen ways. Let's look at two examples of great dreams. One is from the East, and one is from the West.

GENGHIS KHAN'S DREAM: "ONE WORLD UNDER ONE HEAVEN"

The first dream is "One World under One Heaven," and the dreamer was Genghis Khan. He is known as a conqueror and an invader of Korea, but his conquests created a remarkable empire. There are important lessons to be learned by understanding how he achieved his vision and became more than just a conquering warlord.

In the first half of the thirteenth century, he led mobile and disciplined armies of horsemen that burst out in all directions from the Mongolian steppe. Through lightning campaigns he rapidly established the largest land empire the world has ever known, greater than the empires of Alexander the Great or Rome. It stretched from Korea in the east to Poland in the west, and from the Arctic in the north to Persia and India in the south.

He was a brilliant organizer and military strategist. After the First World War, armored warfare specialists studied his campaigns as models for the strategic use of tanks. Jawaharlal Nehru, independence leader and first prime minister of modern India, said, "Alexander and Caesar seem petty before him."[1]

He was, without doubt, a military genius, but that was not what lay at the heart of his success. He grew up in the harsh circumstances of the Mongolian steppe. Its grasslands were populated by scattered, warring nomadic clans, who for generations had lived and died divided by petty tribal rivalries, trapped in a cycle of self-imposed violence.

Genghis Khan himself suffered harshly within this culture. As a boy, he and his mother and brothers were driven out of the clan after his father, the clan leader, died, to live as outcasts at the mercy of any raiding band. Later, his first wife, Borte, was kidnapped by the hostile Merkid clan and held prisoner for some time before he could rescue her.

These experiences marked him deeply, but instead of becoming trapped by his circumstances, he conceived a vision that led him to transcend them. Rather than striving to become just another powerful clan leader, defending his own people and attacking his rivals, he dreamed of ending the centuries-old cycle of conflict and uniting the Mongol tribes. The tribes became a nation, animated by the dream of Genghis Khan, and that nation transformed the Eurasian world for centuries to come.

Genghis Khan's conquests were hinged on the idea that "if one person has a dream, it is only a dream, but if all people share that dream, it becomes a reality." This was the secret of his success. While he used force initially to resolve conflict with rival tribes, that was not the power that united the Mongolian tribes.

There is a saying that "a slave obeys because he is forced to, but a free man follows because he chooses to." Genghis Khan's success lay in his ability to align the will of his followers, as well as others who came into contact with his Mongol bands, to aspire to the same dream that had motivated his conquests. That is how Genghis Khan united the Mongolian tribes and later the Eurasian continent.

The vision guiding Genghis Khan was a simple one, yet with profound significance: there should be "One World under One Heaven." This was the ultimate key to peace, a peace that could become universal in its scope. War and conquest were necessary evils, not an end in themselves. The result of this vision was what Jack Weatherford, in his influential book, *Genghis Khan and the Making of the Modern World*, calls the "persistent universalism" of the Mongol Empire. He credits the Mongols with creating the "nucleus of a universal culture and world system."[2]

The phrase "under One Heaven" was not mere rhetoric but was at the heart of Genghis Khan's vision. He believed in a divinely ordained universal order that was the key to peace and prosperity. Nehru, a great peace advocate, was nevertheless fascinated by Genghis Khan because he realized that Genghis Khan was so much more than a brilliant military conqueror. He was struck by the Mongol leader's belief in "the *unchangeable law* for ever and ever, and no one could disobey it. Even the emperor was subject to it."[3]

Based on this concept, Genghis Khan promulgated simple laws with universal application, rooted in nascent concepts of human rights and fundamental freedoms. Weatherford sees in the laws and systems of the Mongol Empire the seeds of a new global culture that continued to develop long after the Mongol Empire's decline. He finds those seeds in the promotion of "free commerce, open communication, shared knowledge, secular politics, religious coexistence, international law, and diplomatic immunity."[4]

These were the fruits of Genghis Khan's vision. His empire respected the cultures of conquered regions and established freedom of religion in an attempt to neutralize it as a source of oppression and conflict. The Mongols promoted a society in which ability was valued more than social status, abolishing the caste system and breaking the monopoly powers of local elites. This society also reduced discrimination against women and upheld the dignity of all human life, encouraging multicultural, multiracial, and multireligious marriages.

The *Yassa*, or Great Law, as the Mongol legal code was known, restrained the traditional causes of feuding among tribes across the empire and so promoted an era of peace and prosperity. The resulting Pax Mongolica, as it has become known, lasted from the end of the Mongol conquests in the mid-thirteenth century until the end of the fourteenth century, embracing the whole of the Eurasian continent. At that time, there was a common saying about that period that "a maiden bearing a nugget of gold on her head could wander safely throughout the realm."[5]

Marco Polo, the Venetian explorer, was a direct beneficiary of this peace. With free trade and secure travel established across all the regions ranging from Asia through the Middle East to Eastern Europe, he could travel safely to China and record his journeys in a book titled *Travels of Marco Polo*. This sparked a growing European interest in the land of the great Khan.

The Mongol peace combined with their promotion of trade led to the flow of Asian products and technology into Europe and growing cultural exchange between the civilizations of East and West. Europe began to emerge from its long isolation following the fall of the Roman Empire. If it were not for Genghis Khan, the European slumber might have lasted far longer, and the development of the modern world been postponed.

Genghis Khan offers a remarkable example of the power of a dream to see beyond existing circumstances, however intractable they may seem, and envision something better. When that dream was rooted in a compelling vision and was then shared and owned by a clan, tribe, nations, and a continent, it had the power to transform the stark, unenlightened reality of medieval Europe and Asia into embracing a new cultural paradigm and world system. Although we may never know explicitly what truly motivated Genghis Khan's conquest, the historical facts show clearly that the formula to his success was not the lust for power but the universal aspiration, principles, and values implicit in his vision of "One World under One Heaven," the source of that unchangeable and universal law that applied to all people everywhere, regardless of their power and status.

As Koreans, we feel a natural affinity with Mongolia, its people, and its history. We have many common cultural roots and share the blue Mongolian birth spots. This makes the example of Genghis Khan especially interesting for us. Through him, we can learn the power of a great dream to rise above the limitations of circumstance, unite a people into one nation, and transform the world.

This is not just a story in the history books. Tomorrow's history is being made by our choices and actions today. Past history is a source of lessons we can apply to meet and overcome the challenges of our present.

As Koreans, we should reflect on the story of Genghis Khan and ask ourselves: What is our dream today for the future of our country and its role in the world?

THE AMERICAN DREAM AND THE BEGINNING OF THE MODERN AGE

The second dream is the American Dream. It helped give birth to the modern world and modern ideas of human rights and freedoms and remains an active force in the world today. But what exactly is the "American Dream?" Understanding the right answer to this question is important when considering Korea's future direction.

The United States of America has been the leading nation in the world since the Second World War. Today, it is often referred to as the "sole remaining superpower." Its military strength is unrivaled, and it remains the world's strongest economy, a position it has achieved in a little over two hundred years since its founding.

America did not begin as a rich and powerful country. Most of its land remained undeveloped, and, prior to independence, the thirteen original states were agricultural colonies of Great Britain. In relation to the power centers of Europe, America was a backwater. So how did it become the power that it is today?

The European settlement of the Americas was a milestone in the emergence of the modern world. It took place in the wake of a paradigm shift in European worldviews brought about by the Renaissance and Reformation. It is instructive to compare the divergent courses followed by North and South America in the centuries since settlement first began. Although Latin America today is improving economically and politically in many places, its history has been one of stark contrast with North America. Latin America has been marked by political corruption and instability, dictatorships, economic inefficiency, and poverty for vast numbers who were not part of the ruling elites.

The fundamental difference in the course of the two halves of the Western hemisphere lays in their heritage. North America was shaped by the British legacy, which paved the way for the first constitutional government and the recognition of the "fundamental rights" of all Englishmen.[6] The central and southern regions of the Americas, on the other hand, were largely influenced by the more feudal political-religious traditions of the Iberian Peninsula that remained a bastion and champion of old Europe. When those feudal traditions weakened, they were replaced by an absolutist monarchy.[7]

I was born in Korea but received my education in America. I became a keen student of American history, searching to understand the source of America's success and the true meaning of the American Dream. What was it that attracted immigrants to America from all over the world? I came to realize that the essence of this dream was not to be found in externals. It was not about a bigger house, a second car, or a better education for the children. It was to be found in the principles and values that underpinned the American founding and opened the way for a society and nation very different from those of Latin America.

When the thirteen colonies united to declare independence from the British Crown, it marked a watershed in the history of America and the world. Their quarrel with the Crown was that they were being denied the rights guaranteed in England to "freeborn Englishmen." As part of a colony of Great Britain, the colonists, most of whom were of English descent, believed that they were entitled as British subjects to have a representative voice in Parliament. However, they were upset by the fact that they were subject to the arbitrary actions of the Crown without any representation and recourse.

Prior to the American Revolution, there had been many rebellions throughout the world, but none had appealed to universal principles rooted in God. The Declaration of Independence, written and signed by the Founding Fathers of the United States and proclaimed on July 4, 1776, offered a new vision of nationhood. It marked the birth of the American Dream.

The Declaration of Independence was a direct challenge to the arbitrary and absolute exercise of power by a monarch and to the doctrine of the divine right of kings that supported it. The Founding Fathers were able to draw on the British legacy in formulating their principles, because England had already challenged the divine right of kings in a bloody civil war with Charles I (r. 1625–1649) and through the Glorious Revolution of 1688, which established a constitutional monarchy with clearly delimited powers.

In most of Europe, however, absolute monarchy prevailed, reinforced by rigid social hierarchies. The resulting political philosophy was starkly expressed by a minister of Francis I, the last Holy Roman Emperor and emperor of Austria-Hungary until his death in 1835. He characterized the emperor's policy as "unabated maintenance of the sovereign's authority, and a denial of all claims on the part of the people to a participation in that authority."[8]

America's Founding Fathers pioneered a very different course. They rejected the idea that the monarch's authority came from God and was, therefore, absolute. Instead, the Declaration of Independence advocated the theory of natural rights: the notion that fundamental human rights and freedoms are bestowed, not by the state or monarch, but directly to the people by the Creator, and the purpose of government was to ensure the protection of those rights.

Thus, each person has intrinsic value that comes from the Creator and is the basis for the essential dignity of each person and the rights that such dignity naturally entails. It was truly a birth of an enlightened concept of liberty and human rights that pointed the way forward to our modern concept of universal human rights and freedoms.

America's founders also recognized that the principles of equal human rights and fundamental freedoms could only be effective when citizens had the moral character to use them responsibly. A free people must adhere to a transcendent moral standard. In short, a free people must be a self-governing people of virtue. John Adams probably expressed it best when he said, "Our Constitution was made only for a moral and religious people. It is wholly inadequate to the government of any other."[9]

This is why the ideal of religious freedom was so essential for America. It was not just so that people could be free to worship as they choose, but it was also to engender a climate in which the virtues of religion could exert their important influence upon the public square. As George Washington observed, "Reason and experience both forbid us to expect that National morality can prevail in exclusion of religious principle."[10]

Indeed, America conducted an unprecedented and revolutionary experiment by upholding the guarantee of individuals' freedoms and rights as its highest value. This shaped the outlook of newly arriving immigrants and was the vision that fed their aspirations. This is how the goal of creating "One Nation under God" was established.

Many people believe that the strength of America lies in its democratic political process and free market economic system. However, the success or failure of political and economic systems is determined by the principles and values that guide and motivate the people who work within them. A democratic process is no guarantee of freedom. After all, Hitler was elected to power under the Weimar Republic, a democracy. The role of Wall Street finance in triggering the 2008 global financial crisis shows that the same is true of free market or capitalist systems.[11] No process or system by itself, absent ethical standards and a moral people who can give substance to them, can protect those institutions from shortsighted greed or the selfish lust for power.

America's founding principles and values, which have operated throughout its history within its political and economic systems, have shaped this nation into what it is today. Through these principles and values, America has endeavored to build a society full of vitality, opportunity, and freedoms. As George Washington said in his Farewell Address, "'Tis substantially true, that virtue or morality is a necessary spring of popular government."[12] This was the true driving force behind the development of America—a nation that tried to be virtuous and moral by internalizing, substantiating, and manifesting the deeply spiritual principles and values engendered upon its founding.

That is why the Declaration of Independence has been called upon at moments of crisis in America's history, as a touchstone by which to judge the present, and as a guide to a future that is true to its founding.[13] The Gettysburg Address, delivered by President Abraham Lincoln shortly after he emancipated the slaves in Confederate territories, framed the Civil War in terms of the challenge embodied in the Declaration to create a society in which all people, regardless of race, are truly equal.

This theme was carried forth in Dr. Martin Luther King Jr.'s "I Have a Dream" speech at the height of the civil rights movement of the 1960s. In his speech, he reminded Americans of the principles enshrined in the Declaration and asked them to judge the injustices of segregation and racial inequality against those ideals.

In short, the principles and values enshrined in the Declaration of Independence moved American history forward, overcame crises, and united the people of America. Like a compass used to navigate through uncharted waters, the Declaration was the guide that allowed the bold experiment of popular government and free markets to align to a higher ideal and inspire their citizens, the nation, and the world. It became the beacon of hope for all oppressed people throughout the world who sought "life, liberty, and the pursuit of happiness"—in other words, to have the protections, opportunities, and freedoms that they could not find in their ancestral homeland.

That promise was the bedrock of innovation and entrepreneurism, as freedom, initiative, and creativity were celebrated through the rags-to-riches stories of common people who made their fortunes in America. Although the American Dream had a spiritual origin, its expression was substantially manifested in the worldly fortunes of enterprising men and women who dared to dream and take the necessary risks for success that the opportunity of America afforded. These stories and examples were the catalyst for the nation's entrepreneurial and pioneering spirit.[14] It was through that spirit that major railways, highways, and ports were constructed, and the free market economy blossomed, bringing economic prosperity to the continent.

The Declaration of Independence exerts its influence across the world to this day, because the human rights, freedoms, and dignity it upholds are universal. It was not just a declaration for Americans but a declaration for all the world's people. America's independence set the stage for the abolition of despotic monarchies and instigated the modern political drive toward democracy and free markets around the world.

America's principles can be seen in action through its foreign policy after World War II. A victor nation and now the greatest superpower in the world, the United States could have colonized the defeated countries of Germany and Japan—or exacted reparations from them, as Britain and France did from Germany after World War I. Instead, it chose another, unprecedented path: providing its defeated adversaries with aid for their economic restoration, looking to build the foundations for a world of peace and prosperity where such a war could never be repeated.

In the wake of World War II, the United States began to promote its founding principles globally as universal principles. This was the motivation behind the U.S. drive to establish the United Nations, however far that institution may have drifted today from its original ideal. The United States also stood firmly for the independence of new nations in the emerging world and the end of European hegemony. Thanks to America, the era of colonization by great powers came to an end.[15]

America has supported freedom around the world, not just with words, but with the blood of its young people deployed to battlegrounds far from home. It came to Korea's aid in our country's darkest hour. During the Korean War alone, some 40,000 young American lives were lost.

How could American families send their loved ones to foreign battlefields? It is impossible to understand without recognizing the enduring spiritual principles and values that America pursues—that we human beings are endowed by God with freedom and human rights, and that our God-given duty is to protect them, not for ourselves alone, but even for people in far distant lands.

That spirit of self-sacrifice for a noble cause is seriously challenged today in America, which is bad news for the world at large. John F.

Kennedy, at his presidential inauguration in 1960, famously said, "Ask not what your country can do for you, ask what you can do for your country." But today, self-sacrifice is being pushed aside by the spirit of self-indulgence and selfish individualism.

There is a struggle for the spirit of America. The founding spirit is under attack—from a hedonistic popular culture that is the antithesis of virtue, responsibility, and self-sacrifice, and from political philosophies that deny such things as fundamental principles and values. As American popular culture is exported to the world, the image of America becomes distorted, and its influence for the spread of universal principles and values is weakened. To continue to prosper and to exert its moral leadership in the world, America must reassert its founding spirit.

The dream of America's Founding Fathers not only gave birth to a great nation, unique in world history to that point. It also left substantial footprints throughout the world. It set out the ideal of universal human rights, freedoms, and responsibilities and made substantial sacrifices in pursuit of realizing that ideal. If America no longer takes the lead in this endeavor, who else will? Who else can?

What about us, the Korean people? Will we learn from the America whose principles and values led it to strive for human freedom, first for the slaves at home, and then for those oppressed by tyrannies or colonial masters overseas? Or will we be like the America that is in danger of sinking into unthinking consumer comforts and self-indulgence? What footprint are we about to leave on world history?

HONGIK INGAN, THE SPIRITUAL CONSCIOUSNESS OF A PEOPLE AND THE KOREAN DREAM

Surrounded as it has been by great powers, the Korean peninsula has been subjected to repeated attacks throughout its history by continental as well as maritime forces. The history of the Korean people has been one of downtrodden suffering, perhaps more than any other country in the world. We have been the underdogs of history. What type of character have we developed through this kind of experience, and what sort of culture have we created through the course of such a history?

The truth is that suffering forced us to reflect deeply on life and seek spiritual understanding and truth. That impulse is reflected in our uniquely Korean character. The expression "people of *han (恨)*" captures that essence well. *Han* is not about holding grudges or seeking revenge due to injustices and damages received. Rather, it represents the sublimation of resentment into love and forgiveness. This quality was not some exclusive virtue of saintly individuals but a sentiment that all Koreans shared and aspired to achieve. It was openly expressed throughout the daily lives of ordinary people in song, literature, and dance.

Accordingly, Koreans have always been a peace-loving people. We have never attacked or invaded any other country, despite countless foreign invasions and provocations. This is very different from the history of our neighbors. How was such a character cultivated in the Korean people? The answer lies in our unique heritage.

Dangun, the legendary founder of Gojoseon, founded a nation based on the principles of Hongik Ingan (弘益人間), Ido-yeochi (以道如治), Kwangmyung-ise (光明以世), and Jaesae-ihwa (在世理化). This founding spirit can be summarized by the visionary spirit of Hongik Ingan, which means "to broadly benefit all humanity." Dangun aspired to govern the world with "morality and truth" (Ido-yeochi), thereby "enlightening the world with truth" (Kwangmyung-ise) and "creating a world of truth" (Jaesae-ihwa). The dream of building a world of truth rests upon the understanding that the origin of humanity is God and that the Korean people were given a special providential mission by God to live for the sake of all humankind.

I have personally presented the story of Dangun and the Hongik Ingan principles at an international conference that I hosted. The participants, especially two U.S. congressmen, were fascinated by our founding mythology, since the Hongik Ingan vision pursued the same principles and values as did the U.S. Declaration of Independence. They were amazed that a country based on such a vision was founded almost 5,000 years ago.

At that time, and indeed throughout most of human history, the basis of power was force, and loyalties were defined by one's family, clan, and nation. For the ancients outside of Korea, it was unimaginable to govern a nation based upon high moral principles and values and through an exalted vision that reached beyond the tribe and nation to embrace all of humanity.

However, Hongik Ingan is evidence that the Korean people aspired to fulfill such lofty ideals throughout their history. In other words, Korea nurtured modern ideals of enlightened governance before those concepts fully matured in human history with the birth of the United States of America 4,800 years later. This fact alone distinguishes the history of Korea from most other ancient civilizations of the world, for no other country that I know of has this kind of a founding vision and philosophy with such a lengthy history.

My purpose in writing about Dangun and the story of Korea's founding is not to get involved in issues of historical research. Simply, Hongik Ingan is at the root of who we are as Koreans and is a thread running through our people's past, as we continually have internalized it through our historical experiences, cultural heritage, and traditions. As an oppressed people, we sought strength from this past to give meaning and purpose, especially in times of crisis. My conclusion is that the story of Korea's founding is not just an ancient myth but forms the backbone of our actual living history.

Due to the mandate of serving humanity expressed in the vision of Hongik Ingan, Koreans have learned to value human life above all. We have always implicitly or explicitly believed that humanity is equal to and an expression of heaven. The concept of In Nae Chon (人乃天), that has roots in Dangun mythology and was expressed through the Donghak movement in the nineteenth century, represents this tradition well; a world in which people are happy is a world in which God is happy and a world that God desires.

This unique understanding of our humanity and the will of heaven has given the Korean people a deep spiritual consciousness that has shaped our attitudes toward spirituality and religion. I believe that this consciousness, although rooted in our genesis, was forged directly out of our challenging history as an oppressed people who had to endure tremendous ordeals as the object of invasion, oppression, domination, and separation. Because of those challenges, we came to recognize the importance of human life and the importance of our spirit. As a result, the Korean people have a deep spiritual history and an open-minded attitude to different expressions of faith, unlike many similarly homogeneous people.

The acceptance of Buddhism is a case in point. Buddhism was introduced to Korea during the latter half of the fourth century via the former kingdom of Qin. Although Buddhism was a foreign religion, Buddha's teachings of enlightenment and the importance of one's spiritual awakening closely matched the spiritual ideals that Koreans pursued throughout their history. Buddhism brought structure and a tangible regimen of worship that helped establish order without threatening the already rich shamanistic traditions of ancient Korean society. Moreover, Buddhism buttressed the ethical framework of our collective spiritual consciousness, as espoused in the principles of Hongik Ingan.

Like all other foreign religions that were to follow, Buddhism eventually took on a uniquely Korean quality. Korean Buddhism assumed a more holistic approach that tried to explain the inconsistencies seen in other interpretations of those teachings. This internalization of outside faith traditions mixed with the spiritual aspirations of the Korean people to engender a unique relationship between religion and state.

During the Three Kingdoms period (fourth to mid-seventh centuries), Buddhist influence in the religious and political life of the Korean people grew, such that the kingdoms of Goguryeo, Baekje, and Shilla adopted this faith as a state religion. The Shilla kingdom would later unite the peninsula under the era of the Unified Shilla (from the late seventh to the early tenth centuries) by raising the famous "Hwarang youths," based upon Buddhist teachings to be the vanguard force of unification. During the subsequent Goryeo period (tenth to fourteenth centuries), Buddhism became the inspiration not only for a religious life but for higher education and enlightened governance. The evolution of important state institutions under the guiding hand of Buddhist teachings during this period gave stability and legitimacy to our identity as a united Korean people.

The Joseon dynasty (latter part of the fourteenth to the early twentieth centuries), on the other hand, broke away from the influence of Buddhism and accepted a Korean version of neo-Confucianism as its governing idea. Neo-Confucianism was not just a moral philosophy but the melding of Taoism and Buddhism with the teachings of Confucius, creating a unique blend of religion and ethics. This dynasty considered neo-Confucianism to be more conducive to the substantial world of politics and governance than the more meditative and spiritual orientation of Buddhism. The Joseon dynasty particularly experimented with its ethical, family-oriented teachings as the governing political philosophy of the nation, looking at the state as one large extended family with the sovereign as its parent.

The Joseon dynasty followed a pseudo-constitution called the Gyeongguk Daejeon (經國大典), which was a system of codified laws that evolved from the Goryeo period and was enacted in the reign of King Taejo, the founder of the Joseon dynasty. It would be the governing form of law until this dynasty's end in the early part of the twentieth century with the annexation of Korea by the Japanese. However, Gyeongguk Daejeon laid out the framework of an ideal nation governed by laws and principles that promote the common good.

The importance of virtue and good governance during the Joseon dynasty determined the relationship between the king and his retainers in unprecedented ways. A system of checks and balances was created to prevent the ruler from arbitrarily exercising power in his own interests and not in the nation's interests. It can be argued that a limited type of quasi-constitutional monarchy emerged that upheld the ideals of the rule of law and promoted the fundamental rights and freedoms of all Koreans. An amazing fact is that these enlightened ideals of governance occurred in isolation, a continent away and several hundred years before the revolutionary transformation of political thought in Europe that came through the writings of Enlightenment-era philosophers.

Some may argue that the Joseon merely followed the trend of the time and took up Confucianism because the Ming dynasty, then the most powerful nation in Asia, had done so. Of course, no one can say that the Joseon was free from the influence of the Ming, but even when Confucius was alive, Korea was praised as the "country of courteous people in the East." (東方禮儀之國) In other words, apart from questions of cultural or political influence, neo-Confucianism suited the Korean character and was uniquely adapted to meet their desire to create an ideal state, centered upon morality, law, and justice.

Korea also accepted Christianity in unprecedented ways. It has been 200 years since Catholicism was introduced and 100 years since Protestantism first made inroads into Korea. Unlike what occurred in many other nations in Asia, Christianity quickly became a mainstream religion within the span of a century, to the point that a third of its population consider themselves to be Christian. At one time, Pyongyang, the current capital of North Korea, was considered the "new Jerusalem" of Asia, as American missionaries found countless willing converts prepared to receive the Good News.

Given Christianity's relatively short history in the nation, it is amazing that Korea is the leading engine of Christian evangelism in the world today. Korea sends the largest number of missionaries abroad, many times to the most remote and dangerous parts of the world. It has also been an inspiration of the megachurch movement within the evangelical circles of the Christian faith, with many foreign Christian pastors coming to Korea to learn from their Korean counterparts. This level of ownership of a relatively new faith tradition is extraordinary and shows the openness that Koreans have to different expressions of faith, since we are, by our very nature, a deeply spiritual people.

Thus, Korea has become a nation where most of the world's mainstream religions have flourished, supporting a strong and deep spiritual culture. Usually, a country becomes multireligious when different racial and ethnic groups representing different religions live together in a pluralistic society. It is not common for a homogeneous country like Korea to have a multireligious society where people live together in relative harmony and without conflict. The reason is found in our heritage.

The spirit of Hongik Ingan infused a deeply spiritual consciousness in the Korean people, making us aware of religion's important role in guiding our national aspirations to create an ideal nation and be an inspiration to the world. This consciousness was the source of our strength that allowed us as a people to overcome all the challenges thrust upon us throughout our suffering history. Our spirituality shaped an open-minded attitude toward faith as we yearned for truth, not just in the material sense, but more importantly, in a spiritual one.

In our spiritual consciousness, we found the answers and meaning for our tribulations. Here, as a people, we had a sense of divine destiny to serve the world. The Hongik Ingan vision, rooted in truth as a guide to build an ideal nation, defines the enduring hope of the Korean people. It is our essence and DNA.

If the spirit of benefiting all humanity is our essence, then the Korean Dream becomes clear. We should bring peace and prosperity to the peninsula and then, as a united people, live to bring benefit to the region and subsequently the world. We can achieve this by becoming an enlightened nation that advocates peace with the moral authority of our own unification and our desire to serve the world. This is our charge. This is the Korean Dream.

UNIFICATION: THE FIRST STEP IN REALIZING THE KOREAN DREAM

If the vision of Hongik Ingan defines our aspirations as a people, then what should be the first task in achieving it? The answer is obvious, is it not? We must achieve unification.

Although division is our current reality and one that many of us, in the North and South, are resigned to accept, it does not have to determine our future. We should be clear that continued division imposes serious costs and liabilities on the Korean people, the region, and the world. The political and economic instability of the North, combined with its nuclear weapons, presents an ongoing security and economic threat to the South, and to the stability and vitality of the region and the world. Thus, the division of the peninsula is not just a Korean problem but a regional and global one, affecting the future of humanity in this century and beyond. That is why I believe that unification is one of the most important issues for global peace in the world today.

What are we, as Koreans, going to do about it? We stand at the center of this very issue. Before unification can be considered a regional or global issue, it is first and foremost a Korean one. And before it can be considered a political, economic, and military issue for the two governments of Korea, it is a human tragedy that affects our families and, most importantly, our identities as Koreans. Are we to forget our past and where we came from?

Are we to forget the profound dream that animated our ancestors at the beginning of our national consciousness as the Korean people? Are we to accept the circumstances of our imposed division, although we had nothing to do with it? Are we to carry the burden of this division with all its evil consequences and pass it on to future generations? Is there really nothing that average Koreans, North and South, can do about this issue? Is it out of our hands and the sole province of governments and national and regional interests? Are we so inadequate? The questions can go on and on.

I cannot speak for others, but I do not want to live in or accept the reality of a divided Korea. I want to dream of a united Korea, vibrant with hope and pregnant with possibilities. I want this new Korea to set the paradigm of a new enlightened state that reflects the best of the East and West, as well as the past, present, and future. I call this aspiration the Korean Dream. Rooted in our rich and unique past, this vision has the possibility to engage creatively with the modern world.

It is a dream that all Koreans can share, and, if we do, together we can turn it into reality. We can transcend the artificial division of our peninsula and fulfill our providential destiny as a united people and nation, with a moral mission to serve humanity. As the first Nobel Laureate for literature from Asia, Rabindranath Tagore prophesized in poetic prose:

In the Golden Age of Asia

Korea was one of the lamp-bearers

That lamp awaits to be lighted once again

For the illumination of the East.[16]

In our ever-changing geopolitical and economic context, in which the global power centers are moving from the Atlantic to the Pacific Rim,[17] Korea stands in a unique geographic, historic, political, and economic position to shape this shift in real ways. Most of all, it has the opportunity to end the last vestige of the Cold War and bring closure to a terrible chapter of the struggle of Korea and other Asian nations for national sovereignty and self-determination, thereby setting the moral precedent for true peacebuilding beyond all divides that separate the human family. This precedent can be the light for all nations and regions in conflict. As Tagore suggests, the lamp of Korea "awaits to be lighted once again."

In order to realize this dream, we have to start with the end in mind. That end should be the creation of a new nation, rooted in a common past but with shared future aspirations. However, up until now, every discussion on unification has been consumed with the process of unification, usually seen through the lens of Cold War geopolitics and interests, with the assumption that one system or government would win over the other. I believe that such a framework only exacerbates the social, political, and economic divide between the two Koreas, making any sincere efforts for unification next to impossible.

The real issue is whether we, as the Korean people, have a clear vision for unification. The worst scenario would be to have unification forced upon us unexpectedly by circumstances without having formed a clear consensus on the desired outcomes—internally on the peninsula, and externally among the other nations affected. We must not face this issue unprepared. The Korean people must take control of and shape our own national destiny through the unification process and lead our neighbors and the international community to support our efforts.

I believe it is not now a question of why, how, and when we need to consider the unification issue, but a question of what it will look like. South Korea produced the Unification Plan for the Unified Korean Community, while North Korea has the Goryeo Federal System. Both propose peaceful democratic procedures to achieve unification, but they seem far removed from existing reality. Discussions on these proposals have never gone anywhere and seem totally disconnected from actual relations between the two sides. Consequently, nobody believes that these proposals, or any discussion of them, will unify the Korean peninsula.

For any real discussion of unification to begin, we, the Korean people, must identify a common platform through which we can all converge, not as a divided people, but as Koreans. Before we can talk about political and economic systems, as well as institutions of governance, a real discussion should arise around the dream or aspirations of unification and the principles and values upon which a new nation will be built. They determine the nature and quality, good or bad, of any system, institution, or nation, since they are its foundation.

That is why I took such lengths to point out three historic examples, two foreign and one uniquely Korean, to help shape a new framework for discussion on this issue of unification. As I have mentioned, we need to build a consensus on the outcome of unification if the possibility of that event is ever to be realized. Without a consensus, we have no common ground or common objective so all we would do is talk over each other in the world of theory, hypothesis, and conjecture. In that case, unification would be the province of detached academics, think tanks, and policy proponents with little relevance or meaning to average Koreans.

History, however, has a way of making things relevant in a very concrete way. It represents the collective stories of our past, touching the lives of our ancestors, our grandparents, our parents, and ourselves in truly profound ways that shape opinions, perspectives, and understanding on an intimate personal level. By making the events of the world relevant on an individual level, average citizens can be engaged in issues that seem out of their hands and, therefore, disconnected with their daily lives.

For Koreans, all of our personal lives—past, present, and future— have been or will be affected by the current division of our peninsula and our people. Yet, if unification is truly a prize that we seek, then it is paramount to engage the interests, participation, and involvement of the Korean people. Without their involvement, unification is a fanciful dream without real owners who can actualize it into a reality.

All we need to do is look at what happened in Germany with the fall of the Berlin Wall, Mongolia, Tunisia, Libya, and Egypt. Those nations changed in the blink of an eye, to the surprise of all. Even the so-called experts who diligently followed the developments in those respective nations were caught off-guard. No one could have foretold the revolutionary changes in those countries; yet, they happened.

The main instigators of change were the people themselves, not the governments or the heads of those regimes. Change did not happen in some high-level negotiation between state-level actors but through the mass demonstration of people in the streets, a bottom-up change. This is the power of waking the collective consciousness of a people to be change agents. Without them, revolutionary transformation is a fanciful dream. With them, anything is possible.

There is great truth in Genghis Khan's insight that "if one person dreams a dream, it is but a dream, but if a people dream that dream, then it becomes reality." The Korean people, North and South, need to dream the same dream. I believe it should be the Korean Dream. If they have this dream, then unification will come sooner than anyone thinks.

The aspiration that the Korean people have kept alive over 5,000 years resonates with the lofty dream of Genghis Khan to create "One World under One Heaven" and the American Dream to build "One Nation under God." The essence of these visions is rooted in the understanding that certain transcendent universal truths and principles should govern human life and that human dignity, values, and rights are given by heaven or the Creator. The Korean Dream shares this essence in the principles outlined in Hongik Ingan. Building a moral nation centered upon truth and justice and then serving humanity constitute the founding vision of the Korean people and our providential destiny.

Yet, the task of realizing and substantiating that dream rests on the shoulders of this generation of Koreans. Fate has chosen us to stand at an inflection point in the history of our people, our nation, the region, and the world. Will we be the big dreamers who shape our collective tomorrow for the good of all, or will we stand by idly as others shape the future from the void of our inactions? The Korean people hold all the cards. The Korean Dream is ours to realize or to lose. It is up to us.

INTERNALIZING THE KOREAN DREAM AND THE DESTINY OF THE KOREAN PEOPLE

Unification is a major step forward toward fulfilling the Korean Dream. But that dream, as I have mentioned, should be about more than just unification. It is about the destiny of the Korean people and the positive impact they would make on the world. The dream's full implementation can only be realized through creating a united Korea that is aligned with the founding vision of our people. Thus, it must be a noble, enlightened nation that advocates and represents the lofty ideals of Hongik Ingan, which would naturally give it the moral authority to actualize real good in this century and beyond.

Today, however, our most precious resource—our people—is under threat. Although I cannot speak for the North, South Koreans are losing touch with our proud history and sense of identity. The most serious of these problems is the dissolution of the family. The Korean extended family model has been perhaps the most outstanding feature of our culture. It offers a strong, supportive system that is inter-generational and extends outward to the clan, society, and the nation. It has been a powerful social good, nurturing and maintaining the most important qualities of Korean society throughout our history.

Sadly, this sacred Korean institution is being eroded by the impact of rapid modernization and the appearance of Western social patterns.

We see small nuclear families replacing the extended family. Society is becoming more hedonistic, with loosening attitudes toward sex, marriage, and family. As a result, divorce rates are among the highest in the developed world, with an alarming rise in suicide rates and the appearance of deviant sex crimes that were unheard of in the Korea of my youth.

Schools have become memorizing factories that only prepare students for college entrance exams. Many primary schools and colleges never teach their students about moral character and the unique, rich spiritual heritage of their nation. Social trends show the rise of a more self-centered individualism, like the developed countries of the West. The mass media, popular culture, and confluence of technological advancements like the internet, smartphones, and social networking actively promote this trend through commercialization and self-gratifying consumer values.

Politics has lost a sense of national direction, becoming locked in constant partisan disputes between left and right, engaging in populist public debates that generate more discord than solutions. As a result, there is increasing disappointment and distrust in the country's political leaders. The spirit of self-sacrifice that gave rise to industrialization and democratization, leading the South onto the world stage, is not being passed down to today's youth.

All these problems have arisen because we Koreans are losing our connection to the vision that has shaped our identity. Unification offers the opportunity to establish a clear national purpose and, in the process, to recover our Korean identity. It will only be accomplished successfully by returning to the same fundamental spirit that made our unique history possible.

Throughout the twentieth century, Koreans have longed to live in an independent and united nation, yet those dreams were thwarted, first by Japanese colonial rule and then by the ideological and political division of the peninsula within the Cold War context. Although powerful outside forces were at work in both situations, they were exacerbated by disunity among self-interested Korean factions, which ultimately hampered the drive for independence and national unity. This should not happen again if we are afforded another opportunity for self-determination.

As I have mentioned, the Korean people need to be united in our dreams if we are to realize unification and the Korean Dream.

What kind of nation should we build through unification? What will it look like? Any number of outcomes are plausible if we have to come up with an answer in a vacuum. Luckily, we don't. Precedents in our history point the way to what a new unified Korea should look like. In one sense, it will not be a new nation, since its purpose will be defined by the vision of our founding, yet it will truly be a new nation since its creation will realize the Korean people's unfulfilled destiny to serve humanity and the world.

Without going into details about the specific qualities of this new nation, I believe that some defining points need to be mentioned to help articulate a framework upon which it is to be built. As I inferred above, the new Korean nation should represent the best of the East and West and our past, present, and future. Since we are offered the opportunity to create a new nation, we will have a blank slate to learn from the best examples of nationhood as well as our own experiences. As far as systems and institutions, I believe that we should have an open mind with judicious objectivity. Yet, when it comes to our aspirations and the principles and values that this nation should be built upon, it should be defined by our unique historical experiences, culture, and traditions. In other words, a new Korean nation should represent its own unique heritage and not be overshadowed by foreign influences.

First, the nation should embody the spirit of Hongik Ingan, since this is the root of our common history and embodies our common aspirations, principles, and values. In line with this vision, the nation should recognize the sovereignty of God as the basis of humanity's intrinsic value, rights, and freedoms. This approach stays true to the spiritual consciousness of the Korean people, which considers humanity to be like heaven. Thus, no government or human institution can abridge or negate those rights and freedoms because they are endowed by God and would be a fundamental cornerstone of this new nation. As a result, naturally, the nation should be a constitutional form of government that recognizes the rule of law and governs with truth and justice for all its citizens.

Second, the nation needs to represent the wishes of the people, so it should have a popular, representative form of government. It should be made clear that the people are the real stakeholders of Korea and that the purpose of government is to serve them. As a result, there should naturally be a separation of powers so that our new nation will be safeguarded from tyranny through checks and balances. To ensure that government does not become an instrument of suppression and repression but instead safeguards our rights and freedoms, it should be limited to three branches of equal powers but different functions: the executive, the legislative, and the judicial.

Third, our educational institutions, which are the envy of the developed world for training the minds of our children, need to also instruct their hearts and spirits since these determine the character of the people they will become. Therefore, the educational system should encourage our deep spiritual heritage as the ethical backbone of our civic duties and life. This point is absolutely critical to mitigate the negative effects of mob rule to which all representative forms of government are subject.

The political stalemate in Washington, D.C. is an indication that all the best-laid structures break down without virtuous citizens and leaders who restrain their own personal ambitions for the good of the nation. Thus, the goal of education should be to raise the whole person—mind, heart, and spirit—to become someone with character who exhibits moral leadership in every level of society.

Fourth, I believe that communism was indisputably a failed experiment and that the free market system provides the most efficient form of distribution for goods and services. However, we also need to be aware of this system's intrinsic flaws, especially when blind ambition and unrestrained greed are unchecked. One simply needs to look at our global financial crisis. Regulation is one way of control, but there are costs as well, since regulation constrains growth.

The more effective way, in my view, is to raise people of character who would act ethically and morally in the economic life of a nation. The virtue of their character would be the best check against corruption. This virtuous behavior should be rewarded by offering greater opportunities to those who are willing to play by the rules versus those who want to cheat the system. Right now in Korea, the regulatory and economic environment favors the strong and the powerful with little opportunity for the little guy. This environment stifles the innate entrepreneurial spirit of the Korean people and shrinks the size of the economic pie, thereby lessening creativity, participation, and most of all, the incentives to act with integrity. This needs to change.

Fifth, we need to make sure that there is an engaged, objective, and independent media that will speak truth to power on behalf of all the Korean people. One of the most important features of a free society is freedom of speech and the press; yet, today's media is often partisan or, even worse, a propaganda mouthpiece blinded by ideology or special interests at the people's expense. This phenomenon is common in most countries, whether developed or developing.

Therefore, clear standards of journalism with a focus on ethics need to be set in journalism schools, newsrooms, editing floors, and production shops. Such standards should be initiated in the private sector and regulated through associations or other private, industry-specific governing bodies and not by the government, so as to safeguard the media from being an instrument of the state.

Sixth, recognizing the importance of ethics in creating an enlightened model society and nation, we should encourage faith traditions to make their unique contributions in the public square as proponents of moral behavior. Too many developed countries have a distorted understanding of the separation of church and state and misconstrue it to mean that religion should not be engaged with civil society. They fail to realize that this separation was created to ensure that no single, monolithic, state-sponsored religion would abrogate the freedom of conscience and expressions of faith of minority groups. In other words, separation of church and state was set up to uphold religious liberty, not obliterate faith from public life.

Given our deep spiritual heritage, we need to have a mature and insightful perspective on the positive contribution that faith has made throughout our history. Yes, there were abuses, but they pale in comparison to the good afforded us by our spiritual heritage in the direst moments of our history. As the Dangun myth suggests, this heritage embodies our highest ideals and aspirations. I hope that we will not fool ourselves into overlooking the importance of faith in the name of modernity, since faith will be needed more than ever as we take on the challenge of building a new united nation and heal a very deep wound that has divided us for the last sixty-five years.

Lastly, and most important, we need to preserve our most sacred institution: the Korean extended family. The traditional Korean family is the most enduring and unique manifestation of our heritage. It is where we intimately learn our most important lessons that make us who we are, from those we love the most. It is where we learn about our ancestors, feel the warm embrace of our family, experience the diversity of our clan, and know that we are a continuation of an ever-growing network of relationships that defines us, loves us, and is present for us. It is our safety net, far preferable to any government welfare system.

The extended family is where true sincerity is learned, as embodied in the concept of *jeong seong (精誠)*. This ideal of sincerity permeates every aspect of daily family life, from the making of clothes, to food, to housing, and even to work—from the most menial of chores to the most noble of actions. All are taken with a deep measure of sincerity and attendance. As a result, Koreans naturally strive to be the best that they can be in any task and do it with a level of service or self-sacrifice that others might not be willing to make.

Due to this unique Korean character, expressions of devotion like filial piety take on a new dimension of sincerity and self-sacrifice not found in other Asian cultures. Although filial piety might represent an act of courtesy or respect in other cultures, to Koreans it means far more. It represents self-sacrifice of the highest order as expressed through the children's tale of "Shim Cheong," where a daughter is willing to offer her own life to cure the blindness of her father. Through such stories and the examples of our parents, aunts, and uncles, our youth begin to understand the meanings of sincerity and family. In the family, they learn to be Korean.

I hope I am beginning to paint a picture of what a new unified nation might look like. To me, it captures the best of the East and West and aligns with the vision that animated our ancestors while remaining relevant to the modern world. The world is looking for leadership in dealing with the North's nuclear program and the ubiquitous problem of the global war on terror. Unification can immediately solve the first problem and significantly impact the spread and lethality of the second.

Unification will also ensure the economic prosperity of the peninsula, the region, and the world. According to a 2009 Goldman Sachs simulation study on the effects of unification, Korea would be the eighth-richest country in the world, with a GDP per capita income of 90,000 dollars for the South and 70,000 dollars for the North by 2050.[18] As former President Park Geun-hye has claimed, unification would indeed be a jackpot for the Korean people. The North has all the things that the South needs to maintain its economic growth rate in terms of markets, labor, and natural resources; the South has the industrial expertise, technical know-how, and capital to raise the standard of living of the North from its current miserable condition to that of a developed, industrialized state.

Most importantly, unification will set the moral precedent for aligning with our historic heritage and providential destiny. It must be clear, though, that unification begins with the consolidation of our dreams. We Koreans, in the North and the South, must unify our dreams. Unification should inspire and animate *all* Koreans—whether male or female, young or old, living on the peninsula or living abroad—not just the government officials and leaders of the two Koreas.

If all Koreans stand together with this dream in mind, we can mend the ideological, political, economic, factional, and national divide and heal the wounds of division as a united people and nation.

THE KOREAN DREAM AND THE VISION OF "ONE FAMILY UNDER GOD"

A providential moment is here, ready to be seized by the Korean people. Unlike the twentieth century, when we did not have the power to determine our fate, today we hold all the cards. If we are bold enough to dream and substantiate the destiny of our people, it will have a far-reaching impact not only on the peninsula but on the world. Western global leadership and its models of development are being seriously challenged. Some may even argue that they are in the decline. Emerging nations are open to new ideas and paradigms of development. If Korea can realize the Korean Dream, it will be in a unique position to demonstrate such a model.

During the Atlantic era, from the fifteenth to the twentieth centuries, the world was dominated by Western powers that spread across the world through the voyages of discovery and subsequent colonization. That era further developed through the ideas of the Enlightenment and the technological advances of the Industrial Revolution. Today, however, the tide of history is shifting, and we can see the emergence of the Pacific Rim era, in which Asian nations will be increasingly important.

In the context of such a historical shift, Korea is poised to play a unique leadership role. It can stand on the foundation of moral leadership by ending the last vestige of the Cold War and Asia's centuries-old struggle for self-determination outside of Western intervention. This can endear its achievements to other nations that share similar experiences of colonialism and foreign interference. A unified Korea rooted in Hongik Ingan ideals would be a model nation, with a cultural and historic affinity to the many nations that still mistrust the West. Yet, as an enlightened nation in the heart of Northeast Asia, Korea will naturally become the champion of universal human rights and freedoms in the most dynamic and complex region in the world.

Thus, Korea can be a natural bridge between East and West and can offer a uniquely Asian model of development for the world. Nations in the Southern Hemisphere already resonate with and even share Korea's traditional values and extended family structure. Our principles and values, as well as our family model, are not exclusive to ethnic Koreans but are universal in their appeal. The realization of the Korean Dream will give substance to those ideals and inspire other developing nations to pursue them as well.

When those ideals are universalized, as they are through the vision and work of the Global Peace Foundation (GPF) that I founded, they offer a solution to the most disruptive force in the post-Cold War world—namely, identity-based conflicts. The vision that guides my work for peace is that all people—regardless of their race, religion, or nationality—are members of "One Family under God."

This vision resonates with people in every region of the world. In countries wrestling with conflicts and involved in peacebuilding efforts, this message brings power to their efforts by articulating an ideal that transcends ethnic and religious differences.

Through the international work of GPF, I have seen firsthand the global appeal of universal aspirations, principles, and shared ethical values. GPF's work in Korea has become widely known, especially through our role in initiating Action for Korea United, a groundbreaking coalition of nongovernmental and civic groups established to build support for Korean unification guided by the vision of the Korean Dream.[19]

Wherever GPF works, we gather people from diverse backgrounds with wide-ranging areas of expertise to work together on the basis of a universal vision, principles, and values.

Besides Korea, GPF is active in other parts of Asia, in Africa, in North and South America, and now in Europe.

As I travel around the world for GPF, the leaders I meet from the political, religious, business, and nonprofit fields see me first and foremost as a Korean. They understand that the vision I speak about has its roots in Korea. Our Korean history and culture resonate powerfully with the vision of "One Family under God." In fact, a united homeland would be the ideal global advocate for that vision since its extended family model is the best framework for understanding the vision in an intimate and real way. Through our familial framework, one can see the power of sacrificial love centered upon the uniquely Korean culture of *han* and *jeong seong*, bridging the gulf that divides humanity. The Korean Dream embodies that unity and destiny. The realization of that dream will offer a concrete precedent of how a divided people can become one and set the moral precedent for Korean leadership in peacebuilding throughout the world.

Our innate spiritual consciousness within our extended family model has been the most enduring and fullest expression of our living history and cultural heritage. This model has been the basis for raising virtuous individuals and building virtuous families and a virtuous nation throughout our history. That is why we, as a people, loved peace and cherished humanity. As Tagore so prophetically stated, the world awaits Korea's lamp to be lit once more as one of the "lamp-bearers" of Asia. Our providential destiny is to shine the light of hope, opening the path for all people in a world mired in conflict toward the noble goal of building "One Family under God." I pray that we can rise to this challenge as a united people and give substantial meaning to our heavenly charge to live for the benefit of humanity.

The Korean Dream is more than simply an aspiration to unite our peninsula. It is about the destiny of the Korean people, rooted in our founding. That destiny is defined in the vision of Hongik Ingan and manifested in our living history. It is the source of our people's potential greatness and what could inspire us to define the future of our peninsula, the region, and the course of human history. The future is what we determine it to be. That is why now is not the time to stand idly on the sidelines as the tides of history lap against our shores. Now is the time for us to dream big. It is time for the Korean Dream.

CHAPTER 2

Children of a Divided Homeland

"A house divided against itself cannot stand."
—Abraham Lincoln

People are a product of their life experiences, the lessons they have learned, and the legacy they inherit. I am no different. As most Koreans born after 1953, I grew up as the child of a divided homeland. Both my parents were born in the North. My father was born in Chongju, and my mother in Anju, in Pyonganbuk-do. I was born in Seoul, but my ancestral home remains north of the 38th parallel. I still have relatives there, as do the millions of Koreans in the South and the diaspora. This is the shared reality of our people.

Korea still carries the wounds of division, a reminder of its inability to heal the extreme gulf created by the Cold War. After World War II, as the West and the Soviet bloc initiated their ideological struggle, Korea was the first battlefield. Although the eruption of conflict in 1950 was initiated and mostly fought by Koreans, the opposing worldviews of the free world and communism overshadowed the personal ambitions and rivalries of the local actors.[20] The Korean War set the precedent for things to come in Eastern Europe, the Caribbean, Southeast Asia, Latin America, Africa, and the Middle East.

The Soviet Union began declining in the late 1980s and finally dissolved in 1991. In a similar time span, Germany, the only other nation still divided at that point, had heeded the challenge of U.S. president Ronald Reagan to "tear down" the Berlin Wall, which stood as a metaphor for the larger divide between West and East. The German people rose to that challenge and restored their divided homeland. Trials arose along the way, but the last few decades have shown that German unification furthered Europe's prosperity and stability. Today, Germany stands as one of the main pillars of the European Union, as well as a leader in regional and world affairs.

The last century dealt bitter blows to the hope for an independent and united Korea built upon the ideals and aspirations I described in Chapter 1. In light of that history, it is now time for the Korean people to reflect upon our greatest aspiration. Will we continue to accept our divided nation, or will we walk a new, bolder path that will lead to unification? The division of the peninsula is exacting a heavy economic and security cost, but the greater cost by far for Koreans is the human tragedy.

Most Koreans today were born in a divided homeland, a bitter reality that has shaped our lives and our outlook. The risk we face today in the South is that our very prosperity, like a drug, numbs us to the moral dilemma that division brings. If we allow ourselves to be apathetic to the suffering experienced by our siblings in the North, we will be in danger of losing our Korean heritage, identity, and providential destiny.

When America grappled with the moral evil of slavery, Abraham Lincoln stated, "A house divided against itself cannot stand." He uttered those words in the context of a great internal conflict that challenged the very ideals of America's founding and the bold experiment that it represented. Likewise, unless we heal the wounds of our current division, how can we Koreans stand as a united people of destiny? This is the most important challenge that we Koreans face in the twenty-first century, and we must ask ourselves whether we will rise to meet it.

THE TWENTIETH CENTURY: THE HISTORICAL CONTEXT OF DIVISION

The story of our tribulations begins with Japan's annexation of Korea on August 22, 1910. This was the culmination of a series of treaties between Korea and Japan that began first in 1905 when Korea became a Japanese protectorate and then in 1907 when Korea forfeited its right to internal administration. These treaties were designed to wean the peninsula away from the suzerainty of China and bring it within the Japanese sphere of influence after the Sino-Japanese War of 1895.

The Joseon emperor Gojong (1897-1907) considered these treaties to be illegitimate and refused to sign them. Sadly, he had no power to resist their implementation and enforcement. The Western powers, busy with their own colonization, were complicit in the dealings and the Joseon ruler had no support from the international community except for China.

After annexation, Japanese rule became increasingly harsh, prompting the rise of independence movements in Korea, China, and elsewhere. It is not clear whether those movements began with a common aspiration other than their desire to break the yoke of Japanese rule, but the seeds of future division were being sown as different groups looked to different nations, faith traditions, and ideologies for support. Some looked to Soviet communism, some to American democracy, while others, such as Kim Gu, drew from Hongik Ingan principles to shape a unique vision of a future independent nation. The various resistance efforts galvanized popular support throughout the country and culminated in the March First Independence Movement of 1919.

After forcefully suppressing the movement for independence, Japanese authorities moderated somewhat their repressive policies for controlling the peninsula. However, during the 1930s Japan again tightened its grip, seeking to control all major private assets and erase remnants of Korean cultural identity. By 1940, the implementation of a family registry decree compelled Koreans to adopt Japanese names. In 1941, the teaching of Korean language was banned. Japanese businessmen owned and controlled major industries and capital in addition to investments. These onerous measures led about one-sixth of the population, to leave the homeland for China, the Soviet Union, Japan, the United States, and many other countries.

During World War II, millions of Koreans were forced under duress to support the Japanese war effort. Many were exploited as laborers in mines and factories in Japan, Manchuria, and on the peninsula, where a significant number died from poor and dangerous conditions. Even those who had volunteered to go to Japan fared no better. Beginning in 1944, strained with the shortages of war, Japan urgently conscripted Korean males into military service. [21]

An even more egregious crime against Koreans and others was the wholesale exploitation of women during this period. According to UN reports, tens of thousands of girls were compelled to become "comfort women," an innocuous sounding euphemism for what Korean women experienced as the brutal reality of sexual slavery. Many, who were just innocent teenagers, were coerced to have sex multiple times each day; many died from the trauma. [22]

In 1945, with the end of World War II, the Korean people emerged from the nightmare of Japanese colonial rule with a burning desire for an independent and united homeland. This was their heartfelt dream, but, tragically, it has yet to be realized. The divisions within the independence movement were amplified by geopolitical forces emerging in the wake of war.

Two zones of occupation, the Soviets in the North and Americans in the South, were set up after Japan's surrender, yet those spheres of influence hardened as the Cold War worldviews began to take shape in the vacuum of postwar geopolitics left by Japan's defeat. Domestic politics were swept along by these forces and heightened by the individual ambitions and orientations of key Korean protagonists. The dream of a united, independent sovereign state was dashed, and in 1948, two separate governments were established: in the South, the Republic of Korea, and in the North, the Democratic People's Republic of Korea.

When the attempt to unify the country finally did come, it was through force, as the Korean People's Army of the North invaded the South without warning on June 25, 1950, launching the Korean War. Although the war was fought on the peninsula, it became international in scope as China and the Soviet Union supported the North Korean forces, while the United States and fifteen other countries in the United Nations helped to defend South Korea. The war was a multidimensional tragedy.

The cost in lives and injuries was huge. Some half a million South Korean and UN troops were killed, injured, or missing, while on the North Korean and Chinese side, the total was between 1.1 million and 1.5 million. For civilians, the number was much greater—around two and a half million. Homes and infrastructure were devastated. Seoul was leveled. In some areas, half the homes and 80 percent of the infrastructure were destroyed.

We can express these costs in numbers, but there were other, more profound, less quantifiable costs. The sparks of hope for uniting our homeland and establishing a sovereign state with its own distinctive philosophy and character were extinguished.

The twentieth century marked the most brutal and devastating period of world history and Korea experienced the full force of that brutality. The unique Korean identity and sovereignty that were cultivated over five thousand years faced one challenge after another as the peninsula was annexed, liberated, and then divided along the 38th parallel.

All this happened within the span of a half century and continues to this day. The tragedy of these events is multifaceted, but the most enduring aspect is the human element: the continued torment of the Korean people from the deep wounds of division.

For these reasons, we Koreans must consider this history of suffering and division and determine whether we will allow it to continue. To me, the answer is clear. It is a moral imperative that we work, in whatever capacity we are able, to realize unification that embodies the aspirations of the 1919 independence movement and the hope of 1945, thus bringing closure to a division lingering from the last century.

THE SUFFERING OF DIVIDED FAMILIES

The human cost of the war did not end in 1953 when the shooting stopped. The war and the subsequent division of the nation have had a devastating impact on Korean lives and families. After war broke out in the winter of 1950, an estimated 650,000 refugees fled south. A greater number had come south during the three years prior to the war, often leaving family members behind in the North.

In his book *Divided Families: Fifty Years of Separation*, James Foley suggests that, toward the end of the twentieth century, between 500,000 and 750,000 families were divided between North and South. Other estimates—for example, by the South Korean Red Cross—put the number of individuals affected by family separation as much as ten times higher. [23]

Whatever the actual numbers, each one represents a human tragedy. In the chaos of the war, and the rapid advances and retreats in its opening phases, families were often separated—husbands from wives, parents from children, brothers from sisters. Sometimes, families separated, believing they would meet again in a few days. Those days turned into months, then years, which turned into several decades.

Other times, people were swept away with no chance to tell their family members what was happening to them. Both sides then lived for decades with no idea whether their relatives were alive or dead.

I have been deeply touched by the tragic stories chronicled by groups like Divided Families in the U.S. One such story is of Un Chin Lee, who is now ninety years old and lives in America. She went to visit relatives in Seoul and left her three children, ages seven, five, and two, with her mother in North Korea. While she was there, the Korean War broke out, and she never saw her children again. Every night in her dreams, she goes home looking for her children. [24]

The heartache of not knowing the fate of loved ones resonates deeply with me since it is part of my own family's history as well. My father had been imprisoned in the Hungnam labor camp on the east coast of North Korea before the outbreak of war. Hungnam was a particularly notorious forced-labor camp where prisoners were forced to fill sacks of nitrate fertilizers that burned their skin without any protective gear to wear. Many strong men died there within a few months. My father's imprisonment as a "reactionary" meant that the entire Moon family would suffer the pain of being branded in the same way. As a result, the family fortune dwindled to almost nothing. In spite of this, his mother, my grandmother, sold the last cow, so precious for a farming family, to visit her son in prison.

On her way to Hungnam, my grandmother was robbed of all her money. Undeterred, she still managed to visit my father. There, she saw her son—my father—a ragged, scarred, and emaciated prisoner. When she came back to her village, Grandmother cried inconsolably. She would never see my father again and lived with the anguish of not knowing whether her son was dead or alive.

Though my father and his fellow prisoners were liberated when UN forces landed in the area in October 1950, he had to flee south on foot toward Busan, like thousands of other refugees, without having the chance to go north to his hometown and let his family know he was alive. This weighed heavily on his heart.

I recall vividly, as if it were yesterday, my father's tearful face as he told me of his deep emotion when, in 1991, his life came full circle and he was able to visit the family he had not seen in forty years. He met his two sisters, caressing the now-wrinkled cheeks of his younger sister, who was fourteen when he last saw her, and telling her, "How old you've become." He offered his respects at the graves of his parents and visited his childhood home, things he had longed for throughout the forty long years of separation.

When my father visited his mother's grave, he had to stop his heart from breaking; it was so difficult for him to keep his tears from flowing. Rather than focusing on his personal grief, however, he reminded himself of the suffering of his twenty million countrymen in the North. His true purpose for coming to North Korea was for them.

Rather than grieving, he offered a prayer at his mother's grave. He pledged that on the day he completed his mission to obliterate the walls of division and unify Korea, he would return to visit as a son, shed his tears, and offer comfort to his parents. This was his prayer, and it is what defined my father and his sense of mission.

So many Koreans had painful experiences forced upon them by the war and the division of our homeland. Today, some elderly people in South Korea still live with the hope, however slight, that they will meet their relatives in the North at least once before they die. That hope to see their loved ones hinges on the complicated process for limited family reunions that the North Korean and South Korean governments agreed to organize.

The odds are weighted against them under the present circumstances. Before every round of reunions, families have to subject their hopes to the indifferent and often crass judgment of a lottery that will leave many of them disappointed, helpless, and disillusioned. Those who are still healthy enough to hope face long odds of ever seeing their loved ones.

Between 2000 and 2014, only nineteen rounds of family reunions have taken place, and every day more of our elderly pass away with their hopes unfulfilled. By 2014, of the 125,000 South Koreans registered to see their relatives in the North, only 17,100 individuals have been fortunate enough to attend a family reunion. The reunions are always at the mercy of political maneuverings, as in 2008, when North Korea suspended the reunions after Lee Myung-bak was elected president, or the suspension in 2010 after the North Korean shelling of the South. Still, many maintain hope. After a long suspension, another round of family reunions took place in February 2014. Some eighty-three South Korean elders, including a ninety-six-year-old woman and a ninety-three-year-old man, were able to join the tearful reunion with 178 relatives in North Korea.

Reunions are often a bittersweet experience as family members learn who is still alive and who has died. In his book, James Foley recounts the experiences of several South Koreans who took part in the reunions. One man had been separated from his wife when the Chinese entered the war and pushed south. He did not know that she had been pregnant at the time. At the reunion in 2000, he met for the first time the daughter he never knew he had and her adult son. His wife was still alive but had been hit by shrapnel in the fighting and suffered brain damage and memory loss. She had no recollection that she had ever been married. Korea's separated families are full of such heartrending experiences.[25]

For those with families in the North, every report of floods or famine brings new heartache as they agonize over the fate of their relatives. Often they have no idea if their family members are alive or dead. Even for the handful of Koreans who meet their separated family members, the joy of the reunion is mixed with the pain of renewed separation that must follow. The time together is so short, and the parting is, most often, final.

The emotional impact can be devastating. One interviewee said that he had to take mood stabilizers after the reunion because the psychological stress was so great.[26] Another interviewee, a woman, said that she cried and cried for days after her reunion with her brother. Even a year later she would burst into tears when she looked at his photograph.[27]

I saw the same painful longing in the heart of my father. After he met his sisters in his hometown, he felt an even deeper yearning to see them again. At times, he shed tears of sorrow, recalling the face of his younger sister and those he left behind in the North. The memory of those tears is a haunting reminder of the anguish that division has brought upon my family and millions of other Korean families. Healing that division is about much more than politics or economics. These human tragedies are rooted in our personal histories that continue to this day. They are so deeply felt that they cannot be buried and forgotten beneath a thin veneer of material prosperity and the mindless cacophony of modern life.

My father's memories of his hometown and his longing to return there always burned deep in his heart. I heard so many stories of his childhood growing up in Sangsa-ri—fishing in the nearby stream, collecting birds' eggs, or exploring in the mountains. His stories were so vivid that I could imagine the scenes unfolding before my eyes as if I had been there with him. As he told them, he would get a faraway look in his eyes as he reached back into his childhood and to a place and people from whom he had been wrenched away. He used to tell us that people should return to the place where they were born, just like the salmon that makes its perilous journey from the open ocean to the exact place of its birth in some unknown tributary to spawn, and then to die.

As I reflect on the memories of my father, I think of the Korean people who, like the salmon, need to return to their original hometown, the place of their birth, to begin their next cycle of life.

That place begins with the founding mythology of Dangun and is expressed throughout the history of our people in the principles of Hongik Ingan. It finds purpose and meaning in the Korean Dream, to be a unique, united, and independent sovereign nation that can realize our providential destiny to serve and "benefit all of humanity." In order for us to create new life, we need to return to the place of our birth and from there find the inspiration to build a new future.

The North-South division, though, stands in the way. This division of our homeland has not only caused suffering to families, terrible though that is. It has damaged our identity as Koreans and thwarted our hopes of building an ideal, independent, and united nation that could fulfill our providential destiny. In short, it has suffocated our Korean Dream.

My Family Legacy

From an early age, I learned from my father's example and life that Korea's sad circumstances should not define the future of the Korean people. After walking from Hungnam prison to the South, carrying a fellow inmate on his back and on a bicycle, my father built a tiny home of rocks and mud on a hilltop in the outskirts of Busan. It had a packed earthen floor and a roof made of discarded ration boxes from a nearby U.S. Army base. I keep a small, faded, black-and-white photograph of him standing in front of that hut. I do not want to forget where our family began after the war.

Although my father's circumstances were humble, like those of most war refugees who gathered around the port city of Busan during the height of the Korean conflict in 1950, a great dream burned in his heart. On his journey south from Hungnam, he swore to himself and to God that he would devote his life to uniting his divided homeland. More than that, he committed himself to working for world peace and realizing the destiny of the Korean people. Through his own personal yearning to return to his hometown, he came to understand that God also longed for his true home, where he could dwell peacefully with humanity in a world free of war, divisions, and hatred.

The horrors of his incarceration in the North and the ideological system that justified atrocities committed against humanity made it clear to him that communism was the greatest obstacle to achieving the ideal of a peaceful world. The root of the problem was that communism denies God. Denying God meant denying the human spirit, and once the spiritual dimension of human life is removed, there is no foundation for absolute truths that are the basis of human dignity, ethical principles, and fundamental human rights and freedoms. Everything is reduced to matter, including human beings.

In a communist system, people are just another material instrument that can be used and discarded for the purposes of the state. That is why communist regimes and movements have inflicted so many atrocities and crimes against humanity. Sadly, although communism has lost its global appeal, the people of North Korea are still subject to the inhuman realities of a dictatorial communist state.[28]

My father also understood that communism could not be dealt with simply by military force. The falsehood of its ideology had to be exposed. My father launched a worldwide movement to accomplish this. He is widely known as an anticommunist champion, but, strictly speaking, this is not accurate. He wanted not simply to oppose communism but to defeat its ideology through a principled moral vision that recognizes that human rights and freedoms are rooted in the Creator God.

Although my family lived in America, the division of Korea and its underlying ideological conflict directly affected my family. Because of my father's global challenge to communist ideology, he became a target of vicious attacks from the Soviet Union, North Korea, and China, as well as leftist groups in Korea, Japan, and the United States. Young members of my father's Victory over Communism movement effectively debated with leftist student groups on campuses in these countries.

The attacks were not confined to words. At times, my father's life was in danger as a result of his anticommunist activities. In 1988, the police stopped a car on the New Jersey Turnpike driven by a young Japanese man carrying a firearm, bomb-making equipment, and the address of our family home. He turned out to be a member of the Japanese Red Army, a radical and violent communist group with close ties to North Korea, even having an office in Pyongyang. My father was a marked man, and my family was in the cross fire. As a result, I grew up with security guards as a constant presence since the threat of kidnapping or assassination was an ever-present possibility.

I went to school in America and studied history at Columbia University. Through my studies, I came to understand the Western perspective on the modern world. In particular, I learned about America's founding and the importance of the Founding Fathers' appeal to fundamental principles and values as the basis for creating a new nation. I realized that these principles are applicable not only in the American context but are universal. They can be applied to all humanity and thus can be the foundation for guaranteeing human rights and freedoms everywhere. This was the key to creating the world of which my father dreamed.

These studies greatly enriched my perspective. Still, I remain a son of Korea tied irrevocably to its history and destiny through my own family history. In America, I am often asked where I am from. Without hesitation, I always reply, "I am Korean." Although I am an American citizen, I feel immense pride at Korea's achievements in the global arena and shout with joy when Korean athletes win gold medals or set new records.

Yet, as a Korean in America, I am often reminded of the painful current state of our homeland. People who ask me where I am from often then ask, "Which Korea? North or South?" I never know how to reply. I was born in the South, and my parents were born in the North. Are we one family with two different homelands? Such moments are sharp reminders that there are so many Koreans like me who are children of a divided homeland.

This was a reality I could never forget, despite growing up in America. At Columbia, I wrote my honor's thesis on the interwar years in Korea, the period from the end of World War II in 1945 to the start of the Korean War in 1950. Japan's defeat ended colonial rule and brought tremendous hope for the establishment of a new, independent country. Instead, in 1950, Kim Il-sung tried to unify the country by force, which resulted in a split—politically, ideologically, militarily, and economically—that was as severe and absolute as any division in world history. I wanted to understand how such events had moved from the hopes of 1945 to the conflict and subsequent separation of 1950.

Before I went to college, I devoted several years to training as an equestrian. I represented Korea in show jumping at the 1988 Olympics in Seoul and the 1992 Olympics in Barcelona. The Seoul Games were particularly significant beyond the sporting competition. It was the first time since 1976 that the United States and the Soviet Union had participated together in the Olympics. The Soviet Union and its allies had boycotted the 1984 Games in Los Angeles, and the United States had boycotted the 1980 Games in Moscow. The Olympics, intended to be the symbol of a global brotherhood of sports that transcends national and ideological divisions, had become yet another arena of conflict in the Cold War.

My father believed that the Seoul Olympics would mark an important historical turning point. For the first time in twelve years, representatives from the leading countries in the democratic and communist worlds would compete together, and they would do so in Seoul. It was a moment of great significance for Korea and the world. As a result, my father believed that the events in Seoul would herald the end of the Cold War, and that this had to happen before Korean unification could become a real possibility. I rode in those Games with immense pride to be wearing the *Taeguk-gi*, the Korean National flag, on my uniform with a sense of destiny that history was about to change.

Remarkably, shortly after the end of the Seoul Olympics, Mikhail Gorbachev, then general secretary of the Communist Party, became head of state in the Soviet Union and launched the policies of perestroika and glasnost that opened up the Soviet economy and society. These policies swiftly led to the collapse of the Soviet empire, the breakup of the Soviet Union, and the end of the Cold War.

My father did not hate communists, but he hated the godless ideology that had led to the suffering and death of so many millions. As change came to the Soviet Union, he urged the country to replace atheism with a worldview that placed God at its center. To that end, he organized a conference in Moscow in April 1990 during the course of which he met with Gorbachev and urged him to abandon materialism, put God at the center of every endeavor going forward, and institute freedom of religion.

The Soviet press recognized how remarkable the meeting was and gave it extensive coverage. *Moscow News* wrote that my father had been "the most brilliant anti-communist and the No. 1 enemy of the state," saying it was "time to reconcile."[29] As a result of the meeting, dozens of Soviet legislators and officials came to the United States on exchange visits to learn how their counterparts operated in a democratic society. Thousands of Soviet students also came to learn about American culture and, in particular, the principles that underlay American freedom.

If Soviet officials and media were shocked to see the man they designated the "No. 1 enemy of the state" reaching out to them, so were some people in Korea and the West. They saw my father only as an anticommunist in political terms without understanding his deeper spiritual philosophy. In fact, my father's meeting with Gorbachev was completely consistent with his principles. He understood that peace can come only through the power of true love—a selfless, sacrificial love that even embraces one's enemy. Through this power of love, my father befriended his critics and even enemies; yet, such friendship must stand upon a foundation of truth. Truth is what my father spoke to everyone, be they humble workers or world leaders.

The people who were shocked at my father's meeting with Gorbachev were even more shocked when he traveled, via China, to Pyongyang in December 1991 and there met with Kim Il-sung. Given their history, such a journey was hard to imagine. They had diametrically opposed ideologies, and Kim Il-sung had previously attempted to have my father killed. To describe this visit as "bold" is a huge understatement. There was no guarantee that my father would ever return, but his commitment to resolving the division of Korea was absolute and part of the promise he had made to God. With the end of the Cold War, he saw the opportunity to encourage North Korea to take a new direction. He seized that opportunity with no thought for his own safety.

Many Koreans, especially those from the older generation, have told me that my father was truly the pioneer of opening relations between the North and South.[30] I have heard stories of my father addressing the North Korean leadership at Mansudae, their National Assembly. According to all accounts, he spoke for two hours with force and dignity, striking the lectern at times with his fist for emphasis. He told them that, for the future good of the nation, they should abandon Juche ideology and embrace the sovereignty of God.

This was not diplomatic language, but my father spoke with complete conviction because he knew that only through such a change could those leaders save the nation. After such a speech, nobody, except my father, expected that he would be able to meet Kim Il-sung. Yet, on December 6, 1991, he was invited to Kim's official residence in Hamhung for the meeting that supposedly would never take place.

Upon seeing Kim Il-sung, my father did not bow formally or shake hands politely but embraced Kim Il-sung like a long-lost brother. At the same time, he repeated the message he had given at the National Assembly and urged Kim to give up his nuclear project and to allow in international inspectors. He also asked Kim to begin a process of peaceful unification with the simple, human step of allowing family reunions.

Later, during an intimate moment, my father told me that this meeting had been the hardest thing he had ever done in his life. It was not concern for his own safety that he wrestled with but the challenge of embracing, without reservation, a man who had not only plotted against my father's life but had vested untold suffering on the Korean people and nation. Yet, he told me he felt compelled by God to swallow his personal feelings in order to open a door into North Korea.

Through his absolute conviction and complete commitment to this mission, my father possessed a moral authority that moved Kim Il-sung in a way that military force or economic inducements never could. Some time ago, in Korea, I met Congressman Cho Myung-chul, the first defector from North Korea to become a member of the National Assembly. I was surprised to learn from him that his father, who had been a government minister in North Korea, had been present at the meeting between my father and Kim Il-sung. His father told him that Kim had been deeply moved by my father and had opened his heart to him. Kim told his staff afterward that Reverend Moon was the only person outside North Korea whom he could trust.

These experiences are my inheritance. My father's life, my memories of him, the things he spoke to me about in private moments, have all left an indelible imprint on my life. As his eldest living son, I am compelled to carry on his legacy, a legacy that is inextricably tied to the destiny of the Korean people and the Korean nation. For me, that destiny lies with a unified Korea that lives up to its providential destiny.

THE APATHY OF THE SOUTH

To me, a Korean living abroad, with my particular family history, unification seems like a natural and necessary goal. It would heal the wounds suffered by the Korean people as a result of our unnatural division. From a geopolitical perspective, unification would solve so many problems related to prosperity and development and to peace and security.

As a result, I assumed that all Koreans in the South yearned for unification and were actively pursuing it. So I was surprised by the responses I received on the subject from key leaders in Korea. They were quite different from what I expected.

Although the elder generation empathized with my concerns, the younger leaders would remind me that most Koreans, especially the young, are indifferent toward unification. Over the past ten years, a growing number state that they do not want unification, while a vast majority of students are apathetic. Only a small minority see it as a national priority.

According to a *Chosun Ilbo* survey, in 1994, 40.9 percent wanted unification. Twenty years later, that number had dropped by half to 19.9 percent of Koreans. On the other hand, in 1994, only 7 percent wanted to maintain the status quo, but by 2014, that number had risen to 16.8 percent. The youth seem less interested in unification. For those in their twenties, one in four say that they want to maintain the status quo and 35 percent say they are not interested in unity at all.[31]

I guess there are some reasons for this outlook, but I still do not understand it. As an observer coming from abroad, I wonder if South Koreans have become so accustomed to living with the division that they have grown numb to its negative effects. Are they living in denial? Has the possibility of war on the peninsula become so familiar that we forgot its potentially devastating consequences? It seems as if the fear of those consequences has been lost to the younger generations, whose experiences are far removed from the tragic effects of the Korean War.

Yet, this reality imposes a daily cost on the current generation and, if it is not resolved, it will affect future generations. Just think about South Korea's mandatory military service that takes young men away from their homes, their studies, and their careers, all to face their northern cousins across an artificial border with the ever-present possibility of civil war. This affects even the men in the Korean diaspora, who remain eligible for military service up to the age of forty. Huge amounts of resources are spent on the defense of the South that could be more productively invested elsewhere if the threat from the North no longer existed. These expenses are even more unconscionable when one considers that these are not costs to protect the South from a foreign enemy but from our own people, our own relatives across the 38th parallel.

North Korea may be doomed to lose a "hot" war with the South, but who can say that such a war will not happen, given the North's belligerence and instability? What will happen to South Korea's prosperity if, in such uncertain circumstances, conflict arises? How much damage will the North inflict before it is defeated? South Korea today has the fourteenth-largest economy in the world.[32] Where will it rank after a war? The truth is that South Koreans have the most to lose in the event of an armed conflict.

It is clearly in South Korea's material and political interests to safeguard its prosperity from the threat of conflict precipitated by the growing unpredictability in the North. The most effective way to do that is through the wholehearted pursuit of peaceful unification as an urgent national goal.

That pursuit should be rooted in the Korean Dream and draw upon the very best of our ethical and cultural traditions. Even though I grew up in America, my parents faithfully upheld the traditional Korean family model in our household. As an adult, I learned from other Koreans mostly living in Korea that my outlook and customs reflected the perspectives of my parents' generation. In other words, I had been following the "old ways."

Sadly, those traditions are rapidly being abandoned in Korea without their value even being properly understood. In particular, our family values, which have been the cornerstone of a cooperative society, are eroding as we speak. Modern Seoul presents a stark contrast to my father's village, where anyone passing by the family home would be invited in for a meal.

After the war, my parents' generation endured incredible suffering and hardship to build the country up from one of the poorest in the world. They had a vision for the future that drove them on in the midst of misery. Today's generation, however, has become disconnected from the sacrifice of the previous generation that made Korea what it is today. That is a recipe for decline and decadence. A nation can only grow in greatness if each new generation is prepared to make sacrifices for a greater purpose.

Korean identity is molded in the Korean family. Filial piety, together with *han* and *jeong seong*, lies at its core, binding the generations together. It is not only personal in nature between parents and children. A patriotic dimension to it also calls upon today's rising generation to honor the sacrifice of the previous generation and build something noble for the nation. What dream will inspire this generation? How can they lift up Korea to fulfill its providential destiny? My contention is that unification is the great challenge that will define this generation.

Every generation faces a defining moment when it can make its mark for posterity or suffer the dire consequences of an opportunity lost. We Koreans today are standing upon the sacrifice, blood, and tears of the generation before us who seized their moment and were victorious. Today, you and I drink the rich nectar of their sacrifice in a modern, prosperous, and free nation. We owe them so much. Yet, if we have become blind to the magnitude of their toil, how will we be able to recognize the value of the life we enjoy today? Even more sadly, how will we be able to recognize the defining moment of our age when it comes calling? Will we be able to meet that challenge and pass forward an even greater benefit to future generations? The values we choose will determine our path.

THE HUMAN TRAGEDY OF THE NORTH

A powerful moral dimension also exists to the argument for unification. The human cost imposed by the division of the Korean peninsula is not just being borne by the rapidly dwindling number of elderly members of separated families. A terrible crime is being inflicted today upon millions of ordinary people condemned to live in North Korea.

The North is not an area of darkness simply due to the lack of electricity. It has also been an informational black hole from which little precise knowledge emerged of either the mysterious political process or the living conditions of the people. However, the picture has been changing as we learn more from the stories of the 26,000 defectors currently living in the South and various aid and other civic organizations that have gained greater, though uncertain, access to the North.[33]

A mosaic is emerging of life in North Korea; much of the data about the North has been compiled and published by the UN Commission of Inquiry on Human Rights in North Korea, which issued its report in February 2014.[34] The report is unprecedented in its scope, and through it, we know much more about the horrific living conditions for most North Koreans today. I read with horror as the report detailed crimes against humanity and "unspeakable atrocities" resulting from "policies established at the highest levels of state."[35]

The UN Commission called for a global moral response, stating, "The international community must accept its responsibility to protect the people of the Democratic People's Republic of Korea from crimes against humanity, because the Government of the DPRK has manifestly failed to do so."[36]

Much of the very detailed evidence in the report came from courageous North Korean defectors. It is a sad commentary on South Korean attitudes today that many of these defectors face isolation and discrimination as they struggle to adapt to life in a modern industrialized state. In the intensely competitive South, defectors are often regarded as a burden with no useful skills, or as representatives of an enemy nation.[37] They are resented if they receive preferential admission to good universities. Many have rough experiences with coworkers in their first jobs and quit. They learn to keep quiet in subsequent jobs about being North Korean.

I started an organization in Seoul to work with defectors and to help them make the adjustment to life in the South. I have met and spoken with a number of them. One woman in her mid-thirties told me that she had defected from North Korea after her husband died and the hardships of life became too much to bear. Unfortunately, she could not bring her only son with her. She thought she would be able to bring him out later, but security on the border with China had become too tight for a child to slip through. Although life in South Korea was tough for her, the greatest pain by far, she told me with tears in her eyes, was being separated from her child.

North Korean defectors have deep scars and unresolved wounds that are difficult for them to address in the South. They find it hard to trust and even to speak out in public. My organization offers them help to navigate these situations.

Life in the North Korean countryside is hard to imagine for someone living in Seoul. Perhaps many South Koreans do not even want to know. From all accounts, hunger is an ever-present specter haunting the lives of those in the North. When a severe famine hit the country between 1994 and 1998, the government food distribution system broke down,[38] leaving many with no source of food. At least a million people are thought to have died, with some estimates as high as three million.[39] At that time, very little precise information could be obtained from North Korea.

The food distribution system never recovered, so malnutrition and chronic hunger plague the land. Out of the North Korean population of twenty-four million people, two-thirds do not know where their next meal is coming from, according to an Assessment Capacities Report.[40] Twenty-eight percent of children under five years of age are believed to be undernourished. Tragically, when children are undernourished at an early age, there is a high incidence of permanent brain damage. Even if they are well-fed later in life, chances are that the damage has already been done.[41]

Many defectors who end up in South Korea originally crossed into China simply in search of food for themselves and their families. Jinhye Jo (a pseudonym) is twenty-five, now lives in America, and has testified before the U.S. Congress about North Korean human rights abuses.[42] In 1998, her father crossed the border to China in search of food but was then captured, imprisoned, and tortured for ten days. Her mother was also badly beaten for being the wife of such a "criminal." Her injuries were so severe that she could not get up from her bed for two months. Jo herself was arrested in China and repatriated four times between 2002 and 2006, surviving the hunger, filth, and casual brutality of guards in North Korean prisons.

As a girl of fourteen, she often asked why she had been born female and in the North. She said that about 80 percent of North Korean women aged sixteen and over who crossed into China ended up being sold by traffickers into forced marriage with elderly or handicapped Chinese men, or into prostitution. Prices ranged from $300 to over $4,700. Some traffickers pose as guides to help women cross the border into China and then sell them.

Others wait on the Chinese side, even using tracker dogs, to abduct women crossing over. These women are helpless in China. They have no identification, and if they are caught by the Chinese police, they are returned to North Korea and face imprisonment. Jo was in prison with women sent back to North Korea who were impregnated by Chinese men and then subjected to the most primitive, forced abortions.[43]

Children in North Korea have to grow up quickly. One defector, using the name "Mr. Park," told journalist Shako Liu from Connecticut of the police closing businesses and schools and forcing everyone to attend public executions. He was taken with his class to several executions of men accused of stealing state-owned farm animals. "It was all I knew," he said.[44]

Orphans have a particularly harsh time. Yoon Hee, a nineteen-year-old whose story was told on CNN, was abandoned by her mother when she was eight. For the next ten years, she was homeless and lived on the street, begging or working for a little food. One day, she opened the door of a family she knew, and all of them were dead of starvation.[45] "Joseph" was another orphan who was abandoned at the tender age of thirteen and lived the same life as Yoon Hee. "Hope kept me alive," he said. "I don't mean big, grand hope; I mean the kind of hope that the next trash can had bread, even though it usually didn't."[46]

Adult defectors who successfully found their freedom outside of the North's brutal regime suffer other types of pain. Many feel tremendous guilt: for the family they left behind, some for leaving without telling their relatives, many for eating good food while knowing the rest of their family is still starving.

Reflecting on the defectors' experiences, one of them, Lee Hyeon-seo, said, "Everybody dreams, of course, but does anybody want to dream more than the people of North Korea? Their lives are spent inside a virtual prison, without knowing about the truth or human rights."[47] Stories like these are repeated hundreds of thousands of times. Faced with human dramas on this scale, imposed on ordinary people who have little say in their own fate, South Koreans cannot turn away and bury their heads in the sand.

After the genocide in Rwanda in 1994, there was tremendous soul-searching at the United Nations and in the United States about what more could have been done to stop the killings. And yet, in Syria, as of May 2014, the death toll in the civil war had reached 160,000. The U.S. government faces strong pressure from many of its citizens and human rights groups to do more to prevent further killing. Americans feel a moral burden to do something to help the victims of injustice in places like Rwanda and Syria, even though they are a different people in distant countries. How much more should South Koreans feel that it is a moral imperative to bring an end to the injustices being heaped upon our North Korean cousins, who are the same race, speak the same language, and share the same history and culture as we do?

What is it that will allow the people of the North and South to relate to each other and find a common identity? We know that North Korean defectors often feel unwelcome in the South and struggle to adapt to life there. A common bond has to be forged out of something more fundamental than the political and ideological quarrels that marked the division of the past sixty-five years. There has to be a Third Way that can rise above the conflicting systems of right and left by identifying the fundamental aspirations, principles, and values rooted in our common past that should define our future. That is the Korean Dream, the shared history and culture rooted in the philosophy of Hongik Ingan and whose application will allow the original value of all human beings to be respected and to flourish.

Many North Korean defectors, due to their past history and circumstances, are extremely distrustful of other people. Still, the stories of many defectors and the recent reunions reveal that familial tradition and filial piety are still very much alive in the heart of many North Koreans.

In the reunions, families from North and South updated and exchanged family trees. One participant from the North, as an elder son, said that he would perform *jesa,* or ancestral rites, for his parents who had died in the South. He said it had always bothered him that this responsibility had fallen to his elder sister who lived with their parents up until then. Another apologized to his relatives in the South for failing in his duties as an elder brother as he had been absent when their mother died and his siblings got married.

Understandably, the bonds of heart among family members have grown deeper even with the passage of decades of separation, despite the differences of political systems and lifestyles. A North Korean poet told his brother at their family reunion, "Although our ideologies are different, are our tears and warm blood not the same when we embrace?"[48]

A South Korean participant, worried about his brother who now lived alone in the North, said, "Our hopes are that unification will come quickly so that our brother can come and stay in our house and I can go to his house to stay there. How wonderful that would be!"[49]

These stories show the common bond of heart among the Korean people that is based on our shared historic cultural heritage that transcends any ideological or cultural divide. This offers a foundation upon which to realize unification and build the Korean Dream. The inhumane conditions endured by most North Koreans make it a moral imperative to unite. Without unification, the repressive regime of Kim Jong-un will remain a threat to its own people, the region, and the world.

THE KOREAN DIASPORA: CONNECTING KOREA TO THE WORLD

Although I was born in Korea, I have lived most of my life in the United States, so I am part of the diaspora. There are almost seven million of us spread across the world, mostly in the United States, China, and Japan.[50] Koreans in the diaspora suffer from divided families the same as Koreans on the peninsula. We are affected by and engaged in the fate of a divided homeland and often can bring a broader perspective to meeting the challenge of unification. I believe that the diaspora is destined to play an essential role in gathering support and building awareness on a global stage for the unity of the Korean people.

The Korean diaspora is unique in many respects. As globalization has progressed, so have Koreans spread out across the world. Korea's Ministry of Foreign Affairs and Trade in 2013 estimated that Koreans were living in 160 different countries. The major concentrations were in China, with 2.57 million; the United States, with 2.09 million; and Japan, with 893,000.[51] But Koreans went everywhere with an enterprising mind-set. They managed to adapt to local conditions enough to be able to operate effectively while also maintaining their distinctive community identity.

Korea is not a large country, and the overseas populations of Chinese or Indians is much larger. But, remarkably, the proportion of all Koreans, including North and South, who are overseas, is 9 percent, a higher ratio than the proportion of Chinese and Indians. From the 1990s, the focus of emigration shifted from the United States, with increasing numbers of Koreans going to China and countries in the developing world. Koreans seem to have an impulse to reach out to the world, and they make their mark in the countries where they settle.

Koreans in the United States, for example, graduate from college at nearly twice the rate of the average American.[52] Koreans form part of the larger Asian-American demographic, which reports incomes 70 percent higher than the American average according to a 2012 Pew Research Center Study.[53] As highly educated and well-off citizens, Korean Americans are in an excellent position to influence public opinion and their legislators on Korean issues. This influence is likely to be magnified since Koreans in America are concentrated in strong, well-networked communities within metropolitan areas. Koreans in Palisades Park, in Bergen County, New

Jersey, for example, made up a reported 44 percent of the population there in 2010.[54]

Diaspora Koreans are well-placed to build up networks of support in their host countries for unification. It is significant that the three largest diaspora communities are in the three countries—China, the United States, and Japan—whose relationships with Korea will be the most important for the future of the peninsula. Meanwhile, the smaller Korean communities establishing themselves in the developing world will become increasingly important as Korea establishes a global leadership role.

Through figures such as former United Nations Secretary-General Ban Ki-moon and World Bank President Dr. Jim Yong Kim, himself a member of the diaspora, Koreans are demonstrating their ability to exercise responsibility on the world stage.

Koreans in the diaspora often live in strong communities with a much keener appreciation of Korean identity since they have to maintain it while living in a different culture with different values. Many maintain a strong sense of patriotic connection with Korea and the desire to do something for the future of the peninsula and especially for the people of North Korea. Faith is often the spark for the spiritual motivation that leads diaspora Koreans to work for human rights or provide humanitarian aid to North Koreans. While young Koreans born outside Korea may not experience the more formal Confucian aspects of Korean tradition, they do seem to inherit a connection of heart.

Across the world, second- and third-generation Koreans in the diaspora are mobilizing themselves to help separated families and their fellow Koreans suffering in the North. My research led me to some inspiring personal stories. Mike Kim, for example, a second-generation Korean American from Chicago, was running a successful investment business but gave it up to satisfy a growing conviction that he had to do something for North Korean refugees. He spent four years in China near the border helping refugees undertake the six-thousand-mile journey to Southeast Asia, escorted by committed volunteers, along what is known as the "Underground Railroad" to seek asylum in a South Korean embassy.

He wrote about his experiences and what he learned in his moving book, *Escaping North Korea: Defiance and Hope in the World's Most Repressive Country.*[55]

Kim said that, apart from the courage of the refugees, what most impressed him was the great variety of Koreans working at the border and on the Railroad. The list is impressive. There were Koreans from Australia, Canada, China, Great Britain, Japan, Kazakhstan, New Zealand, Russia, Tajikistan, the United States, and Uzbekistan, as well as North Korea and South Korea. They were united by a common purpose: to help those who share their same ethnicity and culture. To them, Koreans are one people bound together by a five-thousand-year-long historic cultural heritage that transcends politics and ideology.

These Koreans from all over the world recognize that separated families and the plight of ordinary North Koreans are both pressing moral issues and human tragedies. Filmmaker Jason Ahn, a third-generation Korean American, speaking about the film *Divided Families*, said, "More than my personal story and the shared experience of tragedy among this generation, I will say that from a moral and ethical perspective [facilitating reunions] is the right thing to do."[56]

Other Koreans of the first generation now living abroad are actively engaged in bringing help to North Korea. These are men such as Dr. James Kim (Kim Chin-kyung), who founded the Pyongyang University of Science and Technology, the first private university in North Korea; and Reverend George Rhee, whose Love North Korean Children charity is based in London and builds bakeries to feed children in the North.

In addition to aiding the plight of North Korean refugees and divided families, diaspora communities around the globe will be essential for the future of Korea through building awareness and support for unification in their respective adopted communities and nations. We already have the historical example of the impact that Koreans overseas made on the homeland with the Korean independence movement in the early twentieth century. Key leaders who became part of the Provisional Government of the Republic of Korea, set up in Shanghai in 1919 after the March First

Movement, spent significant time abroad. Kim Gu was in Shanghai for much of the colonial period. Syngman Rhee studied in the United States and lobbied for U.S. recognition of the Provisional Government. Ahn Chung-ho, also known by his pen name Dosan, was a leader of the Korean-American community based in San Francisco, as well as the founder of the Shinminhoe, one of the leading organizations in Korea that worked against Japanese occupation.

The global footprint of the diaspora can become an invaluable resource for unity and building international support. Unlike the twentieth century, when sentiments in the West were unfavorable to the plight of our people, today, through the diaspora, Korea has valuable allies on every continent for its bid to unify the peninsula; this issue is not simply for those living in the homeland but all Koreans around the world. It is our collective moral imperative.

THE KOREAN DREAM: BUILDING A CONSENSUS TO HEAL A DIVIDED PEOPLE

The twentieth century thwarted the dreams of the Korean people to live in an independent and unified homeland in the harshest way imaginable. Korea became a house divided and remains so today. As a divided nation, we are still paying the price in terms of security threats and lost economic opportunities, but most of all in human suffering. The situation of the Korean people in the North is a challenge to the moral conscience of the world as the UN Commission report states. But, most of all, it is a challenge to the moral conscience of Koreans in the South and in the diaspora.

Do we want to remain known as the last nation still divided from the Cold War era? The eyes of the world will be upon us, awaiting our response. If we can rise to the challenge, we will be able to move beyond the troubled history of the twentieth century and realize Korea's longed-for destiny.

To achieve this goal, we have to create a consensus among Koreans in the South and the diaspora on the principles and moral vision that will form the foundation for a unified Korean people to live together. Unification should become a national priority for South Korea, not just at the government level, but engaging all Korean citizens, civic organizations, and NGOs. It is important to unite disparate factions within South Korea in order to achieve unification and not repeat the divisions within the Korean independence movement that existed during Japanese colonial rule or after World War II.

Still more recently, after my father pioneered an opening to the North through his meeting with Kim Il-sung, we saw the same lack of a national consensus on how to build upon that opportunity. Many South Korean companies and organizations hurried to exploit these changes in relations with the North but without coordination and each in pursuit of their particular interests. No common guiding vision and clear objective existed in terms of what they wanted to accomplish from that engagement.

For ten years, from 1998 to 2008, President Kim Dae-jung and his successor, President Roh Moo-hyun, pursued the Sunshine Policy with the North, seeking to improve relations and induce Pyongyang to change its nuclear and economic policies. It was well-intentioned, but the execution was poorly conceived, and the results were the opposite of what was desired.[57]

Over those ten years, Seoul transferred some $7.4 billion in aid and support to Pyongyang, according to former foreign minister Han Sung-joo.[58] When one includes the further transfer of funds by private businesses, religious organizations, and NGOs, the total amount of money that flowed to the North is even greater. The high point in terms of public relations was the summit between Kim Dae-jung and Kim Jong-il in Pyongyang in June 2000. It was later revealed that $500 million had been paid secretly to Pyongyang beforehand to enable the summit to take place, much of it channeled through the Hyundai Corporation.[59] This transfer of money was the real interest of Pyongyang in the policy.

Ever since the end of the Cold War, Pyongyang has been cash-starved and searching for sources of revenue to replace the discontinued Soviet subsidies. Supporters of the Sunshine Policy compared it to West

Germany's *Ostpolitik* toward East Germany, some even describing it as a *Nordpolitik*.[60] But there were no conditions or controls attached to the aid from South Korea, and the North could use it as it wished. Pyongyang made clear from the start that it would only accept aid on its own terms when it rejected Seoul's proposal to establish a "reunion zone" near the DMZ for divided families. Its actions during the period appear totally unaffected by the Sunshine Policy. In 2003, North Korea withdrew from the Nuclear Non-Proliferation Treaty. In 2006, it conducted its first nuclear test despite having agreed to denuclearize the previous year at the Six-Party Talks.

In effect, North Korea received an unmonitored revenue stream from the South as a result of the Sunshine Policy and offered nothing of substance in return. Whether aid from the South was used directly for the nuclear program is beside the point. North Korea gained support and breathing space during which it could solidify the military-first policy and develop its nuclear and missile programs while Seoul imagined it was making progress toward peace. The lesson from this experience is that engagement must be founded on a clear, overarching vision and pursued through a different strategy in the future.

The importance of the Korean Dream is that it provides the vision that was lacking in the past. On that basis, practical actions can follow that are directed toward a common purpose. My intention in establishing the Action for Korea United coalition in 2012, with nearly 400 civic organizations representing a broad range of political and religious views, was to create a foundation for consensus that can lead to a united approach based upon the Korean Dream. By 2016, Action for Korea United had expanded to almost 1,000 organizations.

That consensus must also reach and speak to the hearts of the people in the North through civil society and NGO initiatives. In 2006, Service for Peace, an NGO that I founded, pioneered exactly this type of initiative through a groundbreaking project in North Korea in the Kumgang Mountain area. The project involved installing more efficient boilers for underfloor heating in North Korean homes, and later the construction of housing.

What made the project unique were the teams of South Korean and international volunteers who came to North Korea to work on the project. This was the first time the North Korean government had ever allowed direct people-to-people contact with North Korean citizens. The volunteers ranged from high school students to pensioners and included officials from Suwon City. Altogether, 2,000 boilers were installed and 150 new houses were built before the project was stopped in 2010 when North-South relations again deteriorated. However, the project remains a model that is scalable and could be resumed at any time.

How we prepare the ground for unification is as important as reaching the final goal. Unification that embodies Korea's historic destiny cannot be achieved by force. It must be built upon a consensus vision of the future among Koreans in the South that can then be extended to Koreans living in the North. Sharing the Korean Dream, reinforced by people-to-people initiatives and aid projects, offers the best prospect of achieving this goal and avoiding conflict. In this way, we Koreans can take control of our own destiny.

We Koreans—across the whole peninsula and throughout the diaspora—are an extended family. That sense of family bond is what motivates those Koreans in the diaspora and in the South to work to help their separated brethren in the North. All the values that have formed our unique identity as Koreans throughout history have been nurtured within the Korean family, which is why it is our most precious cultural heritage.

A divided family cannot endure but will gradually lose the spirit that once made it strong. This is the case with Korea. If we do not take up the challenge to heal the wounds of division and make the Korean family whole, we will be turning our backs on those virtues and qualities that defined our identity as Koreans. We will start to lose our cultural heritage and, with it, the opportunity to substantiate the providential destiny that our founding vision in Hongik Ingan is calling us to fulfill.

Despite the challenges, I do not believe that our current generation will abandon our moral imperative and allow this to happen. We are a resourceful people who do not remain passive in the face of difficult circumstances. The response to the massive oil spill off Daesan in 2007 is a case in point. People did not leave the cleanup to the government, but rolled up their sleeves and got their hands dirty. Within a month, millions of volunteers had come and worked at the cleanup site, an astonishing response.[61] This is the type of response that we, as the Korean people, can muster if we earnestly choose to do so.

It represents the true enduring spirit of our people. All it needs is the right motivation and sense of purpose. That is why our history and the aspiration within Hongik Ingan is so important. It has the power to awaken the collective consciousness of a historically united people, to heal the wounds of our division so that our "house" can indeed stand and we can, finally, realize our historic destiny. All we need is a unifying vision; it is the Korean Dream. If we have the conviction to pursue it wholeheartedly, then we will correct the failures of our past and offer a new tomorrow to future generations of Koreans, Asians, and the people of the world.

This is a lofty vision but a timely one. The political and economic circumstances of the Korean peninsula may appear daunting at first sight but make it ripe for change. The region's geopolitical situation is already shifting in a way that favors a movement for unification as never before. I explore these topics in the next chapter.

CHAPTER 3

The Opportunities and Challenges for Unification

"A pessimist sees the difficulty in every opportunity;
an optimist sees the opportunity in every difficulty."
–WINSTON CHURCHILL

G reat human accomplishments arise in response to great challenges.
They do not come easily. In any worthwhile human endeavor there
is always risk and uncertainty, and plenty of both are on the Korean
peninsula today. I outlined the terrible human cost of division in the
previous chapter and the moral challenge it poses to the conscience of
Koreans everywhere—and to the world.

However, these are not the only costs imposed by the ongoing
division of the peninsula. The political and economic instability of the
North presents a continuing security threat to the South. Missile tests and
artillery bombardments in early 2014 were a chilling reminder of the ever-

present risk of conflict. Because of the nuclear dimension of the North's security threat, that risk is spread to the whole Northeast Asia region, and even globally.

On the economic front, North Korea is a disaster, resulting in severe economic constraints on the South and threatening the future prosperity of the entire region. It is a barrier to free trade and a drag on the economic vitality of the region as a whole. On the other hand, if closer integration was possible, the entire region would be stimulated. These circumstances are a result of geopolitical relationships from the Cold War era and are out of touch with the changing realities of today's world.

The growing indifference among South Koreans, especially the young, to the issue of unification has made the situation worse. This apathy may result from a sense that ordinary citizens can do nothing about these circumstances. So, for them, the response to the security threat is to resign themselves to compulsory military service, though mostly without enthusiasm, perhaps support the building of an antimissile system, and hope for the best. They only see the challenges that the integration of the peninsula will bring and not the opportunities, which compounds this apathy. They draw negative conclusions from the process of German unification, even though the overall result of it has been overwhelmingly positive, both for the new Germany and for the European Union.[62]

This outlook, at least in my understanding, is totally alien to the traditional Korean spirit of rising up to meet and overcome great challenges. This is not the spirit that led my parents' generation to rebuild the country from the ruins and desperate poverty of the Korean War to become one of the world's leading economies. It is not the attitude that drew millions of Koreans to Taean to clean up that oil spill. With the great prosperity of South Korea today, it seems many have become indifferent to our collective history and national identity as Korean people. Many have forgotten the larger sense of social obligation and responsibility that has always been an integral part of our unique Korean cultural heritage.

Many Koreans simply see no way forward out of the existing impasse, with two national governments, two ideologies and political systems, and two military forces starkly opposed to each other with no apparent prospect of resolution. That is why the Korean Dream that I am proposing here is so significant. Through it, we can find a way forward that can transcend the existing, unresolved conflict of rival systems and provide a foundation upon which the whole Korean people can unite. That foundation arises from a vision that connects with and draws upon the rich spiritual and cultural legacy of our common past, while addressing the problems arising from the current impasse in realistic ways.

What we Koreans should remember, especially those opposed or indifferent to unification, is that the risks posed by the North to the security and prosperity of the South are only going to get worse. In an increasingly unpredictable and volatile situation, the status quo is rapidly becoming unsustainable; doing nothing is not an option.

In this chapter, I examine the many risks facing the Korean peninsula and the region today, domestically and geopolitically. I want to show that all of these political, economic, security, and geopolitical risks and challenges also offer significant opportunities. If we are able to grasp these opportunities, they can open the way to peaceful unification. In fact, these opportunities meet the needs of almost all parties involved, domestically in South Korea and North Korea, and internationally among our neighbors and allies. In the current situation, accepting the existing division is likely to prove the most dangerous option of all.

The key to our national transformation is to win the hearts and minds of the Korean people as a whole in support of unification, not just relying on the engagement of the governments in Seoul and Pyongyang. That support must then lead to united action in pursuit of that goal. We are at an inflection point in our history where, if we choose the right path, we can bring the hope of unification to fruition. The frustrated hopes and ideals of all those patriotic ancestors who longed and worked for a free, united, and ideal nation can be realized today. The outcome will depend on our collective efforts. We must no longer be paralyzed by circumstances, like a rabbit hypnotized in front of a snake, but should take command of those circumstances and become masters of Korea's destiny.

RISK AND UNPREDICTABILITY ON THE KOREAN PENINSULA

Ever since Kim Il-sung launched his surprise invasion of the South in 1950, North Korea has always been unpredictable. Under Kim's grandson Kim Jong-un, it has become more unpredictable than ever. He has continued the provocative actions of his late father, such as missile tests into the East Sea, artillery barrages on South Korean islands, and, of course, the development of a nuclear weapon. But he has gone further.[63]

He achieved a new level of savage volatility with the very public and humiliating arrest of his uncle and chief advisor, Chang Song-taek, in December 2013 followed by his execution and vilification in North Korea's media.[64] Although never independently confirmed, South Korea's Yonhap News Agency reported that around 200 of Chang's family members and supporters were executed, sent to prison camps, or exiled.

Kim's action shocked the world; especially for Koreans, this was unimaginable. It violated the most deeply held sacred values relating to bonds of family and the ideal of leadership, rooted in the Confucian ethical influence of our cultural heritage. For Koreans, a ruler is expected to honor the sanctity of familial relationships and act with virtue and wisdom. These were always considered essential qualities of leadership.

As I mentioned in Chapter 1, Koreans have always believed that a ruler should be virtuous in order to bring blessings to his people. If he is depraved, the people will suffer. If they suffer, their bonds to the ruler are dissolved and he loses his legitimacy, or "the Mandate of Heaven." As the supreme leader of the North, Kim Jong-un ordered the execution of his own uncle and regent appointed by his father. This left many Koreans, North and South, questioning his moral fitness and practical competence for that role. For them, what Kim Jong-un did was morally depraved in the extreme.

North Korea is a totalitarian state whose citizens are guaranteed no rights but are subject to the arbitrary will of the leader and his supporting elite who exert absolute power. Kim Jong-un is now exercising his will as leader in a more ruthless manner than we have seen in the past.[65] His capricious character and inexperience, combined with the internal decline of North Korea's economy and society, make the situation of the Korean peninsula more uncertain today than it has been since the Korean War.[66]

To outside observers, the entire Kim dynasty, starting with Kim Il-sung, has been a dictatorship, oppressing and exploiting the North Korean people. But it is important to understand that the picture inside North Korea is very different. Appealing to the powerful Korean cultural reverence for family, the state's propaganda machine has effectively portrayed Kim Il-sung as the father of his nation and its people. [67] At the time Kim Il-sung came into power, the circumstances of the Cold War allowed him to provide for his people's basic needs. At the same time, the absolute control of information prevented North Koreans from knowing the reality of the world around them.[68]

The picture painted by North Korean propaganda of an intimate relationship of ruler and people united together against a hostile world, however fanciful, worked for a time, given the conditions inside North Korea. This began to crumble under Kim Jong-il as circumstances changed, brought about by the end of the Cold War and followed soon thereafter by the great famine. That picture is eroding still more rapidly under Kim Jong-un, who has openly acted against long-held traditional cultural values that his grandfather drew upon in creating his image of the North Korean state.

Today, North Korea is a dysfunctional state that oppresses its people and cannot even feed them or guarantee them work. That was the original implicit social contract between Kim Il-sung's government and the Korean people in the North. The government would rigidly control every aspect of its citizens' lives—where they lived, where they worked, whether they travelled, what they read and thought—and, in return, they would have jobs, a place to live, and a food ration.

This worked adequately at first, and for about two decades after the war, the North Korean economy was stronger than that of the South. Korea was one of the poorest countries in the world and, in those circumstances,[69] a highly centralized government and economy proved temporarily effective in lifting its people up to some basic level of subsistence. Aid and government assistance have their place in lifting people out of destitution until they can stand on their own feet.

But gradually, the North Korean experiment, like the communist experiment everywhere, showed its inherent flaw. Economic growth beyond the provision of the most basic needs is driven by creativity, enterprise, and innovation, qualities that are encouraged within a free market system. Centrally planned economies hit a wall and begin to stagnate because they stifle the initiative that is the engine of further growth. This was also the fate of the Soviet Union and communist systems everywhere.[70]

In the South, there was far greater scope for enterprise, combined with some strategic government direction. The energy and dynamism of the Korean people were released, and in the 1970s, the economy of the South surpassed the North and never looked back.[71] The stagnating North Korean economy was then dealt a further major blow with the collapse of the Soviet Union and, with it, the cessation of the subsidies on which the North Korean economy depended.

With this critical turning point and new historical context, the North Korean leadership was forced to adjust. To adapt to these circumstances would have required dramatic change. They would have had to follow a course similar to Mongolia, which transitioned from a Soviet satellite into an independent democratic state with a growing economy over a twenty-year period. At the very least, they would have had to adopt the Chinese approach to economic reform, as China has repeatedly urged them to do.

Kim Il-sung's successor, his son, Kim Jong-il, was not willing to do that. Instead, he focused on regime preservation, particularly in the wake of the terrible famine in the mid-1990s when he told the leadership elite that they were all in danger of being overthrown and killed and had to focus on clinging to power at all costs. This decision was implemented through the "military-first"[72] policy, a devil's bargain where the military leadership guaranteed support for regime survival in return for being well taken care of by the leadership.[73] This was a fateful and foolish choice. It broke the basic social contract between Kim Il-sung and the North Korean people, however oppressive that had been, and started a downward spiral in the leadership that has culminated in the moral depravity of Kim Jong-un.

Kim Jong-il's policy created a fundamental split between the leadership and the people. The government abandoned any idea of developing the nation as a whole.[74] Rather than providing opportunities for all of its people, it only offered the empty words of its propaganda. It can no longer guarantee jobs or food except to the favored elite on whose support it relies. At least Kim Jong-il maintained a public attitude of filial piety toward his father, Kim Il-sung. When Kim Jong-un killed Chang, his father's brother-in-law, appointed by his father to be his main advisor, the Confucian tradition was broken publicly in the most egregious manner imaginable.

This has resulted in an unsustainable situation. An exploitative elite cannot maintain itself indefinitely at the expense of the general population. Sooner or later, something has to give. The only question is when and how. That is the lesson of the Arab Spring and the way change came to countries like Tunisia, Libya, and Egypt. Kim Jong-un represents a further turn in the downward spiral of North Korea's leadership. An increasingly unstable social and economic situation within the North, combined with an inexperienced, yet volatile and ruthless, leader, is a tinderbox of risk that any spark could set off at any time in unforeseeable ways.

Since no internal disputes ever emerged so publicly and dramatically in the past, the manner in which Kim got rid of his uncle hints at a major factional struggle in the leadership.[75] Whatever the case, the violent and dramatic manner of Kim's assertion of control over the North Korean leadership underscored the growing instability of the state and came at a wider cost to him.

Leaders engaged in the region wondered what sort of individual they were dealing with. China, in particular, was totally taken by surprise at this turn of events.[76] Chang had been the main intermediary between North Korea and China. Apparently, he was working to open up North Korea's economy somewhat, at least in the border regions with China, following the Chinese model. This initiative may be what stirred up the opposition that led to his ouster and death.[77]

Despite the fact that China has been the major sponsor and protector of North Korea since the demise of the Soviet Union, Kim Jong-un did not seem particularly concerned about the impact his execution of his uncle is likely to have on relations with Beijing. At the time, he rarely visited China and, at times, acted as if he could operate in isolation without the need of outside support. This was delusional thinking. It demonstrated that he not only had no sense of humanity or Korean virtues, but also was inexperienced and ignorant of the most basic geopolitical realities affecting his country. His father had ten years of preparation before becoming the supreme leader. Kim Jong-un had almost none.

One wonders what his advisors, who served under his father and grandfather, must have thought when he invited the former professional basketball player Dennis Rodman to Pyongyang. He not only chose one of the most outrageous and controversial characters in all of American sports but then expected him to deliver a message to President Obama.[78] Kim demonstrated how naïve and out of touch he is with the realities of international relations. Under so capricious and inexperienced a leader, the regime's unpredictability is reaching alarming levels. When his control of a nuclear weapon is added to this mix, the outcome can quickly become catastrophic.

Faced with these circumstances, Koreans, especially in the South, must decide how to respond. Do we wait for the bomb to explode, whether figuratively or literally, or do we take action now to defuse it? We can be sure that change will come sooner or later, and perhaps violently. Do we Koreans want to wait passively and allow the course of events once more to determine our fate, as happened repeatedly throughout the twentieth century? Or will we act to direct and influence the course of events toward an outcome of peaceful unification and thus become the masters of our own destiny?

In the course of the first two chapters, I mentioned some features of contemporary life in South Korea that are weakening the type of unified vision for Korea's destiny that is the necessary foundation for unification. The increase in apathy toward unification is part of a wider erosion of traditional Korean values, especially those related to the family. At the same time, the constant political and ideological battles between right and left in Korean society have prevented the development of consensus around a clear national vision. Without this, peaceful unification is unlikely to occur, and then the ideals and destiny to which we are called will remain unfulfilled.

EMERGING OPPORTUNITIES IN THE NORTH

The North's instability has increased the level of risk on the peninsula and in the region, but has also opened up new opportunities that could ease the path toward unification. In the past, the Kim regime held absolute power over its citizens through fear and total control over jobs, food, and especially information. As the situation of North Korea has changed, particularly after the breakdown of the government-controlled food distribution system during the great famine, the ability of the regime to control its people has weakened.

The famine meant that people had to fend for themselves.[79] Many tried and failed, starving to death, but some survived through setting up produce markets or slipping into China to earn money for food. The markets were created on people's own initiative. They existed outside the realm of government control, a first in North Korea. The people who traveled to China brought back information as well as food. Through Chinese media and South Korean television broadcasting in China, they saw a picture of the world very different from the one that the North's state media painted—the only media they previously could access.

Markets and uncensored media were the first cracks in the façade of the People's Paradise, exposing its false pretenses and revealing what it truly is to more and more of its people. After the famine, Kim Jong-il tried to suppress the markets and reimpose previous levels of control. However, since the government could not provide food for all of its people, this effort was doomed to failure.

The attempted currency reform of November 2009 was particularly disastrous. Old currency had to be exchanged for a new, revalued currency, but the amount that could be exchanged was limited, as was the period of time in which the exchange could be made. Part of the aim was to destroy the savings of black-market operators above the relatively small amount that they could exchange.[80] But it affected many ordinary North Koreans, leading to public protests,[81] a loosening of the original policy, and easing of restrictions on markets. An almost unprecedented official public apology was issued, and the unfortunate Pak Nam-gi, the Workers' Party official supposedly responsible for the revaluation, was reportedly executed.[82]

This represented a watershed moment in the history of relations between the government of North Korea and its people. The government conceded, in effect, that it could not suppress or completely control the free markets. The incident also highlighted the growing divergence of interests between the regime and the people. The regime wants to preserve its power, while the people want to feed their families and exercise their initiative to do so, since the government cannot. The regime in Pyongyang is oblivious to such basic requirements for survival. The gulf between the leadership and the people is ever-widening and a sure sign that change, in some form, must come.

Today, markets have become an established feature of life in North Korea, necessary for survival. At the same time, there is a growing market and trade in foreign currency within North Korea, operating outside government control.[83] Apparently, the Chinese yuan is the preferred currency for merchants, especially those operating near and across the Chinese border, while the Pyongyang elites prefer the U.S. dollar.[84]

The spread of information into the North has continued through the greater availability of mobile phones on Chinese networks.[85] North Korea now also has its own mobile phone network, which claims two million subscribers, but service is restricted to within North Korea.[86] In addition, more and more people take the risk of tuning into South Korea TV, a punishable offense.[87] Because the government cannot adequately provide food or health services, the door has opened somewhat for groups offering humanitarian aid to gain access to North Korea. Many of them have direct contact with ordinary citizens, and these channels can begin to have a transformative effect.[88]

The result is that more and more people in the North are becoming aware of the world outside their country. The regime can no longer prevent information reaching them. This is partly a result of technology but also a result of the changing dynamic in the region. Post–Cold War China and Russia, North Korea's neighbors and former backers, are focused on their own economic development and have much freer flows of information than North Korea. They have no interest in helping the leadership there maintain an information firewall to isolate its people. North Korea can no longer rely on the type of support that helped sustain it in the past.

North Koreans have also experienced that the regime does not serve their interests even at the level of basic survival needs, and a growing split is developing between the regime and the people. That was only sharpened by what happened to Chang Song-taek. Some human rights groups in South Korea have secret contact by mobile phone with informants in the North to monitor public opinion there. The widespread reaction to the execution was one of profound shock. People said they had lost confidence in and respect for Kim Jong-un as a leader and felt much more uncertain about the future.

All this adds up to a situation in the North that is riper for positive change and a movement toward unification than at any time since the establishment of the two separate governments in 1948. Koreans in the North are better informed than before and more likely to be taking initiative and exercising responsibility for their own lives, at least comparatively speaking. That has become a simple necessity for survival. At the same time, they are more likely to be aware of how miserable their situation really is compared with even rural China, let alone South Korea. Channels now exist, through media, mobile phones, and the direct contact from NGOs and civic groups, to offer the Korean people in the North a vision of hope for the future.

It is not only among ordinary Koreans struggling for survival that belief in and loyalty to the regime are diminishing. Members of the leadership elite are also looking over their shoulders and wondering how to maintain their privileges in an uncertain and changing environment. One reason that the supposedly illegal trade in foreign currency is unlikely to ever be stopped is that Workers' Party officials benefit personally from it.

North Korean officials often visit Mongolia, which has diplomatic relations with them. One Mongolian government official responsible for North Korean affairs told me how these mostly mid-level officials would ask in a quiet, informal moment about what had happened to Mongolia's Communist Party and its members. The answer was that they had joined the democratic process and had since then been in both government and opposition. This seemed a relief to the North Koreans and gave them a measure of hope. They were obviously contemplating the prospect of change in their own country.

When ordinary people and members of the party elite both start thinking primarily of their own survival, the regime has lost loyalty and unquestioning support. This is what happened with the communist regimes in Eastern Europe. More and more constituencies will be calculating whether the continuation of the regime is in their own best interest for survival.

At the same time, the regime itself has become more isolated. Its Cold War backers, China and Russia, are deeply unhappy with the North's nuclear and missile tests and no longer offer full support. At the same time, South Korea has expanded its own international relationships beyond its traditional Cold War allies to include China and Russia. The economic gulf between North Korea and South Korea is vast, and the current North regime has no prospect of ever competing. Instead, it has resorted to desperate means to generate revenue, including arms proliferation, drug smuggling, and counterfeiting.

This situation makes the regime more unstable and can easily produce a nothing-to-lose mentality in the top leadership that could result in rash and provocative actions. As a result, the overall situation on the peninsula has become much more volatile. But at the same time, it offers a real opportunity for change if people on both sides of the 38th parallel can grasp the unifying vision of the Korean Dream and act upon it.

SOUTH KOREA'S ECONOMIC CHALLENGE

When we shift our focus to South Korea, we see that the dynamic economic growth of past decades is beginning to slow. The future material prosperity of the South is facing real constraints that are exacerbated by the division of the peninsula and the character of the regime in the North. An Organisation for Economic Co-operation and Development (OECD) report projects that South Korea's annual growth rate will begin to fall, averaging only 1.6 percent from now to 2060.[89] Thus, Korea is in danger of falling into the "Japan trap" of low growth and long-term stagnation.[90]

This prospect is aggravated by an aging population, increasing competition for natural resources, and the danger that the Korean economy becomes squeezed between the larger economies of Japan and China. People over sixty-five years of age make up 11.1 percent of the population today, according to Statistics Korea's Estimate of Future Population 2011. But that proportion is expected to increase to 20 percent by 2026 and increase still further thereafter. By the time today's elementary school students retire, half the population will be over sixty-five given current demographic trends.[91]

As a result, the labor force will be limited, and welfare spending will have to rise under the existing system to provide for the vastly greater number of elderly. This rise in welfare costs will result in rising taxes, which will, in turn, lessen capital investment siphoning from the private to public sector and slow the growth rate of the South's economy, which is primarily fueled by the private sector. Research by the Korea Institute of Public Finance in 2012 estimated that this would increase the annual budget deficit, the gap between government revenue and expenditure, to 8.3 percent of GDP. The institute projects that the overall national debt will rise to 137.7 percent of GDP by 2050.[92] A greater financial burden would fall on the working-age population, who would have to support a larger pool of retirees than today's workers. Korea would be forced down the unsustainable path already followed by the welfare societies of the West.

This is one of the reasons I am reminding Koreans so strongly of the virtues of our traditional extended family structure. The extended family offers a natural caring environment for elders as an alternative to institutionalized government welfare, with its ever-rising costs imposed on a shrinking working population. It makes much more sense for the government to provide incentives for extended families to care for elders as this would be a practical contemporary application of the traditional Korean family model.

Another constraint on the Korean economy is the lack of natural resources. Korea has to import much of its energy needs and other vital resources to sustain the economy. International competition for these resources, especially with the rapid industrialization of China, which has been called a "black hole"[93] for resources, pushes up prices, threatening the profit margins of Korean industry. Some economists fear that Korea could then become the "nut stuck in the nutcracker," losing out to China in economies of scale and to Japan in certain areas of technological innovation.

Finally, Koreans in the South have to consider the ever-present security threat from the North and whether they want to live with it, and all the uncertainty it brings, indefinitely. Nobody believes that the North could win a "hot" war with the South and its American allies. Its military is large in terms of manpower at around 1.2 million,[94] but its equipment is aging[95] and the overall destitution of the economy has taken its toll on military efficiency, too. However, the North could cause terrible destruction to Seoul and other areas in the South before being defeated.[96] One of the best-maintained parts of the North Korean military is the long-range artillery,[97] with some 10,000 barrels and rocket launchers sheltered in deep underground bunkers that are able to reach far into South Korea, not even mentioning the nightmare scenario of the use of nuclear weapons as a last desperate measure by the regime in a confused scenario of collapse.

THE GEOPOLITICAL RISKS AND OPPORTUNITIES

Of course, the security threat posed by North Korea extends far beyond the peninsula itself, affecting the whole region and, through the proliferation threat, spreading out to the world. North Korean nuclear and missile capacity is a direct threat to Japan as well as South Korea. The North has test-fired missiles across Japan, as well as into the East Sea west of Japan. It also aspires to create a credible nuclear threat against the United States.

A report in 2014 from the North Korea–focused think tank 38 North suggests that the North may have a functioning version of the KN-08, a road-mobile intercontinental ballistic missile (ICBM) that could reach the U.S. West Coast, although it has yet to be tested.[98] North Korea is thought to have designs for miniaturizing a nuclear warhead to fit on a missile that it obtained from A. Q. Khan, the rogue Pakistani nuclear scientist.[99]

Proliferation is the other dimension of the North Korean nuclear threat and is global in scope. After the latest North Korean nuclear test in March 2014, the UN Security Council unanimously passed sanctions against Pyongyang; even China, the North's supporter and benefactor, backed the resolutions. The sanctions called for the complete denuclearization of North Korea and an end to all arms proliferation from the country.

North Korea is suspected to have supplied Libya under Muammar Gaddafi with uranium hexafluoride,[100] used for the uranium enrichment needed to produce nuclear reactors and nuclear weapons, through the A. Q. Khan network.[101] In an April 2014 report, the Congressional Research Service reported North Korean "nuclear technology cooperation" with Syria.[102] More recently, American experts have found evidence that suggests Iranian scientists are working with North Korean counterparts on the North's nuclear program.[103]

Desperate for revenue from any source, North Korea has shown itself ready to sell conventional arms, missile technology, and military training to any country.[104] It has also shown its willingness to deal in nuclear technology with countries in the increasingly volatile Middle East.[105] The regime in the North clearly believes that Gaddafi would still be in power if he had not given up his nuclear program.[106] In a 2011 article by *Asia Times Online*, "North Korea Laments Gaddafi's Nuke Folly," Donald Kirk wrote:

> No way, they [North Korea] are saying, would the U.S. and others have dared to attack Gaddafi's forces if he had had the nuclear deterrent needed to strike back ... [North Korea] found plenty to report about "the Libyan crisis" for "teaching the international community a grave lesson." A Foreign Ministry spokesman, quoted by Pyongyang's Korean Central News Agency, said the bombing [of Libya by the U.S. and others] "confirmed once again ... the truth that one should have power to defend peace."[107]

The danger is that North Korea could help Iran with the technology to acquire a nuclear weapon, which would further destabilize the Middle East. Worse still, a North Korean nuclear device might end up in the hands of a terrorist group such as al-Qaeda or ISIS. Although the risk might be small, the consequences would be cataclysmic.

The security threat posed by North Korea's nuclear program is a direct consequence of the end of the Cold War. The DMZ is a remnant of that era, but the geopolitical context is changing and being replaced by new realities. The North's nuclear threat is one result of these changes, but the changes also offer new possibilities for international relations in the region. These represent an opportunity for peaceful development in Korea and the region that we need to understand and act upon.

The two ideological blocs—of communism, headed by the Soviet Union, and democracy, headed by the United States—have disappeared, and most of the region is now interested in economic development and the political stability needed to pursue it. When the Soviet Union collapsed, North Korea lost not only the economic subsidies it relied upon but its main security guarantor. Thinking in Cold War terms, Kim Jong-il feared that the North's new weakness might invite an American assault. After all, it was probably what he would have done if the situation had been reversed. Not wanting to be too heavily dependent on China for security, Kim pursued a much more self-reliant and aggressive defense strategy that gave birth to the military-first policy and the nuclear and missile programs.[108]

China has traditionally viewed North Korea as a buffer, insulating China from the presence of American troops in the South. "Lips and teeth" is the metaphor the Chinese use for the relationship. If the lips (North Korea) are gone, the teeth (China) feel the cold. This outlook is also a remnant of the Cold War but has been surprisingly persistent as a basis for Chinese policy.[109]

On Kim Jong-il's death in 2011, China mobilized troops and held military exercises along the Yalu River. When Seoul protested, Beijing responded that the troops were there to prevent mass defections.[110] Unofficially, however, the Chinese informed Seoul that they had no intention of taking over North Korea but could not be unprepared in case U.S. forces moved north of the demarcation line in the event of regime collapse. China's basic policy toward the Korean peninsula has been to maintain peace and stability there,[111] and it has done this through supporting the Kims' regime as the least bad option, at least until recently.[112]

Recent North Korean actions are forcing China to reconsider its policy and recognize that circumstances in the region have changed radically from the Cold War relationships. As a result, China is starting to reassess whether backing a nuclear-armed Pyongyang that does not listen to China is the best option for the region's peace and stability.[113]

China needs stability in order to manage its meteoric economic growth in an ordered and peaceful way. At the same time, it aspires to emerge as a major nation that exercises increasing global influence. It has the second-largest economy in the world, and many economists project that it will overtake the United States and claim first place some time before 2030. The OECD projected the overtaking date as early as 2016.[114] Of course, all these projections are based on assumptions, and much can change over time. But they do indicate that China is a significant power in the world with global ambitions.

But to exercise global influence, China will have to be seen by other nations as acting with a certain degree of moral authority, not just with economic and military power. Such an aspiration is delegitimized by too close a link with North Korea, a rogue nation that acts with extreme disregard for international norms. China's pursuit of peace and stability calls for a nuclear-free peninsula, yet North Korea persists in its nuclear program and nuclear tests, despite Chinese protests.[115]

China's leaders have to start weighing the possibility that a nuclear North Korea is a greater threat to the stability of the region than the prospect of change in the North. The North Korean nuclear program, especially taken together with missile tests that splash down in the seas around Japan, is a factor in strengthening the Japanese political right and fueling a push for Japanese militarization. The last thing that China wants to see is resurgent militarism in Japan, still less a Japanese nuclear weapon as a response to the threat from North Korea. However, China's aggressive actions to expand its influence in the surrounding seas and airspace are counterproductive and only further exacerbate the tension.[116]

China's policy has not yet changed, but a growing number of signs indicate that its attitude is shifting. After the second North Korean test, in 2009, China urged a soft approach. Although it supported the UN Security Council resolution against North Korea at that time, it urged more diplomatic approaches to Pyongyang and less reliance on the sanctions imposed by resolution 1874.[117] However, when North Korea conducted its third nuclear test in February 2013, despite explicit Chinese warnings, China took a more active role, working with the United States to draft the resolution of the UN Security Council condemning the test and imposing wide-ranging sanctions.[118]

The state-run Chinese Academy of Social Sciences (CASS) put the possibility of reunification of the Korean peninsula firmly on the table of Chinese policy options in its "Annual Report on Development of Asia-Pacific" (2014) that examines possible Chinese strategies in the region over the next five to ten years. The report said that "in 10 years, the key issue in North and South Korean relations will be the unification issue" and warned Pyongyang to "dispel the miscalculation that China will not abandon North Korea, no matter what the situation."[119]

It is clear that Chinese policy circles are beginning to consider whether unification is not a better guarantee of regional security than maintaining North Korea as a buffer between Chinese and U.S. forces. The report says that this shift was made possible after South Korea abandoned the old doctrine of "unification by force" and began pursuing a peaceful unification policy since President Park Geun-hye. The report also pointed out a growing mutual inter-dependence between China and South Korea because of the North Korean situation, Japan's resurgent militarization, and growing economic relations.[120] South Korea's trade with China was more than $270 billion in 2013,[121] more than South Korea's trade with Japan and the United States combined.[122] In comparison, North Korea's two-way trade with China is worth only approximately $6.45 billion.[123] The CASS report says that changes in administration in Seoul are unlikely to alter this growing connection. More suggestive of China's reevaluation of its approach to the peninsula is the April 3 editorial in the *People's Online Daily*, an official mouthpiece for Beijing. It was published in response to Pyongyang's threat to conduct a fourth nuclear test. It condemned the North's nuclear program as a sign of weakness, saying, "Nuclear tests and missile launches have become Pyongyang's only diplomatic cards, which is unfortunate for Pyongyang and the entire Northeast Asia." It then broadened its criticism to the state of the regime and the country as a whole, observing, "If Pyongyang continues to follow this [nuclear] path, it will suffer long-term isolation by the international community and the country's poverty will never be eliminated. The risks these factors pose to the Pyongyang regime can hardly be offset even if North Korea truly becomes a nuclear state."[124]

China's exasperation with Pyongyang translated not only into a general deepening of relations with Seoul but also into specific support for Park Geun-hye's approach to unification.[125] President Park made her initiative for progress toward peaceful unification of the peninsula the central theme of her visit to Germany at the end of March 2014. She drew inspiration from Germany's own history, saying, "Germany is an example and a model for a peaceful reunification of our own country."[126]

During that trip, President Park met with Chinese President Xi Jinping at the Nuclear Security Summit in the Netherlands. In the course of the meeting, President Xi expressed his support for an "independent and peaceful reunification" of the peninsula.[127] This was reinforced the following week at a press conference in Beijing by a spokesperson of China's Foreign Ministry who stated, "China always supports the ROK [South Korea] and the DPRK [North Korea] in improving their relations through dialogue, promoting reconciliation and finally realizing an independent unity."[128]

If China's rethinking of its strategy toward the Korean peninsula is related to its broader geopolitical ambitions, Japan's concerns regarding North Korea are more narrowly focused primarily on its own security, although the resolution of the issue of Japanese citizens abducted by North Korea is a major concern of the Japanese public. With its missile tests, North Korea has demonstrated that it poses a direct threat to Japan. Japan's leverage with Pyongyang is limited, particularly since sanctions have reduced the level of economic interaction. Consequently, Japan is focused on developing a military response to the missile threat and working in alliance with the U.S. and South Korea to contain it.[129] At the beginning of April 2014, Japan's defense minister ordered the Maritime Self-Defense Force, Japan's navy, to shoot down any ballistic missiles launched from North Korea.[130]

The threat from North Korea has had a destabilizing effect on the region as a whole and, along with rising tension in the region with China, has led to calls for the wholesale remilitarization of Japan and the conduct of military exercises with other countries. This is an extremely sensitive issue for both China and Korea because of the unresolved historical issues arising from Japan's actions in both countries before and during World War II. Whatever the strategic and geopolitical arguments for Japan to play a greater military role in the region, there are clearly unhealed wounds from Japan's military actions in the past that must also be addressed.

Unlike in Europe, where Germany was never allowed to forget its war guilt by worldwide Jewry and those nations occupied by Nazi Germany,

many feel that Japan has never completely accepted responsibility for its crimes during the war to the same extent that Germany did. Germany clearly repudiated its Nazi past and paid billions of dollars to Israel in reparations for the Holocaust. Although Japan apologized for her conduct during the war and paid compensation, her recent actions are causing Korea and China to suspect Japan's sincerity. For example, the Japanese government approved textbooks for school students that portray the war years in a positive light. This incenses both Koreans and Chinese, and the prospect of a remilitarized Japan in this historical context causes great anxiety and increases tension in the region.[131] The actions of North Korea are the source of this confrontation and, no doubt, they feel that to foment conflict among their neighbors helps their own survival.

During the Obama administration, the impact of the push for Japanese militarization in the region was exacerbated by the direction of U.S. policy. The "pivot to Asia," later renamed a "rebalance" toward Asia, became a buzzword in U.S. foreign policy circles after Secretary of State Hillary Clinton's article "America's Pacific Century" appeared in *Foreign Policy* magazine in November 2011.[132] However, countries in the region, in both Northeast and Southeast Asia, didn't see a great deal of substance to this shift. Cuts in defense spending prevented significant increases in U.S. military presence in the region.[133] Both the State and Defense Departments remained largely focused on the Middle East, managing the withdrawal from Afghanistan, Iran's nuclear ambitions, Iraq's civil war with Sunni extremists, continuing hostilities between the Palestinians and Israel, as well as the terrorist threats from places like Yemen and the lawless Pakistani border regions. To these were added the situation in Syria and Russia's adventurism in Ukraine.

This left little time and insufficient funding for a major Asian initiative.[134] U.S. President Obama, in his 2014 State of the Union address, said almost nothing about the rebalance to Asia. In fact, he said very little about foreign policy at all.[135] This approach reflected the lack of leadership and disengagement from the rest of the world under his administration that created new regional power vacuums in the wake of America's retreat in the Middle East, Eastern Europe, and Northeast Asia.

For Asia, this situation had serious implications. Traditional U.S. defense policy has been built around a capacity to fight two wars simultaneously. But with defense spending cuts, would an America engaged in a Middle East war still be able to undertake an Asian war in support of its Korean and Japanese allies should an emergency arise? It was highly doubtful, and, as a consequence, the Asian allies, and Japan in particular, realized that they should rely less on the United States and make greater provisions for their own defense, an additional impetus behind Japanese nationalists pushing for remilitarization.[136]

From the perspective of domestic U.S. politics, this might have seemed like a good thing since defense costs would be shared more broadly with America's allies. However, what this view failed to recognize was that America has been a stabilizing force in the region since its presence has assured regional security. As it reduces its defense profile, that stability becomes threatened as historically based conflicts and grievances resurface. Regional anxiety at the prospect of a more nationalistic, militarized Japan set America's two allies, South Korea and Japan, against each other, and led China to view Japan as more of a threat. Chinese leaders might do well to recognize that a strong U.S. presence in the region has acted as a restraint on the need for Japanese defense spending and rearmament.

Nevertheless, America's lower profile did have some positive aspects. Its policy toward North Korea has been described as "strategic patience,"[137] which basically means ignoring the North except when it makes military threats and letting South Korea take the lead in dealing with the North on other issues. This outlook is a result of the frustration experienced in the course of both the Clinton and George W. Bush administrations when neither carrots nor sticks altered Pyongyang's behavior in any significant way.

The result was that many U.S. officials and foreign policy experts began to think that the only way to make progress is through unification. Victor Cha, the director of Asian Affairs on George W. Bush's National Security

Council, wrote in his book *The Impossible State* that "the embracing of unification ... stems from a rational realization that after decades of unsuccessful negotiations, the only true solution to tangible problems like nuclear weapons, human rights abuses, and the conventional military threat is through unification."[138]

The failure of nuclear negotiations with North Korea in the past together with America's global pullback meant that unification offered the best prospect for progress on the peninsula. In fact, there has been a growing convergence among the United States,[139] China, and Japan on this issue as a solution to both the nuclear threat and the region's economic development. Increasingly, they have been coming to accept that South Korea should lead this process.

Russia, with its annexation of Crimea and fomenting of Russian ethnic separatism in eastern Ukraine, raised global concerns about the scope of its revivalist ambitions. Russian President Vladimir Putin told the Russian Parliament in April 2005[140] that he regards the "demise of the Soviet Union as the greatest geopolitical catastrophe of the twentieth century."[141] His aim was to revive Russia's former glories, and in a speech in May 2012, at the start of his third term in office as president, he promised to project Russia's power onto the world stage.

Under Stalin, the Soviet Union had territorial ambitions in the Far East, and Putin's new assertiveness raises questions about what this might mean for the geopolitical balance in East Asia. However, Russia's policy interests on its European borders and in its Far East provinces are separate and very different. Historically, Russia has always been more focused on its borders with Europe than on its Asian regions. Given Putin's desire to revive Russia's former glories, many experts believe that he saw the push of NATO and the European Union ever closer to Russia's borders as a challenge.

Historically, countries like Ukraine and Belarus have been considered by Russia to be part of its sphere of influence. In his 2005 speech, Putin also said of the demise of the Soviet Union, "As for the Russian people, it became a genuine tragedy. Tens of millions of our fellow citizens and countrymen found themselves beyond the fringes of Russian territory." John Bolton, former U.S. Ambassador to the United Nations, observed of Putin's actions in Crimea and the Ukraine: "It's clear that he wants to reestablish Russian hegemony within the space of the former Soviet Union."[142]

The context of the Russian Far East is totally different. Korean unification presents no security threat to Russia. In fact, Russia's main interests in the region are economic. At the time, faced with the debt crisis in Europe, traditionally Russia's top trading partner, Putin launched in 2012 a Look East policy, an economic pivot to Asia. In the *Wall Street Journal* of September 6, 2012, Putin wrote, "Russia has long been an intrinsic part of the Asian-Pacific region. We view this dynamic region as the most important factor for the successful future of the whole country, as well as the development of Siberia and the far east."[143]

Russia's trade with European nations has been in decline since 2006, while the growing trade with Asia-Pacific Economic Cooperation (APEC) nations could amount to one-third of its total trade by 2025, according to Andrey Kostin, CEO of VTB Group, the country's second-biggest lender.[144] Russia wants to export more of its oil and gas resources from Siberia to China, Japan, and South Korea. As a result, its goals in the region are to promote trade liberalization, regional integration, food security, and transportation.

These goals require peace, stability, and cooperation among the nations of the region. Russia is strongly opposed to the nuclearization of the Korean peninsula[145] and fears proliferation in the region if Japan and South Korea choose to develop their own nuclear deterrent should no solution to the threat from the North be found. Russia also needs to develop pipelines for the transport of its oil and gas. Several proposals are being considered, including one that would run through North Korea into the South. But having a major energy pipeline in the hands of the highly unpredictable Kim Jong-un would be extremely risky.[146] All in all, North Korea in its present form represents a major obstacle to Russia's goals and stands in the way of the regional integration necessary for successful economic development.[147]

So far, I have discussed the outlook of the nations other than South and North Korea that have been involved in the Six-Party Talks about the Korean peninsula: China, Japan, Russia, and the United States. I want to add one more nation that is centrally engaged in the region and can play, I believe, an important bridge role in its peaceful future development. That nation is Mongolia.

CONCRETE APPROACHES TO UNIFICATION

Mongolia's relations with North Korea go back to the Soviet era, when Mongolia supplied the DPRK with livestock during the Korean War.[148] Those relations continued even after the Soviet collapse and Mongolia's challenging but ultimately successful transition out of the Cold War framework to democracy and economic prosperity. They wisely kept the door open to North Korea despite the new difference in political systems and now maintain embassies in both Pyongyang and Seoul.

Although Mongolia's trade with South Korea has soared while trade with the North has contracted, it still has significant contact with North Korea. Officials come from Pyongyang to meet their counterparts in Ulaanbaatar, and there is a bilateral agreement by which 5,000 North Koreans work in Mongolia on a temporary basis. Mongolia is seen as nonthreatening by Pyongyang, unlike the powers involved in the Six-Party Talks, and can draw on the experience of its own successful transition from communist totalitarianism.

As the one democratic country that has relatively open relations with North Korea, Mongolia is in an ideal position to serve as a neutral mediator in a wide range of discussions. Mongolia has already played that role when it invited Japanese and North Korean officials to Ulaanbaatar in 2012 and mediated their discussion about the Japanese abductees.[149] Professor Charles Armstrong of Columbia University said, "Mongolia had done a good job portraying itself as an honest broker on the Korean peninsula issues. It is probably the only country that both North and South Korea can be said to trust."[150]

Former president of Mongolia Tsakhiagiin Elbegdorj is a very good friend of mine. We have talked several times about his country's role in East Asia. I reminded him of the long and deep historical relations between Mongolia and Korea and told him I thought Mongolia was in a unique position to play the role of a regional broker in relation to North Korea and to unification.

Since Mongolia had abandoned communism and embraced the free market without bloodshed, I urged him to use his country's example to encourage North Korea to accept economic reforms and transition to a market economy. I also said I thought that Mongolia should be involved in the Six-Party Talks should they ever resume. It would serve as a neutral seventh nation mediating between the old Cold War lineup of South Korea, the United States, and Japan, facing North Korea, China, and Russia.[151]

The next year, in August 2011, I organized a Global Peace Leadership Conference[152] in Ulaanbaatar on the theme "Peace in Northeast Asia and the Unification of the Korean Peninsula." The conference was held in the Government Palace and was sponsored by the Mongolian government. One purpose was to position the government for the type of role in the Six-Party Talks that I had discussed with President Elbegdorj.

Consequently, the message that the Mongolian president delivered in Pyongyang on his visit there in October 2013 was no surprise to me. He was the first head of state to visit North Korea after Kim Jong-un assumed power, and he spoke very frankly to an audience of faculty and students at Kim Il-sung University. His goal was to present his country's history as an example of how to achieve sovereignty and economic development without relying on the use of force.[153]

He explained the importance of freedom, not just for prosperity, but as a fundamental aspiration of human nature. "No tyranny lasts forever," he said. "Freedom is an asset bestowed upon every single man and woman. Freedom enables every human to discover and realize his or her opportunities .... It is the desire of the people to live free that is the eternal power." The president also quoted a Mongolian saying that it is "better to live by your own choice however bitter it is, than to live by others' choices, however sweet."[154]

He also explained that the share of the private sector in Mongolia's GDP had risen from a mere 10 percent to over 80 percent in the last twenty years. Although Mongolia is surrounded by two mighty nuclear and economic powers, China and Russia, it exists with a perfect sense of security without its own nuclear weapons. In fact, it declared itself a nuclear-free territory. The message to the Pyongyang leadership was clear. Whether the North heeds Mongolia's message is another matter, but the example for the regime is there.

The conference in Mongolia was just the beginning of a series of initiatives I launched to place the issue of Korean unification squarely before the Korean people and our neighbors in the region. In December 2011, I held the third annual Global Peace Convention in Seoul on the theme "Peacebuilding in East Asia and the Reunification of the Korean Peninsula." At that time, many experts advised me against it, arguing that unification was unrealistic. They said it was a story for the distant future, holding little interest for Koreans. I heard that it would be better to focus discussion on welfare, as that was the subject of most topical concern to Koreans at the time.[155]

Despite these objections, I moved forward with the event because I believed that a unified Korea is fundamental to fulfilling the destiny of the Korean people. Participants concerned about the impact of Korea's division on peace regionally and globally came from twenty-eight countries. They represented a broad coalition of interests that embraced political figures, scholars, policy experts, faith leaders, and the NGO/nonprofit sector.

At that time, I presented the idea that Koreans of the North and South must come together on the foundation of a common vision for a united Korea. I believed the time was ripe for Koreans to ask seriously what vision they had for reconciliation and, ultimately, unification.[156] Jose de Venecia Jr., founding chairman of the International Conference of Asian Political Parties and the Convention co-chair, called for "creative, pragmatic methods to further North-South reconciliation without letting ideology get in the way." Dr. Cho Myung-chul, chairman of the Education Center for Unification at the time, reminded participants that universal rights and freedoms had to be guaranteed in a future reunified Korea.[157]

About two weeks after the Seoul conference, on December 17, 2011, the chairman of North Korea, Kim Jong-il, died. Since his death, there have been many changes in North Korea, and the perspectives and policies of neighboring powers on North Korea have changed as well.[158] Faced with such changes, the people of South Korea were forced to take a renewed interest in relations with North Korea. Unification became a hot issue and is likely to remain so.

Recognizing the opportunity and the need, I had the Global Peace Foundation in Korea work with partners to create a broad-based, grassroots coalition to engage with the Korean public on the issue of unification. Action for Korea United (AKU), as I mentioned earlier, brings together nearly 400 civic, religious, and humanitarian groups and NGOs from across the political and religious spectrum. It is nonpolitical and nonsectarian. It was publicly launched in August 2012 with a rally in Yoido Hangang Park that attracted 20,000 people and was aired live by Chosun TV.[159]

The rally was jointly hosted by Action for Korea United and Korean Sharing Movement, which represent the center-right and center-left groupings of NGOs. The rally was sponsored by the Ministry of Foreign Affairs and Trade and the Ministry of Unification, the *Daily Chosun*, and TV Chosun. Kim Deok-ryong, head of the Korean Council for Reconciliation and Cooperation; Park Se-il, head of Greater Korea United; Lee Gi-taek, executive advisor of the Korea NGO Association and former president of the Democratic Party; and Young Dam, the executive representative of the Korean Sharing Movement, participated as co-conveners of the event.

Prominent political figures addressed the rally, including Hwang Woo-yea, chairman of the Saenuri Party; Kim Moon-soo, governor of Gyeonggi province; and Cho Myung-chul, member of the Saenuri Party and a defector from North Korea. Congressman Eni Faleo Mavaega represented the United States.

AKU's purpose is to create the basis for a unified approach to Korean unification that embraces all sectors of Korean society and bridges differences of political ideology and religious belief. This is an absolute necessity. As I explained in Chapter 2, the lack of a clear national vision and common strategy after my father's breakthrough 1991 meeting with Kim Il-sung led to piecemeal and uncoordinated initiatives. The result was that the North exploited the lack of cohesion in the South's policies. The South Korean government held talks with and sent aid to the North, which in effect funded Kim Jong-il's military-first and nuclear program.

That is why it is so important to establish a clear national vision that can focus and guide all the efforts for unification, both governmental and private. The Korean Dream can unite all Koreans, including those in the North, around a common understanding of Korean identity and destiny. Upon this vision, a broad-based grassroots movement such as AKU can create the practical organizational framework for approaching unification. It is unprecedented in its character and scope as it unites so many organizations representing all aspects of Korean society willing to work together toward a common goal. AKU is also well-positioned to create a partnership between civil society and government to advance unification. In order to achieve this historic national goal, all Korean people must be engaged and fired up by a common vision.

REALIZATION OF THE KOREAN DREAM: THE CREATION OF A NEW NATION

Throughout the twentieth century, as I have described, Korean aspirations and dreams were at the mercy of circumstances beyond our control. Our fate was largely in the hands of geopolitical forces and more powerful nations. This situation is not destined to continue indefinitely. Although the risks and challenges laid out so far in this chapter are complex and serious, they do not have to determine our fate. The environment today is significantly different from that of the twentieth century, dominated as it was by colonialism, followed by Cold War political alignments.

History is transitioning away from these structures toward something new that is still to be determined. In other words, history has arrived at a point of balance where the Korean people can act decisively to determine the future direction of their nation. We can take our fate out of the hands of others and shape our own destiny. Through the creation of a new and unified Korean nation, founded upon the Korean Dream, we can substantively address all the risks and challenges facing us, on the peninsula and in the region.

In the first place, unification and the building of a new nation would resolve the security threat from the current regime in North Korea. It is clear from past negotiations that Pyongyang has no intention of giving up its nuclear capacity, which is their ultimate insurance policy to ensure regime survival. Neither negotiations, sanctions, nor Chinese warnings have made any difference. Only changing the playing field will make a difference, and that can result from a concerted, peaceful push for unification with the united commitment of the Korean people and support from the international community.

This would benefit South Korea and each of the other Six-Party nations. In a unified nation, the perpetual threat of armed conflict looming over South Korea's prosperity would be removed. Resources could be released from defense needs to more constructive purposes, while the North's military-first policy would end and resources would be redirected toward reconstruction.

The Six-Party nations and other international actors involved in the region have two main concerns about the current situation: security risks and economic development. Unification, by removing the security concern, would open the door for much greater regional economic integration and development. It is thus worth looking at the security and strategic implications of ending North Korea's nuclear and missile threats.

The direct threat to Japan would be removed at a stroke through unification, based upon the ideals of the Korean Dream, since this would result in a Korea free of nuclear weapons. As a result, the power of the nationalist right in Japan and the impetus for militarization would be diminished.

For China, it would solve their strategic dilemma over North Korea and help them to finally emerge from the last vestiges of a Cold War outlook. For China, stability in the region is necessary for continued economic growth, while keeping U.S. forces at arms' length. Until recently, China propped up the Kim regime in North Korea as its best bet for stability. However, like every other nation in the region, it opposes the nuclearization of the peninsula. Now that it is clear that Beijing cannot make Pyongyang give up its nukes, China has to determine the greater threat to stability: the existence of nuclear weapons in the North or a move to unification of the Koreas.

As we have seen, China is now leaning toward support for President Park's unification initiative as the best prospect for peace on the peninsula. Unification would drastically alter the geopolitical dynamic of the region in a way that helps China. Currently, South Korea, Japan, and the United States have been drawn into a tighter alliance in response to North Korea's threatening actions. This makes China nervous and tends to reinforce old Cold War–legacy fault lines. The creation of a new Korean nation would change the regional context.

U.S. troops in Korea, who guarantee the American commitment to defend the South against attack, would no longer be needed. Any withdrawal of U.S. troops should be contingent upon the demilitarization of the North and the achievement of a certain level of political integration on the peninsula, but movement in this direction would greatly reassure the Chinese. The issue could be discussed informally between the United States, South Korea, and China, and a tacit agreement reached that would ease the path to unification. Ultimately, Korea and other nations in the region will have to balance their relations with both China and the United States. The fundamental issue is that unification must be Korean-led and free from controlling foreign influences.

The more that the initiative for unification is Korean-led and driven, the easier it will be. The ultimate result would be that international relations in the region will be removed from the old Cold War context and can begin to be refashioned toward common regional goals of peace, stability, and economic development. The new Korean nation, having opened the door to this refashioning of relations, will play a leading role in the region.

For the United States, its security concerns will be met. The threat to its treaty allies, the ROK and Japan, will be removed. More importantly, since the United States remains heavily engaged in the Middle East and in the global war on terror, unification will end the greater threat, from an American perspective, of nuclear proliferation from the North. Stability in the region would also free Russia to pursue its economic development goals for Siberia and its Far East provinces. With the security threat gone, economic development in the region, which is each country's primary goal, could move forward unhindered.

This is true of the peninsula also. In 2014, President Park said that unification would bring an economic "bonanza" to Korea.[160] A number of studies have supported her forecast, pointing to the synergy between the capital-intensive, technologically advanced South and the labor-intensive, resource-rich North. The Goldman Sachs report on the economic prospects of a unified Korea projects that it would surpass Germany and Japan by 2050.[161]

For many Koreans, however, especially the younger generation, the glass appears half empty. In 2013, Seoul's Ministry of Strategy and Finance estimated that unification would cost $80 billion annually, or 7 percent of GDP, for a decade.[162] They think of unification as a huge financial burden that they will carry over many years rather than seeing the opportunities it presents—opportunities that Korea needs if it is to continue to prosper.

The unification of Germany is often cited as a cautionary example, especially since the population ratio between North Korea and South Korea is very different compared to that between East Germany and West Germany. Also, the income difference is much larger. The per capita GDP ratio between South Korea and North Korea[163] (on a purchasing power parity basis) is estimated to be 18:1.[164] In the case of Germany, it was only 3:1.[165]

However, the reality is that predictions of the economic cost of unification are guesstimates and rely on widely differing assumptions.[166]

Andrei Lankov, a Russian specialist on Korea and author of the book *The Real North Korea*, counted over thirty serious attempts to calculate the costs of unification since the mid-1990s. There was a twenty-five-fold difference between the low estimates ($200 billion) and the high estimates ($5 trillion). This is to say, the calculations are largely guesswork, and the actual cost will depend to a great degree on the particular policy choices made to bring about economic integration.[167]

In the years since 1989, German unification has been a net positive. Germany today stands as the economic engine of the European Union and a model to aspire to. Even so, there are lessons to be learned from the German process. The 1:1 exchange rate between West and East German marks, for example, was unsustainable given the much lower level of productivity in the East.[168] Korea can learn from the German experience and from other examples of unification, such as Vietnam. Goohoon Kwon, author of the 2009 Goldman Sachs report, points to Hong Kong and China, as well as Eastern Europe, Vietnam, and Mongolia, as better models. He suggests that there are other, more effective ways to unite the two nations and move from communism to democracy than the German model.

In the end, the estimates that unification will incur huge costs is an excuse for doing nothing but becoming the passive victims of circumstance. There is no certainty in any of these estimates. What is certain is that North Korea has assets that complement the South Korean economy and address its limitations.[169]

In particular, it would help with the aging population, dwindling workforce, and lack of natural resources in the South. The North Korean population can provide a pool of new labor for the economy of a unified Korea. Its workforce is literate, disciplined, greatly underemployed, and much younger.[170] As their income level gradually rises, they will also offer an expanding market. South Korean capital, entrepreneurship, and technology can combine to offer the North Korean workforce far more productive opportunities.[171]

Mineral resources in the North are far greater than in the South[172] and access to them would insulate the Korean economy and industry from price fluctuations on the global market. South Korea has relied heavily on imports of iron ore, zinc, and copper. North Korea's reserves of iron ore are between 2.4 billion and 5 billion tons, some seventy-seven to 150 times greater than South Korea (32 million tons). Copper deposits are eighty-three times larger than those in the South, and zinc deposits are fifty-three times greater.

Overall, the value of mineral resources in North Korea has been estimated at $9.7 trillion, twenty-one times higher than South Korea.[173] North Korea has significant deposits of magnesite and is thought to have rare earth deposits large enough to double the world's known reserves.[174] The labor pool and natural resources of the North complement the technology, capital, and enterprise of the South. The result over the mid-term would be to push back the current constraints starting to squeeze the Korean economy and provide for a new burst of growth and development. The Goldman Sachs report says that Korea can become the eighth-largest economy in the world.[175] Personally, I believe this projection is too conservative and that a unified Korea can become one of the top five economies in the world.

The economic benefits will extend throughout the region. President Park told the 2014 World Economic Forum in Davos, "As unification can provide the Northeast Asia region with a fresh growth engine, I think unification will be a jackpot not only for South Korea, but also for all neighboring countries in Northeast Asia."[176] She said that unification would open the door for major international infrastructure investment in the North, as well as encourage new investment in the neighboring regions of China and Russia.

All the countries of the region would benefit as new trade routes would open up and the North Korean regime would no longer be an obstacle that had to be worked around. China could develop its border provinces in cooperation with its Korean neighbor without having to worry about setbacks arising from upheavals in the North Korean leadership and subsequent unforeseen shifts in the rules governing their trade and investment. Russia could pursue a pipeline through the Korean peninsula should it wish without any of the current concerns. Japan, whose trade with North Korea is now minimal because of sanctions, would have a new market for trade and investment.

THE DILEMMA OF THE NORTH KOREAN ELITE

In North Korea, Kim Jong-un's harsh efforts to consolidate his rule suggest there may be divisions within the ruling elite. Many members of the elite are very likely anxious about their own survival. This was the pattern among the party bureaucrats as the Soviet Union and its communist empire in East Europe fell into decline. They certainly realize that the regime's last survival card is the threat of nuclear-armed conflict, but that if they ever launched a hot war it would mark the end for them and the country. Unlike in the Cold War, they would receive no support from either Russia or China.

For them, the best hope of survival is to engineer a change within the North that would lead to serious discussions on a process of peaceful unification. The North-South Joint Communique of 1972[177] already provides an agreed foundation of principles upon which talks could proceed. The alternative for them is grim, and in this they can learn from the historic precedents of transition from communist regimes.

In Mongolia, where there was a bloodless transition to democracy, the communist party changed its name and some of its ideas and joined the democratic process. Since then, as the People's Party, it has been in both government and opposition.[178] Even in countries in the former Soviet Union and other communist countries that guided their own transition from communism, the party leadership mostly survived in a new form.[179]

However, if members of the elite in the North resist to the bitter end, they can expect a very different fate. After a government collapse in the North or a chaotic transition, members of the elite would face trial and imprisonment for a wide range of crimes, including crimes against humanity, documented in the UN Commission of Enquiry report. For most of the Workers' Party elite, their best hope for their own survival lies in cooperating in the transition from the current system toward a unified nation.

For South Korean society, the commitment to create a new nation on the peninsula based on the vision of the Korean Dream would create a renewed sense of national purpose that can dispel the growing apathy toward unification and Korea's cultural identity. This needs to be a national movement that engages the whole population. The unification initiative of President Park is timely, but it does not give enough attention to public support of and involvement with the process.[180] In a democracy, the will of the citizens is central, and without broad-based citizen support, a government initiative of this scope and significance will not succeed.

A VISION THAT MEETS ALL CHALLENGES

The challenging circumstances of Korea today are, in fact, ripe with opportunities. The greatest opportunity, if Koreans are ready to seize it, is the creation of a new nation, a Korea that exemplifies the Korean Dream, rooted in our common history and shared cultural identity. The creation of this new Korea would address existing challenges and meet the aspirations of Koreans both North and South, as well as of our neighbors in the region.

For Koreans in the North, it offers a way out of their current impasse, especially for members of the leadership elite that are, nevertheless, quintessentially Korean in character. For Koreans in the South, it offers a way out of shortsighted consumerism and political bickering by establishing a clear national purpose based upon the essential features of our Korean cultural identity and history. For our neighbors in the region, it removes the major threat to security and stability and thus stimulates greater economic prosperity, which is what they all desire. In sum, it is a solution that meets everyone's needs.

The opportunity is real, but it will not last indefinitely. The security threat from the North to South Korean prosperity is real and, with growing uncertainty, will only become greater. The flow of information into the North, the military-first policy, and the appearance of markets have all divided the people from the regime, making it less secure. When you add to that the international isolation of the North, even from its former allies, and the inexperience and unpredictable character of Kim Jong-un, you have a volatile mixture where Kim may start a conflict feeling he has nothing to lose.

That is why Koreans both North and South must seize the moment to act and preempt such a possibility by promoting a principled unification. We cannot afford to wait passively for events to unfold and possibly bury us.

This moment is an inflection point in our history, a moment of transition from past structures and relationships. It offers the Korean people a unique opportunity to determine our own destiny. Whether we seize it or neglect it will determine the path of our future for better or worse for a long time to come. The emergence of a new Korean nation will close the door on an old history by removing the last vestige of the Cold War and the dynamics of confrontation in the region that were based upon it.

It will also close the long chapter of the Asian struggle for independence and self-determination free of earlier colonial and geopolitical influences from outside. This step is necessary as the global center of gravity shifts eastward from the Atlantic region to Asia and the Pacific Rim. In the course of this shift of balance, a new Korea, built upon universal principles and having achieved unification peacefully, will exercise tremendous moral authority. It can use that authority to act as a bridge nation in the region, mediating historic disputes, promoting regional cooperation, and advancing the ideals of human rights and freedom.

For North Korea, the writing is on the wall. In its current state, the country cannot endure. Its best hope for survival lies in supporting a peaceful transformation on the peninsula to bring about the unification of North and South. To achieve that, we need a vision that unites us as a people and transcends present political squabbles. If we can unite and act upon the vision of the Korean Dream, we can reverse the painful history of the twentieth century, where Korea was often the plaything of fate.

More than that, we can become a light in the region and the world. The Korean Dream, rooted in Hongik Ingan principles and substantiated in a new, united nation, will give Korea the foundation to be the link between the nations of the Asian continent and those of the Pacific Rim. Since Hongik Ingan embodies universal principles of human rights that are also reflected in the European Reformation and Enlightenment traditions, Korea will be uniquely placed to also be a bridge between East and West. The destiny that calls to us is astonishing in its scope.

We can act decisively to take control of our destiny free from the domination of others. If we fail to act, however, outside forces will once again determine our future as they did so often in the twentieth century. The key is to act not just from political and economic calculation but in a manner that is true to our identity as a Korean people. I examine that identity in depth in the next chapter.

CHAPTER 4

Discovering Our Future Through Understanding Our Past

"I wish my nation would be a nation that doesn't just imitate others, but rather it be a nation that is the source of a new and higher culture, that it can become the goal and an example [for others]. And so true world peace could come from our nation. I wish peace would be achieved in our nation and from there to the world. I believe that that is the Hongik Ingan ideal of our national ancestor Dangun."
–KIM GU, BAEKBEOMILJI, 1947

Prolonged division has created many differences between North Korea and South Korea. Our language and lifestyle have developed distinct qualities. Some people believe these differences are too big to overcome, and that the goal of ending the division and achieving unification is unattainable. Yet, seventy years of separation is nothing compared to the 5,000 years of our shared history. The real problem is that Koreans in both the North and South are losing their connection to that shared history and, as a result, are losing their Korean identity. In the North, totalitarian rule and a materialist ideology have eaten away at it; in the South, the materialism of a consumer society has had the same effect.

Korean identity, originating in the Dangun founding story and the Hongik Ingan ideal and forged through harsh historical experience, is inseparable from Korea's destiny. Hongik Ingan laid out the principles that took root in the Korean consciousness, leading Koreans to aspire to high-minded ideals and adopt a fundamentally spiritual outlook toward life. On the level of society, this produced the desire to establish an ideal nation and to become a source of inspiration and learning for the rest of humanity. This type of hope is clearly expressed in the opening quote of the chapter from the great independence leader Kim Gu.

These characteristics run like a thread through Korea's history and point us toward our unfulfilled destiny. They have given us the capacity to embrace a wide range of religions and ethical systems—Buddhism, Taoism, Confucianism, and Christianity—yet always being able to adapt them to correspond with our unique spiritual consciousness, one that has been forged and tempered by a Korean reality and a pursuit of our destiny.

Unification is the next significant step toward realizing that destiny. However, to successfully achieve it, Koreans must revive those core ideals that still burn deep within the Korean consciousness and are an essential foundation of our Korean identity.

For this reason, it is critical to understand the history in which the Korean identity was molded and given expression. As the saying goes, "There can be no future for a people who have forgotten their history." Unfortunately, the emphasis on Korea's unique history is being neglected within the education curricula for the youth in the South. The subject is only an elective for university entrance exams, something many foreigners find hard to understand. Knowledge of our history is an essential part of understanding what it means to be Korean. In this chapter, I want to examine our people's historical goals and the culture we developed to pursue them, especially the unique Korean family culture. I also want to show how they relate to our current situation and the path we must take to fulfill Korea's destiny.

THE DREAM OF BUILDING AN IDEAL NATION OF HONGIK INGAN

Historically, we have been invaded countless times, and the entire peninsula has been occupied by foreign powers several times. What then was the force that made it possible for us to stay together as one people on this land without losing our identity? Normally, people who are invaded become assimilated, losing their distinctive historic and cultural identity. Some civilizations have ceased to exist, even after building massive empires that spanned vast territories and endured for centuries. But we have lived together on this peninsula as a cohesive homogeneous people for thousands of years, although we were invaded and attacked repeatedly throughout our history.

I personally believe that the Hongik Ingan ideal of benefiting all humanity is the true strength of the Korean people and what allowed us to endure throughout our challenging past. These ideals, tempered by national tribulations, have been internalized by our people to create a deep spiritual consciousness that guided us on a unique historical path of enlightened governance and providential destiny. Looking back in our history, whenever we faced a significant turning point, such as the founding of a new dynasty, we always went back to the roots from which our people sprang. If we were to encapsulate our history in one phrase, we could say that it was "a history of aspiring to build an ideal nation."

All the kingdoms established during Korea's history looked back to Gojoseon as their origin and drew legitimacy from it. The thirteenth-century manuscript *Samguk Yusa* recounts the legendary founding of Gojoseon by Dangun in 2333 BC. The first contemporary written records of the kingdom are Chinese and appear in the seventh century BC. In the second century BC, Gojoseon fell to invasion by the Han Chinese and a turbulent period of clan warfare followed until the emergence of the Three Kingdoms in the middle and later part of the first century BC. However, each of these kingdoms sought to inherit the mantle of Gojoseon and looked back to Dangun as their founder.

The story of Jumong, which has become immensely popular through the TV drama both in Korea and worldwide, recounts the genesis of Goguryeo (37 BC–AD 668). Jumong is the legendary founder of Goguryeo, who tries to inherit the legacy of the Dangun myth of creating an ideal homeland for the Korean people. Thus, Goguryeo was formed to reclaim the territory that had formerly belonged to Gojoseon. This same impulse can be seen in the early history of both Silla (57 BC–AD 935) and Baekje (18 BC–AD 660), the other two of the Three Kingdoms.

Their founding stories share the same theme that we are a people descended from heaven with a providential mandate to benefit all humanity. Kingdoms built upon such a foundation would naturally seek high spiritual aspirations, principles, and values. Goguryeo, Silla, and Baekje all developed Buddhism and Taoism as the foundation of their spiritual culture and consciousness on top of the already rich indigenous traditions. In addition, they incorporated the ethical and moral elements of Confucianism as the foundation of their political ideology.

While other East Asian nations were influenced by these religious and ethical traditions to some extent, few, if any, other nations integrated and developed them the way Koreans did. The spirit of Hongik Ingan made our people very receptive to seeking spiritual truths, righteousness, and good governance—the origin of the Korean spiritual consciousness that has developed throughout our history. This consciousness assimilated the various traditions, learning from them and shaping them in pursuit of Korea's broader destiny.

The Hwarang system, developed in the sixth century AD under Silla, played an important role in unifying the Three Kingdoms. This system selected high-born youth to become leaders of character dedicated to the service of the nation. These youths used the duality of nature's challenging environment and serene beauty to train their bodies in the martial arts as well as to cultivate their minds and hearts through the study of philosophy, religion, and ethics.

Won Gwang (AD 542–640), teacher of Hwarang and a Buddhist priest, established the Five Commandments for Secular Life (世俗五戒): loyalty to one's lord (事君以忠), love and respect for one's parents and teachers (事親以孝), trust among friends (交友以信), never retreat in battle (臨戰無退), and never take a life without just cause (殺生有擇). These were the practical virtues of Hwarangdo that all Hwarang youths were to exhibit.

The Five Commandments for Secular Life incorporated elements of the Taoist, Buddhist, and Confucian traditions in a uniquely Korean manner. Its special characteristic was that the practice of personal ethics was ultimately infused with the motive of the creation of an ideal nation. It could be considered a code of conduct for the establishment of an ideal Hongik Ingan nation. When Silla unified the peninsula, the Five Commandments became our people's unique ethical philosophical tradition. As a result, the moral standard of the later Goryeo and Joseon periods can also be explained using the Five Commandments for Secular Life as the standard.

Choe Chiwon (857–?) said the following about Hwarangdo in his "Nallangbi Seomun (鸞郎碑序文)":

> Our nation has a deep and mysterious form of enlightenment (玄妙한 道), which can be called a form of refinement (風流). The details of this spirit are written from our early history in *Sunsa* (仙史; "History Book of Sunga"). It truly embraces the three religions and it edifies (敎化) the people. It is the same as what Confucius teaches in Confucianism in that one must pursue filial piety (孝) in the family, and be loyal (忠) to the nation; it is the same as Lao-tzu's Taoism in that it teaches action through non-action (無爲), and teaches actions without words; it is the same as the Buddha's

Buddhism in that it guides us to pursue every goodness (諸善) instead of all evil (諸惡).[181]

According to Choe Chiwon, our people originally had a "national spirit," which he described as aligned with the essential spirits of Confucianism, Buddhism, and Taoism.[182] He said that the spirit of Hwarangdo is the systematization of the spirit that our people have cultivated since our genesis. In other words, the ideals of Hongik Ingan spawned a spiritual consciousness that resonated with the universal truths found in those faith traditions that Hwarangdo helped shape into a substantial expression of Korea's national spirit and identity.

However, the Unified Silla dynasty eventually declined due to internal divisions and the extravagant lifestyle of the king and aristocracy. It marked a period of internal struggles during which our people, although unified, lost sight of our unique heritage and providential destiny. Faced with such circumstances, General Wanggeon (877–943) established Goryeo (918–1392) with a call for national unification, centered on the historic aspirations of the Korean people to create a model nation.

Unfortunately, throughout this dynasty, Goryeo had to defend itself from the invading army of Mongols (1231–1270), as well as continuous attacks from other nations. Due to those struggles in this period, there was an even greater impetus to turn to our spiritual consciousness and yearn to establish the ideal nation that Dangun envisioned. *Samguk Yusa*, written by the Buddhist monk Iryeon (1206–1289) and *Jewang Ungi* by Yi Seung Hyu (1224–1300) both hearken back to our founding mythology to find guidance and instill a sense of national destiny. It can be assumed that such historical texts were widely distributed since printing was invented in Korea around that time.[183] However, toward the end of the Goryeo period, the incompetence of the rulers and the corruption of the aristocrats (權門勢家, Kwonmunsega) once again—like Silla before it—diverted this dynasty from its original ideals, and later it fell into disorder.

As a result, Goryeo collapsed, and Yi Seonggye (1335–1408) then established a new dynasty called Joseon. The new dynasty aimed to establish an ideal Confucian nation. Once again, the legitimacy of the newly founded state was based on the aspiration of the Korean people to create an ideal nation alluded to in our founding mythology. Even the name of the new nation, Joseon, was a means to clearly show that its roots lay in Dangun's Joseon. The new dynasty built shrines and altars—in Mani Mountain, in Kanghwa Island, and all around the nation to honor Dangun as our national ancestor.

More than ever before, true to Hongik Ingan ideals, Joseon's political system was based on a people-centered philosophy (民本主義) that had a clear guiding purpose: "The ruler is not more important than the nation, and the nation is not more important than the people." In other words, very similar to the ideals upon which modern Western democracies were formed, there was a social contract between the ruler and government and the people, in which the people's happiness and well-being were the objectives of good governance and why the ruler and his government had power. This bond was melded further through the lens of the Confucian family ethic, in which the monarch was looked upon as the father of the nation and, thus, had a moral obligation to take care of the people as his extended family—with virtue, wisdom, and justice.

The reign of King Sejong the Great (1418–1450), the fourth king of this dynasty and the most celebrated monarch in Korean history, exemplifies this well. Among his greatest achievements was the creation of Hangul, the phonetic alphabetic system that became the basis of the Korean language. For decades, the king personally led the effort to develop the easiest system of reading and writing, to help his mostly illiterate and uneducated people. At that time, literacy and education were the exclusive province of the aristocracy and not of common people. Hanmun, the Chinese system of characters, was cumbersome and difficult to learn, reinforcing the social divide between the classes. The creation of Hangul fundamentally changed the social landscape, offering those in the lower classes opportunities for advancement.

In addition to this achievement, Sejong and his retainers debated intensively on how best to govern for the benefit of the people. Sejong is largely recognized as mainstreaming the Confucian ethic and ideal not only into government but gaining wide acceptance in the common everyday life of average Koreans. He strengthened the military and had several diplomatic victories that expanded Korea's national territory. Even the advancement of science and technology, as well as the issuing of regulations, fell under the responsibility of the king who created the Hall of Worthies (集賢殿), consisting of the best scholars at the time for the development of those areas. Scholars and thinkers continuously wrote and advised him and future monarchs to ensure that they ruled according to moral principles of good governance.

The tradition of a people-centered philosophy (民本主義) was not just a virtue required of the king, but it was also considered the core spirit for all government officials. This trend led to the emergence of Shilhak (實學), the Realist School of Confucianism, a social reform movement during the late Joseon that tried to tackle the real problems of good governance. It was a response to the more metaphysical and structural orientation of neo-Confucianism. This movement's proponents advocated the importance of human equality by reforming the rigid Confucian social structures, promoting land reform, encouraging science, and developing technology, as well as pioneering empirically based methods of engaging social problems. In addition, it promoted a Korean-centric historic worldview in line with Hongik Ingan ideals.

Jeong Yakyong (1762–1836), the most prominent scholar of this movement, presented a detailed theory of the responsibilities and duties of government officials toward the people. Deeply concerned about the widespread poverty of many Koreans during the late Joseon period, Yakyong authored the influential work the *Mokminsimseo* (The Mind of Governing the People), in which he outlines the role of government and its bureaucrats in dealing with this issue in service to the least fortunate. His most influential book, the *Gyeongse Yupyo* (Design for Good Governance) became his seminal work, which outlined a blueprint for the ethical management of the nation. It would have an enduring effect throughout the later Joseon period well into the modern era.

Jung Dojeon's (1342–1398) *Joseon Gyunggukjeon* (1394) proposed a framework for Joseon's legal system. The publication underwent extensive revision until it was finally completed as the *Gyeongguk Daejeon* in 1485 during King Seongjong's rule. This was the Joseon tradition of royal politics based on a people-centered philosophy (民本主義的 王道政治), which meant that a ruler could not govern by arbitrary decree but had to govern through consultation centered upon a framework of law.

In effect, Korea developed a quasi-constitutional system of checks and balances as early as the fifteenth century. It covered not just the power of the king himself but also the state bureaucracy with emphasis on good governance for the sake of the Korean people. What is remarkable is that this system emerged independently of any Western influence and three centuries or so before European philosophers of the Enlightenment era such as John Locke, the father of modern liberalism, introduced the ideas of liberty and social contracts that birthed modern Western political philosophy. Even later, Montesquieu began writing about the separation of powers that became the hallmark of all constitutional democratic states after the founding of the United States.

Thus, Hongik Ingan represented the enduring vision of our people and the basis of our deep spiritual consciousness that sought to build an ideal nation based on high principles and values. Due to this, we embraced the universal truths in various faith institutions and ethical philosophies and internalized them to fit our unique Korean aspiration. We developed a people-oriented philosophy in which the purpose of the king and government was to provide for the well-being of the larger populace at a time when absolutist monarchies were the norm both in Asia and Europe. As a result, our ancestors established a limited quasi-constitutional form of government during the Joseon dynasty that had many of the features found in modern democratic free market states centuries before they appeared anywhere else until the creation of the United States.

A Nation for the People and to Serve the World

The tradition of a people-centered philosophy did not suddenly appear during the Joseon dynasty. Politics for the sake of the people has been a long-established Korean tradition. One striking piece of evidence for this principle is that all the dynasties founded by our people lasted for at least 500 to 1,000 years. Historically speaking, in both East and West, it is hard to find dynasties that have lasted for more than 500 years; even China, which has a similar long history, averaged 200 to 300 years per dynasty. Why were our dynasties able to continue for so long? If the dynasty ignored its people or if the ruler acted like a despot, then the dynasties would not be able to sustain themselves for such prolonged periods. This characteristic of our history is very special. And it was possible because they engaged in governance with a mind to benefit the people in the spirit of Hongik Ingan.

There were many different dynasties and nations formed by our ancestors after Gojoseon. Although there were examples of despotic kings throughout our long 5,000-year history, it would be fair to say that most were tempered by the unique Hongik Ingan legacy, making their actions somewhat benign compared to other extreme examples of the time. Yet, the majority of Korean rulers practiced the spirit of living for the people (為民), believing that they should engage in politics and govern based on a people-centered philosophy in their attempts to establish a Daedong Segye (大同世界; a concept of an ideal form of nation during the Joseon period).

This orientation of governance for the sake of the people naturally elicited a long-standing tradition of loyalty to the ruler and nation. That is why our citizens are very patriotic, believing that they share in responsibility for the well-being of their country along with their king and his government. This spirit shined exceptionally brightly when we were invaded by outside forces. The Sambyulcho resistance (三別抄 抗爭) that lasted forty years during the Mongol invasion of Goryeo was a popular movement. The same was true during the Japanese invasion of Korea (壬辰倭亂, 1592–1598) and the second Manchu invasion of Korea (丙子胡

亂, 1636–1637). On each of these occasions, armies raised in the cause of justice (義兵) were created by people all over the nation. They stood up to defend the country when the government could not. The strength that sustained us for half a millennium was due to our people's ownership of Hongik Ingan and the aspiration to create an ideal nation.

Although Koreans emphasize patriotism as an important value, we have a special view of state power in that, throughout our 5,000-year history, we never developed the type of totalitarian rule that forcibly sacrifices the individual for the benefit of the state. This attitude among our citizens found its source in the relationships within the Korean family. We considered putting one's family before one's self as the highest ethical expression, and this spirit then naturally extended to the community and nation. Unlike in totalitarian regimes, emphasizing the community was done freely by patriotic citizens who acted as owners of the nation's destiny.

Our people's religious culture is also based upon such a sense of community and view of the state. The faith traditions that our people accepted were focused on the well-being and development of society and the nation, rather than focusing solely on individual spiritual development. This religious tendency in Korea strove not simply to influence the ethics of the individual but, more importantly, to influence the morality of society and the nation. Throughout most of our history, this was true not only of Taoism and Confucianism but also of Buddhism.

Korean Buddhism readily embraced much of Confucian teaching, with its emphasis on social ethics. The Five Commandments for Secular Life of the Hwarangdo, similar as they are to Confucian ethical principles, capture the character of our Buddhist tradition. Whereas traditional Buddhism tended to emphasize the individual's search for spiritual enlightenment through meditation and introspection, Korean Buddhism gave a higher priority to the community and the nation. As an example, although Buddhism has an unwritten rule against the taking of life, when our nation was invaded by outside forces, even monks and priests would take up arms in its defense. That is why in Korea we speak of "Buddhism that defends the state" (*Hoguk* Buddhism; 護國佛敎).

Our people actively accepted Confucianism, Buddhism, and Taoism, and then wove them into a unique spiritual culture centered upon our core idea of Hongik Ingan. This was the foundation upon which we accepted new religions, cultures, and knowledge from outside. With our innate spiritual character and open-mindedness to different faiths, we took the best aspects of those we encountered and made them part of our own spiritual tradition. In the process, we shaped and developed our own distinctive Korean identity throughout the course of our challenging history.

The tradition of the people-centered approach to governance that emerged so early in Korean history combined with the people's commitment to preserve the nation is striking. It seems to be a characteristic of well-functioning modern democracies that uphold fundamental human rights and freedoms. Since I received most of my education in the West and am familiar with Western history, particularly the evolution of democracy there, I was intrigued to compare Korean history to that of America. The United States pioneered a new constitutional democratic republic that far outstripped Greece and Rome in terms of protecting individual liberty and freedoms and limiting the power of government through the separations of power; in turn, the United States became the "beacon on the hill" to which flocked millions of immigrants who could not find those rights and freedoms at home. Upon becoming citizens, they would fiercely fight for what America stood for.

Like Korea's long-standing tradition, America adopted a truly people-centered political philosophy with the "inalienable" rights of its citizens endowed by a Creator and not by any human being, institution, or government. According to the Declaration of Independence, the purpose of government was to protect those rights and freedoms for its citizens and not for its own sake. As President Abraham Lincoln famously described in the closing of his Gettysburg Address at the hallowed grounds of the Civil War's greatest battle, the American experiment was to show the world that a "government of the people, by the people, for the people" shall "long endure." These similarities to Korea's people-oriented philosophy are striking, considering the influence of the United States in shaping the direction of world attitudes and history over the last quarter millennia in their advocacy of constitutional popular government. In other words, those are universal ideals whose time has truly come in the modern era, yet they have been part of Korea's history for thousands of years.

As a nation that aspired to high principles and values, Korea never undertook a policy of military intervention or conquest, although attacked and threatened countless times by its neighbors. Nor did the intense patriotism of our people lead us to develop an aggressive nationalism, as was the case for many of our neighbors. Instead, we developed a culture in which the value and dignity of the individual and the needs of the nation existed in harmony, bound together by a common destiny (共同運命體). That destiny was firmly rooted in the Hongik Ingan ideals of creating a model nation that would benefit all humanity.

Thus, Korean foreign policy was relatively benign in an intensely contested region, with powers such as China to the west and Japan to the east, as well as the Mongols, and later Russians, to the north. Korea was caught in a cauldron of violent interventionist maneuvering among all its neighbors, but somehow Korea was able to persevere without abandoning its high-minded ideals and losing sight of its destiny. Our track record is unique among nations, especially those that have a long history. With an emerging global consensus against aggressive interventionism, and among nations with such pasts, our history is something to be proud of. It gives us the moral authority to champion issues of peace and stability as well as to build nonthreatening relationships of trust and mutual benefit.

Although Korean history ran independently from that of the United States until the turn of the twentieth century, these two nations have much in common. As I have mentioned above, both nations adopted a people-oriented philosophy in which the well-being and rights of its citizens were the purpose of government and not the other way around. In order to safeguard against the misuse of power, both developed the idea of separation of powers with clearly delineated limits to the authority of government institutions. Most importantly, both nations aspired to high-minded ideals that uplifted human value with a divine providential mission to serve humanity. The only difference was that Korea set these precedents thousands of years before the creation of America.

These similarities were not unknown to our ancestors in the beginning of the twentieth century, when Koreans first met American Christian missionaries spreading the Good News. Catholicism was present in Korea a century prior to this new wave of American Protestant evangelism, but proved not to have Protestantism's mass appeal. Unlike people in other Asian nations who rejected Christianity outright as a threat to their national identity, many Koreans, especially the royalty and aristocracy of that time, embraced this new faith from the West. Although one could conjure some cynical political reasons for it, I believe that acceptance of this Western faith tradition aligned with the innate aspirations of the Korean people, very much like Taoism, Confucianism, and Buddhism did earlier.

Christian teaching, with its emphasis on selfless love and service for one's fellow man, fit nicely with the Korean character molded throughout the millennia by the ideal of Hongik Ingan. The notion of divine providence naturally complemented the Korean understanding of their special mission "to serve humanity." Most importantly, the Korean term for the Creator, Haneunim, fit well with the Christian understanding of God. As a result, although Christianity came from the West, to many Koreans it complemented the already existing beliefs, characteristics, and qualities that they had cherished and cultivated.

By accepting this new faith, Koreans made a bridge to the West unlike other Asian countries, except the Philippines. However, in the case of the Philippines, Catholicism was forced upon the population through Spanish conquest and colonization. The situation with Korea was very different; Protestantism was readily accepted by many Koreans, to the point that today one-third of the population is Protestant. Since American missionaries made inroads in Korean society, Korean Christianity has a special relationship with the United States. Thus, not only does Korea bridge East and West in general, but in particular it has a unique relationship with America and the principles and values it espouses, especially since America's values resonate with our own national aspirations.

Thus, Hongik Ingan set the stage for a people-oriented philosophy that allowed Korea to develop in ways not found in other Asian countries. The high-minded ideals of its founding set it on an independent path from its neighbors by developing a deep spiritual consciousness that sought to find truth, enlightenment, goodness, and virtue, embracing foreign religious traditions with an open-mindedness not found in many other countries. Independent of the social transformations that would come in Europe during the Reformation, Renaissance, and Enlightenment eras many centuries later, Hongik Ingan ideals allowed Koreans to have an enlightened view of humanity and its relation to heaven. Thus, our political, religious, and social orientations reflected a philosophy that exalted the human dignity of our people as well as the rest of humanity. Central to the Korean story was its mission to create an ideal nation and live for the sake of all mankind. We were specially chosen for this task. It defined us and gave our people meaning.

FINDING OUR PEOPLE'S DREAM AGAIN IN MOMENTS OF CRISIS

During the nineteenth century, the light of the Joseon dynasty started to dim as the country was embroiled in peasant rebellions due to wholesale corruption, political intrigue, and intrusions from foreign powers. In addition to what was happening inside Korea, the world, especially China, was being carved up by the imperialist policies of the great Western powers. To many Koreans, the subordination of China, which had historically been Korea's suzerain, to the West was unimaginable. This confluence of factors presaged the impending doom of the dynasty and revolutionary changes to come in Korea.

Under these challenging circumstances, our people sought direction and meaning by returning to our original ideals. One prominent new indigenous religious movement arose out of this vortex of turmoil and confusion. In 1860, as a reaction to Seohak (西學; Western learning), Choe Je-u, inspired by his own revelations as well as Korea's founding heritage, rich spiritual traditions, and elements of Christianity, created a new religion unique to our people. He named it Donghak (東學; Eastern learning). He spread the idea of In Nae Cheon, which declared that "people are heaven" (人乃天) and that "Heaven's heart is the people's heart" (天心 則人心). Through his teachings, Choe called for the realization of heaven on earth, in which all people could live with human rights, dignity, and equality, echoing the aspirations of our people in Hongik Ingan ideals.

Daewongun, the regent father of King Gojong, saw the meteoric rise and popular support of this new faith as a threat. In particular, his administration took issue with Choe's prediction that the Joseon dynasty would end in its five-hundredth year in accordance to his belief in dynastic cycles, which many scholars of the period also shared. By 1863, a rushed mock trial was held, and he was convicted of practicing Catholicism and sentenced to death the following year. However, his martyrdom only secured the future of his new religious movement as his teaching resonated with the plight of the peasantry caught under the yoke of increasing corruption among the aristocracy and government officials, as well as the continuing pressures of foreign influence. Thus, the Donghak faith had a widespread grassroots base throughout the southern provinces of Korea.

The death of Choe only helped hasten the end of the Joseon dynasty as his dynastic prediction came true. Ironically, the new religious movement that he founded became the catalyst for geopolitical events that were to fundamentally change the future of Korea during the twilight of the nineteenth century. In 1894, an insurrection against the despotic rule of the Gobu county magistrate led to the Donghak Peasant Revolution (東學農民運動). This rebellion, motivated by the ideals proposed in the Donghak religion, developed into a political and social movement to fundamentally reform the nation from foreign influences and inner corruption, although the rebellion stated its continuing loyalty to King Gojong.

Due to the scope and intensity of the uprising, however, King Gojong requested and received military assistance from the Qing emperor of China in quelling this rebellion. This step eventually set the pretext for Japanese involvement in Korea. Under the Convention of Tientsin in

1885, China was required to inform Japan of troop movements on the peninsula, which it failed to do when sending aid to quell the uprising. This became grounds for the Sino-Japanese War, which Japan won on every front—on sea and land. Later, in 1894, the Donghak rebellion was crushed by Japanese and government forces, eventually securing Japan's position in controlling the peninsula and setting the stage for events to come in the early part of the twentieth century.

The first of these events was the official end of the Joseon dynasty. In 1897, King Gojong, the twenty-sixth ruler of that dynasty, declared the creation of the Great Korean Empire. He would be the first emperor, taking the title of Emperor Gwangmu. He hoped to create an independent Korea strong enough to rival China as well as fend off Japanese and Russian attempts to control the peninsula. Yet, in the end, all his efforts turned out to be futile as he increasingly succumbed to unfavorable negotiations with both Japan and Russia, which in 1904 led to the Russo-Japanese War.

With Japan's victory a year later, the Meiji government forced Emperor Gwangmu to receive permanent pro-Japanese advisors into his Imperial Court to administer the country. Later, in 1905, with the Protectorate Treaty between the empires of Japan and Korea, Korea forfeited its diplomatic sovereignty to Japan. Two years later, the first emperor was forced to abdicate his throne to his son, Sunjong, due to his efforts at the Hague Peace Conference to gain international attention for the plight of Korea and the ambitions of Japan in Asia. Yet, Sunjong's reign was short-lived, as three years later the Annexation Treaty of 1910 brought an end to the Korean Empire and Japan took total control of the peninsula. For the first time in our 5,000-year history, our people lost their independence, sovereignty, and control over the future of our nation.

Under Japanese colonial rule, movements for independence sprang up across the entire nation and the Northeast Asia region. Unlike other efforts, the Korean independence movement strove to create a model nation in line with its founding ideals and not to reestablish the old order. As a result, it possessed higher aspirations than simply to gain national sovereignty, achieve political independence, or seek vengeance upon

Japan. Through this movement, Korean activists sought to build a nation that could be the perfect embodiment of our people's national spirit (民族精神) as embodied in Hongik Ingan.

An event that clearly reflects this spirit was the 3.1 Independence Movement of 1919. Thirty-three leaders representing Christianity, Buddhism, and Cheondoism, the native Korean faith that grew out of the Donghak movement, gathered at Tabgol Park in Jongno to deliver to the Korean people and their Japanese overlords their Declaration of Independence. This was an unprecedented show of unity among people of different faiths, social classes, and backgrounds, brought together by the common fact that they were Koreans. Thus, it was a striking expression of our Korean identity and solidarity. The Declaration opens by stating:

> We hereby declare the independence of Korea and that Koreans are a self-governing people. We proclaim it to the nations of the world affirming the principle of the equality of all people, and we proclaim it to our posterity, preserving in perpetuity the right of national self-determination.

> We make this declaration upon the authority of five thousand years of history as an expression of the devotion and loyalty of twenty million people. We claim independence in the interest of the eternal liberty and development of our people and in accordance with the great movement for world reform based upon the awakening conscience of mankind. This is the clear command of Heaven, the course of our times, and a legitimate manifestation of the right of all nations to coexist and live in harmony. Nothing in the world can suppress or block it.

The reason the Shanghai Provisional Government, Korea's government in exile during Japanese rule, changed the name of the country from "Great Korean Empire" (大韓帝國) to "Great Nation of the Han People" (大韓民國) was that the goal of independence was not to establish a "nation of an emperor" but a "nation of the people." They expressed their determination to form a government for the people based on the Hongik Ingan spirit. Kim Gu, as the head of the Shanghai Provisional Government and leader of the independence movement, prefaced his 1947 collection of essays, "My Desire," with this paragraph:

> If God asked me what was my wish, I would reply unhesitatingly, "Korean independence." If He asked me what was my second wish, I would again answer, "My country's independence." If He asked me what was my third wish, I would reply in an even louder voice, "My wish is the complete independence of my country Korea."[184]

His collection of writings that begins with the paragraph above finishes with the essay "The Nation I Dream Of." He had a very clear vision of the type of nation that he wanted to establish through the independence movement and was willing to risk his life to pursue it. It was a model nation built upon Korea's own unique aspirations, heritage, and culture and that could serve to inspire others. Korean independence to him meant fulfillment of the Hongik Ingan ideal. I started this chapter with this quote but it is worth mentioning again here. Kim Gu states:

> I wish my nation would be a nation that doesn't just imitate others, but rather it be a nation that is the source of a new and higher culture, that it can become the goal and an example [for others]. And so true world peace could come from our nation. I wish peace would be achieved in our nation and from there to the world. I believe that that is the Hongik Ingan ideal of our national ancestor Dangun.[185]

His eternal optimism in the destiny of the Korean people is apparent when he explains that the time was ripe to create such a nation and that the Korean people had the necessary qualities and character, forged through history, to accomplish this task. He then says:

And I believe that our people's talents, spirit, and our training from the past is sufficient for us to accomplish that mission, and that our nation's location and other geographic conditions also allow for it, that the demands of the human race that went through the First and Second World Wars also require it, and that the spirit of the times during which we who are newly establishing our nation also asks of it. Can't you see that the day our people will stand on the world stage as the protagonists is right before our eyes?[186]

The activists who sacrificed their lives for the independence movement had a vision greater than just national self-determination. Theirs was a lofty vision of creating a new nation that was true to the founding ideals of the Korean people. They were able to look beyond the precarious state of occupation to hope for an opportunity to create a model nation based upon high aspirations, principles, and values that would be an inspiration for other nations to emulate, with a larger goal of contributing to world peace. Their optimism in the face of tragedy reveals the enduring spirit of our people and the dream that kept it alive. That dream, as I have framed in this book, is the Korean Dream, rooted in Hongik Ingan ideals. That is why independence was so emotionally charged: it was rooted in the very origins of our historic and cultural identity.

Unfortunately, with the end of World War II and the end of Japanese occupation, the hopes of independence were dashed as the peninsula was not wholly independent but under two separate zones of influence. It was divided along the 38th parallel and sucked up into a larger geopolitical divide between the West and the Soviet bloc. By 1948, each side chose the political and economic framework of their sponsors and the subsequent antagonism of the two opposing ideological blocs. Thus, instead of the Korean people being the masters of our own united destiny, realizing the dream that animated us throughout our collective history, we were divided artificially and forced to view our brethren as our enemy in a larger geopolitical conflict beyond our control. That reality continues to this day.

We, as the Korean people, need to ask ourselves whether we will continue to fight a foreign conflict that has nothing to do with our collective historical aspirations and heritage. This conflict is even more ridiculous given the end of the Cold War with the collapse of the Soviet Union. However, both South and North lay claim to the legacy of Gojoseon and the Dangun mythology. The government of South Korea chose "Hongik Ingan" as its education ideology, and the North Korean government used the name "Joseon" as part of its official national name. Although their choices differed, in their own way, each side believed that the structures they chose would help them construct the ideal nation that our people have dreamed of for five millennia. Yet, today, it is clear that both structures have flaws that can be remedied by creating a new nation centered upon the Korean Dream.

Dangun's founding spirit penetrates Korea's history and has shaped our identity, as well as inspired our dreams. The recurring desire to establish an ideal nation built upon Hongik Ingan ideals is the historical expression of our inherent spiritual nature seeking to fulfill our destiny. That destiny looks to the future, to the creation of a new nation with the sort of global moral influence that Kim Gu prophesied. It has nothing to do with returning to a worn-out world of the past, be it 1910, 1948, or today. It has everything to do with creating a new future for the Korean people, the peninsula, the region, and the world, centered upon our unique providential destiny.

THE DEVELOPMENT OF KOREAN FAMILY CULTURE AND ITS CONFUCIAN ROOTS

A model nation based upon Hongik Ingan ideals can only make the transition from a dream to a reality when virtuous citizens and leaders of character own the Korean Dream and set the proper precedents for what those ideals should look like. As in all cultures, the family, being the smallest and most intimate social unit, has played an essential role in nurturing the values that society deems important. Throughout our long history, our unique Korean family culture (家族主義) formed the essential core of the Korean character and identity by nurturing virtuous human relations aligned to our high-minded aspirations.

Confucian thought played a central role in the development of Korean family culture. The ideal that Confucius envisaged was a world of Daedong Segye (大同世界),[187] in which all humanity lives as a family. It is where the intimate love and order within the family are extended into the larger society, nation, and world. The words "Sushin-Jega-Chiguk-Pyungcheonha" (修身齊家治國平天下) summarize this understanding well. Taken literally, it means that one should discipline oneself, establish a good and virtuous family, govern the nation wisely, and have peaceful dominion over the world.

Thus, self-discipline, morality, and virtue became desirable qualities expected of anyone in a position of authority, power, or respect. It was expected for a leader to live with humaneness, righteousness, propriety, and knowledge (仁義禮智) in order to become a moral person. In other words, he should aspire to be a *gunja* (君子), a "lord's child" or "gentleman." Likewise, since the nation and the world should be governed with virtue (德) and propriety (禮) (德治와 禮治), the ruler should set the best example of a *gunja*. Moreover, the best place to initially learn and practice all of these virtues was in the family.

Koreans have been very passionate about realizing these Confucian sentiments, even more so than Chinese, who live in the birthplace of Confucianism. Being part of the same Chinese cultural sphere, our people accepted its moral and ethical frameworks at the time it was emerging in China. Confucian ideas were already adopted as the guiding political ideology during the Three Kingdoms period, and educational institutions were established at that time that taught from Confucian texts.

In the view of many scholars, Koreans actively accepted Confucian sentiments about the family because of old, established traditions that long predated Confucius. Historians claim that our people's notion of family virtue and respect for our ancestors is related to our distinctive shamanistic beliefs and that this is part of a deep Korean spiritual consciousness. Indeed, the claim that Confucius himself was influenced by the culture and etiquette of our people, known then as the Eastern barbarians (東夷族), is gaining more credence today. Which one came first is not important here. However, by looking at the result, it is clear that the unique Korean family culture took shape because of these influences, centered upon the idea of virtuous human relationships.

Some may argue that this culture took root because Korea was an agricultural society. However, most societies before the nineteenth century were no different. Nevertheless, no other nation developed the Confucian family model to the extent that our ancestors did. In addition, what made our family culture unique, even in Asia, was the way we expanded this notion to the clan, society, and even to the level of national government as systematically as we did.

For example, during the Joseon period, our unique family culture was strongly promoted by its rulers, adapting the Confucian family ideals to Korea's system of governance and political philosophy. Joseon rightly claimed to be the ideal Confucian nation of the East, recognizing that such a nation must stand on a foundation of strong and virtuous families. Consequently, the dynasty led national reformation efforts to strengthen family culture through measures such as the completion of the clan rules system (宗法制度), centered on the family shrine or *gamyo* (家廟).

During the mid-Joseon period, the *jibsungchon* (集姓村; a village where people from the same clan live together) system was established, centered on the family shrine. It consisted of about 100 households and was the smallest political unit. It was also an economic unit that engaged in buying and selling, as well as a religious community that conducted religious observances centered on the family shrine. Although everyone was related by blood, the norms of behavior that an individual had to follow were very clearly delineated. The result of this effort was the expansion of family ethics and order throughout the entire society.

Through this process, the Confucian moral teaching of *Samgang Oryun* (三綱五倫), or Three Fundamental Principles and Five Moral Disciplines, took deep root in Korean culture. *Samgang* was advanced for political purposes and so is often criticized for causing patriarchal and authoritarian excesses, but *Oryun* is from Confucius's original teaching and contains elements that are important for everyday life. These are the Five Moral Disciplines:

- *Buja yuchin* (父子有親): Between parent and child, intimacy.
- *Kunshin yuui* (君臣有義): Between ruler and minister, righteousness.
- *Bubu yubyeol* (夫婦有別): Between husband and wife, distinction.
- *Jangyu yuseo* (長幼有序): Between elder and younger, ranking and order.
- *Bungwu yushin* (朋友有信): Between friends, trust.

These five disciplines are the virtues that our people considered most precious and have internalized in our culture. Intimacy between parent and child meant that the parent should give compassionate love to the child, which the child reciprocates with filial piety. Righteousness between a ruler and his ministers implied that the ministers' duty was not simply to obey, but to uphold justice and goodness. Distinction between husband and wife delineated the different roles of a father and a mother, essential in raising healthy and balanced sons and daughters. Ranking and order were necessary preconditions to establishing value and social cohesion where elders should be treated with respect and younger ones taken care of. Finally, trust should not only apply between friends but should be the basis for all human relationships.

The Kunsabu Ilche (君師父一體) ethics equated the roles of the king, the teacher, and the father. It was based on the vertical culture of filial piety toward one's parents and respect toward one's ancestors. The idea that the king is like a parent meant that filial piety toward a parent became patriotism toward the nation. The extension of filial piety into society offered a pattern for the ideal nation that Joseon sought to achieve.

As a result, Joseon gave public recognition to those who were exemplary models of ethical family behavior. They erected monuments to people who exemplified the ideals of filial piety and built memorial shrines (忠臣閣) to those who embodied patriotism. Monuments were also built for women who were models of love and fidelity toward their husbands (烈女碑). Loyalty, filial piety, and fidelity (忠, 孝, 烈)—all of which stemmed from our family culture—were regarded as the highest moral virtues.

In Korea, moral virtues grow in the context of two quintessentially Korean spiritual dispositions: *han* (恨) and *jeong seong* (精誠). Korean culture has been called the culture of *han*. The word is impossible to translate into English, so rich and complex is its meaning. The typical translation as "resentment" or even "grief" is totally inadequate. The old proverb, "When a woman has *han* there will be frost in summer," suggests this type of meaning but there is much more to it than that.

Han is the beginning of a process of spiritual growth whereby a person seeks to digest an injustice or injury internally rather than react in an angry, vengeful manner. Through wrestling with difficult emotions, the person can attain a deeper understanding of the human condition and a new level of spiritual maturity. *Han* should not end with the wrestling but should give birth to the inner realization to forgive, love, and embrace those who have done us wrong.

I know this adds a new dimension to the way we understand *han*, but I believe it is one to which our identity and history as Koreans is directing us. It is an understanding that resonates closely with the teachings of Jesus, although it developed independently. Perhaps it explains why so many Koreans have taken so quickly and wholeheartedly to Christianity.

Through facing the challenges of history and struggling to digest them internally, as well as meet them externally, Koreans have deepened their spiritual consciousness. We have grown as a people, prepared by the difficulties we have undergone to meet the challenge of this age. This spirit is then translated to and passed on through individual families, which is where Koreans learn to be Korean.

Korean family culture is also unique because of the other quintessential Korean attitude of spirit, *jeong seong*. The virtues that are modeled and learned within the family, such as filial piety, loyalty, and fidelity, are all practiced with *jeong seong*. That is, they are practiced with a degree of sincerity and wholehearted devotion that lifts self-sacrifice to a higher, nobler level. This quality is taught by the living examples of one's family members and through many forms of popular culture. Children's stories like those of "Shimcheong" (沈淸) and "Chunhyang" (春香) are deeply moving, instructive tales that convey powerful life lessons on the importance of *jeong seong* in living a virtuous, noble life.

"Shimcheong" is a story of a daughter who sells herself as a sacrifice to the sea gods in order to get money to cure her father's blindness. Her heart of filial devotion ultimately moves the dragon king, and she is saved and returned to land where she eventually becomes a queen. "Chunhyang" depicts a girl risking her life to remain faithful to her absent husband in the face of threats from a corrupt magistrate who wants to make her his concubine. In the end, Chunhyang's fidelity is rewarded when her husband returns from Seoul as a royal emissary.

These stories are part of the *pansori* (a Korean genre of musical storytelling performed by a vocalist and a drummer) tradition. Our ancestors brought the essential qualities of Korean family culture to life in vivid ways in paintings and in song, through the *chang* (唱; a song which a vocalist sings in pansori) and *pansori* styles. Our people have laughed and cried through these images and stories. Ultimately, those familial virtues did not just arise from the ethical teachings of scholars who studied Confucianism. Nor were they exclusively the province of the ruling elite. They were cultivated in all Korean families and celebrated widely through popular culture, becoming an ideal to which all people adhered, even those commoners who lived in small towns and farms.

The moral power of these virtues, practiced with *jeong seong*, has often made a deep impression on foreigners—from East and West, past and present. There is a very moving story of a Japanese general who became a Joseon citizen during the Japanese invasion of Korea in 1592. According to accounts at that time, General Sayaka was successfully leading 3,000 soldiers against the Joseon Army. Nevertheless, he was so moved by the steadfast virtue of the Korean people that he concluded that their slaughter would make him worse than an animal and surrendered to his Korean counterparts, although he was on the verge of victory. He would later teach our ancestors how to use matchlock guns and would fight with the Joseon Army against the Japanese invaders. He would ultimately be recognized for his actions and is known and honored in our history as General Kim Chungseon (1571–1642).[188]

More recently, a widely told anecdote recounts that Arnold J. Toynbee, the eminent British historian of civilizations, wept during a lecture on the virtue of filial piety while on a visit to Korea. Afterward, he was reputed to have said that this virtue would contribute greatly to world history if Koreans could spread it globally.[189] Whether this story is true I am not sure, but similar reactions are often seen in foreigners who had direct experience with our family culture. One often hears stories from Westerners about how moved they are to see younger Koreans showing respect on the street to the elderly whom they don't even know, especially since those customs have rapidly eroded in the West.

Thus, the Korean family culture is rooted in Confucian familial ideals, yet it took on unique characteristics when married to the concept of *jeong seong*. The virtues of loyalty, filial piety, and fidelity were elevated to new levels of devotion and sincerity. The amazing thing about this culture was that all Korean families tried to embody these ideals as they were considered to define our common humanity. As a result, the standard by which we determined moral and ethical behavior that differentiated us from animals naturally exhibited these sentiments. In short, it was a standard that we all strove to fulfill in our daily lives in order to be Korean.

KOREA'S FAMILY CULTURE: THE MANIFESTATION OF OUR DREAMS

Our Korean family culture defines our identity by connecting our daily lives to the high and lofty aspirations of our founding. By internalizing our aspirations through the social norms and etiquette of our families, our ancestors strove to manifest our founding ideals—first, through devotion and sacrificial love for our immediate family members and, second, expanding it in the greater community, society, nation, and world. As a result, it can be natural for us to see humanity as one large extended family, peacefully coexisting based upon universally shared aspirations, principles, and values, since that is what we try to accomplish in our daily lives. This is an exceptional point about our family culture in that it becomes the school where we develop the people of character who can truly own the Hongik Ingan ideals and Korea's providential destiny.

As a result, we habitually call people *hyung*, *nuna*, or *dongseng* (older brother, older sister, younger brother or sister, respectively), even though they are outside our family circle. We show our respect to older people by addressing them as *ajeossi* (uncle) or *ajumoni* (aunt). This is not just a matter of terminology. The most intimate human relationships through which we learn the deepest virtues are those within the family, which then forms the framework in which we view all human relationships. For example, of a close friend we might say, "I love him like a brother." A young person might describe a relationship with a teacher or mentor by saying, "He is like a father to me." As the similes show, the most intimate relationships are viewed within the familial context. There we experience the deepest bonds of love while having real living examples of proper relational integrity and decorum.

Koreans raised in this tradition view all human relations from a virtuous family perspective, which means that when familial relationships are based on sacrificial love, then family members will view all of humanity through the lens of that type of love and thus exhibit the highest expressions of virtue. Thus, how we relate to humanity is a direct reflection of what we have learned within our families. A person who violates this standard is subject to strong ethical criticism not only for his or her behavior but also for the lack of education within that person's family. The person might hear that his or her actions are not those of a proper human being, meaning that there are universally accepted truths and standards of ethical behavior and decorum. Kim Jong-un exposed himself to such criticism by his treatment of his uncle.

The same principle is applied in politics throughout the Korean dynasties, especially in the Joseon era. As I mentioned above and in Chapter 1, the king was viewed through the lens of the family. In other words, he was seen as the father of the nation and judged according to the standard of virtue a father should display. Even today, Koreans view politicians and government officials in this context. Political leaders are expected to display the qualities and virtues of good parents. From this perspective, despotic acts or blatant corruption are unacceptable because they violate the moral laws of family relationships (天倫) in which parents are supposed to care for their children with compassion.

In recent history, the decisive events during the April 19 and June 10 pro-democracy resistance movements of the 1980s followed revelations that the government abused its power by killing a young man by torture. This led people from all around the country to join the demonstrations. They were expressing moral outrage because the nation was violating its sacred duty of protecting its citizens, as if the government were an immoral and depraved parent who was abusing a child. The ethical standard that Koreans demand from their political leaders is very high, even today.

We need to recognize the unique and attractive qualities of our family culture. In an increasingly secular and cynical world, traditional Korean families, with their emphasis on moral character, sincere virtues, and deep, enduring relationships, are like an oasis in the desert of shallow, petty consumerism and an outrageous, vulgar, and often violent popular culture. Korean family culture offers a wholesome message of what humanity can and should aspire to, rather than appealing to its most base elements. Therefore, it could hold tremendous global appeal.

The clear evidence for this is the Korean Wave, which is expanding all over the world. It is not only reaching other Asian nations with similar cultural and religious influences but is currently spreading across every continent. Korean TV dramas are conquering living rooms everywhere. What could possibly explain this unexpected phenomenon? The appeal of the Korean Wave, especially the TV dramas, lies in the unique level of devotion, or *jeong seong*, expressed in sacrificial love within Korean family relationships that the stories feature.

The most popular Korean TV drama internationally was *Daejanggeum* (大長今). Since its first airing in 2003, *Daejanggeum* has been shown in more than ninety countries. One remarkable fact is that viewer ratings in Muslim nations like Iran and Egypt were above 90 percent, and it also set an extraordinary record of 90 percent viewership in Buddhist Sri Lanka. There are stories of youth in remote areas of Africa gaining the inspiration to pursue their dreams after watching *Daejanggeum*. The drama focuses on young Janggeum, who perseveres through tremendous hardship to untangle the *han* (恨) of her mother. She becomes one of the most important women at court, in charge of the royal kitchens and preparing food for the king himself. She also treats any women of the court who fall sick and performs all these tasks with the highest level of sincerity and devotion.

Daejanggeum clearly displays the spiritual culture of Korea manifested within the family. It shows the process of maturing internally and overcoming *han* through love and forgiveness, rather than through hatred and seeking revenge. It also shows the culture of attendance and sincerity (精誠), a unique aspect of our culture. Korean people believe in the phrase "sincerity moves heaven" (至誠感天). In other words, if one devotes all of one's heart and effort with absolute sincerity, that action will even touch heaven deeply. Since Koreans view humanity in terms of family relationships, they also consider the relationship of heaven to humanity as that of parent and child. The child's total expression of sincerity and devotion can thus move the heart of the parent—that is, of heaven itself.

The producer of *Daejanggeum* said that never in his wildest dreams did he imagine that his drama would touch so many people worldwide since he made it strictly for a Korean audience. However, while the story of *Daejanggeum* is uniquely Korean, the moral character and virtues that it portrays have universal appeal that speaks to the hearts of people worldwide. *Daejanggeum* is not the only example. Korean dramas typically portray a unique depth of heart in family relationships that is expressed through lives of moral nobility. Parents sacrifice themselves for their children's future, while children strive to resolve their parents' *han* and devote themselves to achieve their parents' dreams. In addition, Korean dramas, whether classical or modern, not only portray love within a family but also show the protagonist acting in ethical and patriotic ways for the sake of the society and nation.

The appeal of Korean dramas abroad lies in their portrayal of the most intimate human relationships, especially within the family. They touch upon the most fundamental and universal qualities that make us human, expressed with *jeong seong*, a standard of sacrificial love and total devotion. A drama such as *Winter Sonata* portrayed the purity of love possible between a man and woman, free of any selfish motivation. Japanese women in the tens of thousands became entranced by *Winter Sonata*. In fact, people everywhere yearn for this type of sacrificial love, and when they see it, they recognize it and are drawn to it. This quality of love has emerged from the Korean family model and makes it unique.

THE DESTRUCTION OF FAMILY VALUES AND THE PROBLEM OF THE NUCLEAR FAMILY

Living in America, I have heard many moving stories from Americans married to Korean women about their wives' relationships with their American parents-in-law. As you may know, the culture of sons and daughters taking care of their parents at home is disappearing in America. When children become adults, they leave their parents' house. And while the parents are no longer responsible for their children, the children do not feel the sense of ethical and virtuous obligation to care for their parents beyond their physical needs, which has always been part of Korean family tradition.

The average American retires in his or her mid-sixties and then enjoys what they can of the remainder of their lives. Many then move into a nursing home when they can no longer take care of themselves and end their lives there. While there might be some practical convenience in such an arrangement, it presents a very cold image of human life, especially for Koreans. No matter how useful the facilities of a nursing home may be, it is a very lonesome and sad affair to pass the last moments of life isolated in such a place apart from one's family. Most Americans will do their best to see their aging parents well cared for in regard to their health. But they seem to forget that human beings are far more than a collection of physical needs. We are spiritual beings who need love and emotional support, especially toward the end of our lives when we yearn for the love of those closest to us: our families.

But a daughter-in-law raised in the Korean tradition is well-acquainted with the ethical virtue of taking care of her parents-in-law. I heard of many American parents who were so moved by their Korean daughters-in-law because of the wholehearted effort they invested into caring for them with a heart of filial piety. Korean daughters-in-law approach married life with the thought of supporting their husbands, including their husbands' families, and educating their children well. How beautiful is this? For Korean people, at least in the family traditions we inherited, this is just the normal way for people to behave. I believe that the Korean family culture is our unique and precious heritage, one that we should export to the rest of the world as a way for us to bring benefit to all humanity.

Unfortunately, traditional Korean virtues are under threat today. We are witnessing the destruction of family values in our society—values that our people have historically regarded as the highest virtue, viewing the whole of society as they did from a family perspective. Confusion in sexual morality is damaging the relationship of trust and fidelity that couples should share, and neglect of family values is resulting in high divorce rates. The culture of filial piety and attending to one's parents is disappearing, and with it, respect for the elderly is becoming a dim memory. Young people are no longer being properly educated in these values, a serious issue eroding our Korean identity and jeopardizing the future of our society.

Many people believe that the collapse of sexual ethics and the loss of traditional values are an unavoidable consequence of modernization. Free sex, homosexuality, and divorce are considered to be phenomena symptomatic of modern life. After industrialization drew large numbers from their farms and villages to flock to the cities, it became more common to think of family as an old-fashioned institution belonging to an earlier age.

But how modern is this phenomenon in reality? The truth is that this type of decline in moral virtue has occurred in a wide variety of societies in both East and West throughout history. The Roman Empire is one prime example, in which the powerful family ethic of the early Roman Republic gave way to the moral corruption of the ruling elite under the empire. It requires a spiritual foundation and moral effort to uphold ethical family values and transmit them from one generation to the next. When permissive sexual mores take hold, they threaten the trust and sacred relationships of the family and are the prelude to social collapse. Whether we look at world history or our own Korean history, it is undeniable that one of the major reasons for the collapse of dynasties has been the moral depravity of the leadership, which led to social division and confusion. The corruption of those in power brought about upheaval in all of society.

At the core of that corruption has always been the collapse of family virtue and, with it, of sexual ethics. On the other hand, the beginning of a new era would almost always be marked by the reformation of moral standards. The course that Korean society takes in the future will depend upon our choices. Nothing is predetermined. We can accept the dissolution of the traditional extended family and its virtues as natural or inevitable, or we can recognize the unique cultural and ethical value of such families and create a virtuous society based on it.

The traditional Korean family is an extended family, and, within it, a child learns the virtue of sacrificial love through a wide range of relationships. As I outlined in Chapter 1, within the Korean family, the basic ethical standards of social behavior taught in the Confucian ideal were lifted to a whole new level. The virtue of *jeong seong*, investing in every action and relationship with total sincerity and devotion, encouraged self-sacrifice of the highest order. Through its family relationships, not only with parents but also with grandparents, uncles, and aunts, a child would learn this virtue by example until it became second nature. The standard of relationship learned within the family should then extend naturally to the clan and the wider society. Today, with modernization and urban living, such families are disappearing and with them go the rich moral and spiritual heritage they passed on to each new generation. They are being replaced by the so-called nuclear family.

The "nuclearization" of the family is currently taking place in Korean society without much resistance. The nuclear family is defined as one in which parents live with their unmarried children. No longer do three generations live together under one roof. In fact, our whole concept of what makes a family is changing, which has important cultural consequences. If we look at Western societies, we can see a clear progression in the dissolution of the family. Extended families were replaced by the nuclear family, but the process did not stop there. Instead, the nuclear family itself began to dissolve, being replaced by single-parent families, a rise of illegitimate births, children with two (or more) sets of parents as a result of divorce, siblings with the same mother but different fathers, and a growing variety of other arrangements. This family dissolution has serious social, economic, and moral consequences that advanced societies are only just beginning to recognize, let alone address.

With these examples before us, this is a path that we Koreans would be wise to avoid. We should consider what we are losing with the spread of the nuclear family in terms of the transmission of traditional virtues and the quality of human relationships. We also need to realize that the social and cultural transformation brought about by the spread of nuclear families brings with it a new set of socioeconomic problems.

In the past, the extended family took care of all its members and so played the role of social safety net that today has been transferred to government. However, unlike modern government, extended families take care of all the needs of their members viewed as whole human beings. Members of an extended family support one another spiritually, psychologically, and emotionally, in addition to taking care of the material needs that government welfare programs address.

The structure of the extended family with its many different roles creates a framework for intergenerational cooperation and a wide variety of relationships through which we can cultivate the best elements of our humanity. Within an overall atmosphere of love and mutual respect, family members can observe and then practice such qualities as self-sacrifice, sincerity, hard work, the pursuit of excellence, and responsibility. They also learn a sense of decorum and respect for boundaries that becomes an ingrained sense of what is right and wrong in human relations. These lessons, taken to heart by each new generation raised within the extended family, allow us to relate to other human beings in a cooperative, peaceful, and cohesive manner, whether in the smallest social unit of the family, or the largest: the global community.

In contrast with the three or more generations present in extended families, in the nuclear family, there are only parents and children. Even then, the two generations are really a temporary phenomenon from the birth of the child until she or he reaches legal adulthood at eighteen or twenty-one years old. In the United States, parents often expect their children to leave home once they become adults. The children, for their part, think the same way. Once they are legally adults, they feel they can live however they want, making their own choices without consulting their parents.

So, although there are two generations in the nuclear family, their roles and relationship are defined legally. At a certain age, the child is considered an adult, and at that point, the mutual responsibility and obligation between parent and child end. How strange is that? Instead of the deep, eternal relationship that should be the natural human connection based on an ideal concept of family, the law is shaping our concept of value in human relationships. This is the exact reverse of the proper natural order in which our laws should reflect our deepest and most precious human values, not determine them. In these circumstances, it is hardly surprising that we are seeing a generation gap—the rift between generations in contemporary society.

The consequences of this cultural shift regarding the family are both moral and practical. The pressure on parents raising children in a nuclear family, without the presence and support of grandparents, means that couples tend to have smaller families, with only one or two children, and leave the children in daycare centers while they are working. This may enable the family to live at a comfortable level of affluence, but it produces poverty in deep familial emotional bonds and the virtues of character that one learns through them.

Many children have no sibling relationships but only relate to their parents. Children grow and develop within a certain culture of loving relationships, and in the nuclear family, these are limited. To develop a mature and rounded character, a child needs to receive and learn to give different types of love, not only with parents, but also with grandparents and siblings. The love of grandparents adds a dimension that connects children with their heritage and thus strengthens their sense of identity. Parents alone cannot provide this.

That is why children today don't know how to respect their elders. Character education is becoming a problem in schools today because of the loss of the natural teaching of moral virtue within the family that has resulted from the nuclear family model. Our reality is that parents are afraid of sending their children to school because of bullying, school violence, and shunning (왕따). Even teachers now suffer violence at the hands of their students, something that was unthinkable in the past.

Nuclear families produce a rupture in the transmission of tradition between generations because of the absence of grandparents. Children should grow observing how their parents treat their own parents, the grandparents, with proper manners and etiquette and with an attitude of filial piety. One has to learn these habits and qualities naturally through family culture. They cannot be taught theoretically. If parents do not live with the grandparents, then it becomes very difficult to teach children about filial piety, manners, and etiquette in a way that takes root in their hearts. But the nuclearization of families has torn grandparents from their grandchildren, creating a disconnect between past and future. If this trend continues, we can foresee a future in which our society has become cut off from our traditions, meaning the loss of heritage and identity that our people have cultivated for five millennia.

As the contemporary perspective on the family has narrowed from the broad, intergenerational framework of the extended family, so also have views on marriage changed. Current popular views see it as "the meeting of a man and a woman," an encounter involving only two people. Romantic love between two people is elevated as the most important aspect of marriage, and this attitude is reflected throughout popular culture, in literature, movies, drama, and song. What this wave of sentiment overlooks is that marriage is much more than the coming together of two individuals. It is the meeting of two families, demanding greater responsibility from the couple than just caring for each other.

The woman does not simply become the wife of a man, but also the daughter-in-law to his parents and a member of his extended family. Likewise, the man does not simply become the husband to a woman, but also a son-in-law to her parents and a member of her extended family. So a married couple not only has to raise their children but also be responsible for the parents and other family members. In this way, marriage establishes a broad set of dynamic and loving social relationships. Thinking of marriage primarily in terms of romantic love damages family culture and increases divorce; it's a focus on just two people's feelings, which means that they have no reason to stay together if their feelings change. Emotional and physical separation is not so easy when the couple also must consider all their relationships with extended family members.

The stress of managing life in a nuclear family and the limited scope of relationships compared with an extended family may well have a negative impact on psychological health in the longer term. Recently there has been an increase in cases of depression and bipolar disorder. Suicides are also on the rise. These phenomena might be considered the secondary effects of the nuclear family where the emotional support from a broad range of loving family relationships is missing.

Korea has also experienced a spate of scandals related to moral corruption in public life. In 2011, South Korea dropped seven places, from thirty-ninth to forty-sixth, on Transparency International's Corruption Perception Index. Koreans lost $857 million in the savings bank scandal that has led to twenty banks being closed and hundreds of indictments. We have seen the chairman of a major *chaebol,* family-run industrial conglomerate, convicted of embezzlement only to have the court suspend his sentence, judging him "too important to serve time." With the *Sewol* ferry disaster, we learned that the owners were warned of the ship's instability but ignored it. The ship nevertheless passed a 2013 safety inspection by the Korean Register of Shipping, which was investigated by prosecutors. As Confucius observed, a well-ordered nation must be built on a family foundation. Widespread public corruption points to a breakdown of education in moral virtue in the family, at least when it comes to extending the practice of those virtues to the whole society.

The changing family pattern in Korea also has a more immediate social impact with serious economic consequences for the future of our society. In the past, extended families provided the social safety net by taking care of their members, especially the elderly. As nuclear families proliferate and more elderly people live alone, this responsibility is being passed to the elderly themselves and increasingly to the government. In addition, where there are no grandparents in the home, working parents have to rely on daycare facilities and will increasingly look to government to subsidize them.

Government spending on welfare will have to rise to meet these new demands, which simply will not be sustainable in the future. Advanced Western societies are already facing this serious issue—namely, that they will soon be unable to pay for all the welfare they are committed to provide. This problem will strike Korea in a particularly severe way for a number of reasons.

In the first place, nuclear families seem to encourage couples to have fewer children, a particularly acute phenomenon in Korea. The fertility rate in Korea has ranked as one of the lowest in the world for more than a decade, according to Andrew Mason of the East-West Center in Hawaii. In 2014, the Ministry of Health and Welfare announced that the rate had fallen to 1.18 children per woman.[190] The impact will be that the population will start to decline and the proportion of the population who are of working age will shrink.

The decline was projected to begin from 2018, and by 2050, there will be almost 6.4 million fewer people in South Korea than today, according to a 2009 report from the National Statistical Office.[191] This will mean a reduced labor force, as I mentioned in Chapter 3. The Deputy Prime Minister and Minister of Strategy and Finance, Oh-seok Hyun, estimated a shortfall of 2.8 million workers after 2030.[192] Fewer people will also mean a smaller domestic market and a shrinking tax base at a time when demand for welfare spending will be rising.

While the overall population is decreasing, the proportion who are elderly will grow, until by 2050 almost 40 percent (38.2 percent) will be sixty-five years or older. By then, Korea will have the most aged society among developed nations. I raised this issue in the previous chapter in the context of the negative impact of a reduced labor force on the Korean economy. But there are also serious social consequences. By 2050, the burden of paying for welfare is likely to become crushing as the working-age population will have to support more elderly through higher taxes. Currently, every 100 Korean workers support fifteen senior citizens, compared with the average of twenty-four among OECD (Organisation for Economic Co-operation and Development) member countries. But by 2050, 100 workers will have to provide for seventy-two elderly people, compared with the predicted OECD average of forty-five.[193]

These economic issues do not even begin to address the emotional and psychological concerns of an aging society built around nuclear families, concerns that are naturally taken care of within the extended family. One example is loneliness. In 2010, the number of senior citizens living alone was 1.06 million. That represents more than 20 percent of our entire senior citizen population. It is not uncommon to hear the news that an elderly person living alone died and the body was not found for months.

As we have seen, the form of the family, society's most basic unit, has a huge impact on every aspect of the life of that society. Politics, economy, culture, and education are all affected. More important still, the form of the family determines the moral character and core identity of each new generation as members take their places as citizens of the nation. To create the ideal nation that our ancestors longed for and to realize the Korean Dream, we need the type of family that can nurture people rooted in the tradition of sacrificial love and who can become virtuous citizens.

We have analyzed the shortcomings of today's nuclear family in the economic, moral, and emotional spheres. We should realize that the Korean extended family is a unique and precious cultural heritage that has shaped and sustained our Korean identity over millennia. It is the most important legacy that defines us as Koreans and is something ready to be shared with the world, as the global response to Korean Wave dramas demonstrates. Our government should devise policies and create incentives to preserve and promote the unique value embodied in our traditional family culture.

UNIFICATION: AN OPPORTUNITY TO RECOVER OUR IDENTITY AND FULFILL OUR DESTINY

Problems relating to the spread of the nuclear family, growing materialism, lack of national purpose, and indifference toward the fate of people in the North have arisen because Koreans are losing sight of the vision that has shaped our history and our identity as a people. The prospect of unification of the country offers us the opportunity to recover that vision and create a nation that reflects its founding aspirations. That is why the movement for unification cannot occur only on the level of governments and of political and economic negotiations. Unification has to engage the Korean people as a whole and involve serious reflection on our identity as Koreans and the destiny to which it calls us.

The key to knowing how to move forward and bring transformation to the peninsula is to understand how our history has formed our unique Korean identity. We have to look back to our past, to historical precedents, to see clearly our path into the future. This is what I have outlined in this chapter, together with the critical role of the rich and unique cultural legacy represented by the Korean family model that embodies our most precious values and traditions.

As I have emphasized before, our unique character finds its origin at the very founding of our nation in the Hongik Ingan ideals of Dangun. It has shaped our outlook throughout our history, guided our response to great challenges, and made us a people who live for a greater goal than just our own happiness, or even that of our nation. For our patriotic ancestors, independence was just a means to an end. The end was to establish an ideal nation and create a higher culture that would be an example to others and bring peace to the world.

It is easy to overlook just how remarkable the Dangun story and Hongik Ingan ideals are. But the truth is that nothing anywhere else in history is like them. Prominent figures from other cultures have remarked on this. Former French president Jacques Chirac said of Dangun and Hongik Ingan, "A saint is born out of hard times in other countries, but it was a saint who founded the nation of Korea."[194]

From this root emerged a spiritual consciousness that became a fundamental aspect of Korean character. We saw how this consciousness developed through the experiences of history and how it drew on a wide range of spiritual and ethical systems to strengthen it and further its pursuit of an ideal nation built upon principles of justice, human dignity, and social harmony. Principles alone, however noble, guarantee nothing unless they become embodied in people's lives and how they relate together as communities and a society.

The Korean Dream is fulfilled when Hongik Ingan is wedded to Korean family tradition. One complements the other. Hongik Ingan sets out the vision of a people that lives for the sake of all humanity, an expression of the virtue of living for the sake of others on a global level. People who practice this virtue first learn it within the bosom of the family, and nowhere has the practice of sacrificial love been more wholeheartedly pursued than in the Korean extended family that developed in the course of our history. The uniqueness of the Korean character is defined by the fundamental spirit that emerged at our origin, together with the family culture that nurtured virtuous human relationships and passed on that spirit to each generation. The founding spirit gave us the aspiration to build an ideal nation, while our family tradition cultivated people of moral character who could sustain it as righteous citizens.

This is the key to our Korean identity and what makes it unique. Unification is not just about resolving several decades of political and ideological division. It is the opportunity to fulfill a destiny for which the 5,000 years of Korean history has been preparing us. Through it, we can rediscover and take pride in our identity as Koreans. The time is calling us to undertake a real transformation and reconnect ourselves to the essential spirit and ideals expressed in our history and through our family culture.

Such a movement among the Korean people can naturally become the source of inspiration for other countries. The Korean identity is uniquely positioned to be a bridge between East and West. Constantine Virgil Gheorghiu, a Romanian author, said in his book, *Beyond 25th Hour to the Land of Morning Calm*:

> Dangun is king, father and owner of Korean people. The constitution he gave to Korean people can be described in one word. That is Hongik Ingan. It means give blessing to as many people as possible. Since then Koreans received many other religions. Yet the law of Dangun is being maintained for 5,000 years. It's because his law doesn't contradict any faith. Hongik Ingan is the ideal state of all religions or philosophies...[195]

Western political philosophy has advanced the notion of liberty and human rights as a universal principle. The contribution of the American founders was especially important, as I noted in Chapter 1, because it grounded the notion of "inalienable" rights in a Creator. In other words, our innate human dignity and value came from God and not from any human ruler, institution, or government. In the concept of In Nae Chon that I referred to earlier, and that grew from the Hongik Ingan tradition, we Koreans have a similar understanding that developed independently of Western thought. The idea that humanity is equal to that of heaven uplifts mankind's intrinsic value upon an absolute spiritual foundation of universal truths.

Western thought tended to frame rights in relation to the individual citizen, although that does not mean it was individualistic in the modern, self-centered sense. As I noted earlier, George Washington and other presidents stressed the need for moral virtue among the citizens of a nation if it was to endure. Extended families were also the typical pattern during the pioneer period and among the large immigrant communities of the early twentieth century in America.

These patterns only began to change significantly after World War II and particularly with the emergence of the so-called counterculture in the 1960s. A robust, self-reliant individualism had been prized in America's pioneering past. This type of individualism, which helped define the American character, was rooted in a deep sense of individual responsibility for the benefit of the wider community, society, and nation. In the 1960s, an extreme form of self-centered narcissism emerged that turned its back on traditional norms and, especially, social responsibilities in the pursuit of self-indulgent experience. Its spirit is perfectly captured in the popular motto of the time: "Do your own thing." This sort of selfish individualism brought moral confusion with it through the questioning of all standards of right and wrong. If young Koreans start to follow this path, it would be disastrous for Korea's future.

Korean family culture, if we are wise enough to preserve it, is the best antidote to this type of selfish and rootless attitude. It also complements and balances the focus of Western thought on the individual citizen. Oriental culture views human beings not as independent individuals, but through relationships. In Chinese, the character for "human" (人) is represented as two people supporting one another. The word for "human being" (人間) means the "relationship between two people." In the East, roles and responsibilities are determined within relationships, and that's how one's identity is defined.

These relationships begin in the family, and all social relationships mirror family relationships. As the saying goes, "A patriot is born in a house with children of filial piety." The family is the institution that generates citizens who are responsible for the society and the nation. The family is the place where moral education to raise future citizens takes place, and it does so at a level of intimacy that develops the most deeply rooted moral qualities.

In Western family culture, it is not common to find an ethic that connects one's family to the public domain of community and nation. There is much wisdom in the Confucian ideal that I mentioned earlier: to change the world, you first have to change the nation, and to change the nation, the family must be properly established. Confucius goes on to say that to establish the family, the individual must train himself, but of course, much of that training will take place in the family where he or she grows up.

Confucian tradition is not perfect. Nor am I proposing a retreat into the past. There are many positive aspects of Western individualism that encourage independent initiative and responsibility for larger purposes from which Asian tradition can learn. Wrongly understood, Confucian family tradition can be patriarchal in a way that subordinates the role of women and those who stand in subordinate positions. As a result, it can also become overly hierarchical and authoritarian in a way that stifles creativity and initiative to the detriment of society. This culture has led to fatal results, for example, in airplane crashes in which flight crew members failed to warn the captain of a problem out of a misplaced sense of deference to authority or where the captain ignored warnings when they were given.

If the best elements of Eastern culture and tradition can combine with the best elements of Western thought, an ideal union will emerge through which each complements the weaknesses of the other. Such a union can form the spiritual, cultural, and philosophical foundation for a truly global civilization that transcends existing divisions and conflicts and makes world peace possible. This was the vision Kim Gu had, expressed in his quote at the beginning of the chapter. He believed that Korea had a unique contribution to make to the world and could become instrumental in bringing world peace.

I am convinced that the Korean people are uniquely positioned to play such a role and give substance to this dream. In the Hongik Ingan ideal, we have the vision; through the history I have described, we have the character; and through our family culture, we have formed the spiritual and moral foundation to make it possible. This is our heritage, and through owning it, we can reclaim our Korean identity and look forward to fulfill our destiny, the realization of the Korean Dream that I described at the beginning of the book.

Through the Korean Dream, we can bridge East and West and draw on the past to build a new future. For the Korean peninsula, it offers the chance to make a fresh start. It will enable the Korean people of both North and South to move beyond the past and the conflict that was largely imposed upon us by forces we could not control. Through claiming our common Korean identity and recognizing the destiny for which our history and culture have prepared us, we can come together, not as North Koreans and South Koreans, but as one Korean people.

CHAPTER 5

People Power Is the Path to Unification

"I alone cannot change the world, but I can cast a stone across the waters to create many ripples."
—ANONYMOUS

In the last chapter, I reviewed our history and the unique precedents set by our people in trying to realize the aspirations of our founding. Korea, especially in Northeast Asia, clearly championed a people-oriented philosophy that exalted humanity as being equivalent to the value of heaven. As a result, our ancestors pioneered systems of governance and moral and ethical traditions rooted in the family to manifest that aspiration in everyday life. In addition, they developed a rich, spiritual heritage of open-mindedness, as well as a collective consciousness recognizing the importance of faith as an instrument in realizing the Hongik Ingan ideal of benefiting all humanity.

Today, Korea stands at a transformational moment in its history. The challenge posed by North Korea through its threats and instability is becoming unavoidable, and the unification issue is now a matter of urgency. The question is: How do we bring it about in a peaceful manner? My argument throughout this book is that the prospect of unification offers the Korean people a golden opportunity to reclaim our identity as Koreans and move closer to the destiny toward which our legacy is calling us.

This opportunity is expressed through the Korean Dream that I have been describing. For that dream to become more than an abstract ideal or utopian hope, it needs the broad popular support of the whole Korean people. Only in that way will great transformational change come about. Remember the words of Genghis Khan with which I opened the first chapter: "The dream of just one person is only a dream but if is shared by a people it becomes a reality." This, then, becomes the challenge to every Korean: to contribute to the process of change, to make a difference by becoming part of a broad-based movement for unification based upon the Korean Dream.

Popular movements exert a tremendous power for transformation in all societies but especially in democratic ones. The key to whether such movements are a positive or negative force is their motivation and guiding vision. Without a vision, a mass movement can quickly become an angry mob. Positive change comes about through a guiding idea that is rooted in truth and hence has a moral authority that resonates with the conscience. Large numbers of people, driven by their conscience, are then motivated to act in concert to bring about change based upon that idea and the principles it encapsulates.

Yet, large numbers of people engaged in the process of social and national change are but the by-product of personal initiatives and ownership of the cause. For unification to truly be realized, the individual citizen first must be inspired, motivated, and passionate about that goal. Citizens must have their own stake in the game. Although it may be but a small piece of the overall puzzle, personal ownership will be absolutely essential since it is the sum of all those individual pieces that will create the necessary critical mass for people power to bring about fundamental transformation. The quote that opens this chapter—"I alone cannot change the world, but I can cast a stone across the waters to create many ripples"—captures this idea perfectly.

At this pivotal moment in the history of our people, we, as Koreans, should ask ourselves: What "ripples" shall I make for unification and the realization of the Korean Dream? How will I contribute to the story of our people? What legacy will I leave in the realization of our founding ideals? These types of questions are what we should be considering for the sake of our people, our homeland, and our destiny "to benefit all humanity." This chapter explores the role of people power in bringing great change in the history of Korea, as well as examples from other regions in the world. It will identify the key ingredients for successful transformation, such as moral authority rooted in universal truths that are the basis of humanity's fundamental aspirations, principles, and values. It will then analyze the effects of the communications revolution on social movements worldwide with the advent of the internet, social media, and smartphones and the opportunities that the communications revolution gives to individual participation, more so than ever in human history.

THE KOREAN PEOPLE MAKE KOREAN HISTORY

Korean history is full of examples of popular movements formed to fight injustice or defend the nation in pursuit of a higher ideal. Chapter 4 highlighted several of these, telling how, for example, popular resistance to the Mongolian invasions lasted forty years. It was built upon the grassroots cooperation of local farmers inspired by a patriotic ideal of the nation. In Chapter 4, I also described the emergence of the Donghak movement in the late nineteenth century in response to the unjust oppression of peasant farmers by aristocratic landowners. This movement was not just based on anger and resentment but was guided by principles rooted in the Hongik Ingan tradition. These asserted the inherent value and spiritual dignity of every person no matter their social status.

The March First Independence Movement was also guided by principles and, as expressed in Kim Gu's outlook, a vision for a Korean future that transcended even national independence. The Korean Declaration of Independence itself appealed to human equality, liberty, and conscience, as well as to Korea's 5,000-year history.[196] The students who drew up the declaration were also inspired by U.S. President Woodrow Wilson's Fourteen Points presented at the Versailles Peace Conference in France that outlined the principle of national self-determination.[197]

The reading of Korea's Declaration of Independence at various sites around the country drew large numbers of people to demonstrate peacefully in support of it. The Japanese, fearful of the sheer size of the marches, reacted with harsh repression.[198] The spontaneous popular response to the reading of the Declaration nationwide illustrates a basic character of our people. Koreans will mobilize in support of a vision and idea that they know in their hearts to be right and true. This impulse was also a feature of the development of democracy in Korea in more recent times.

Student activists had been at odds with President Chun Doo-hwan's military rule for some time before the June 10, 1987 pro-democracy demonstrations. They represented a range of political views, some extremely radical. But all of them wanted to see reforms to the constitution and direct election to the presidency instead of the system of indirect appointment that essentially allowed President Chun to appoint his successor. At that point, although there was a certain level of sympathy among the broader population for these demands, there was not yet active popular support for them.[199]

What made the difference was the news that student activist Park Jong-chul had been tortured to death by security forces. He died on January 14, 1987. The government tried to conceal the facts, but the truth came out.[200] News of Park's death struck a chord with a much wider public.[201] The government's treatment of Park outraged most Koreans since it violated their deeply held belief that the nation is the cradle of the larger Korean family and must be governed with virtue and respect for human life. To most, a virtuous parent could not treat one of his children that way. This sense of outrage was heightened after Yonsei University student Lee Han-yeol was fatally injured by a tear gas canister at a demonstration on June 9, dying on July 5, 1987.[202]

A broad sector of the Korean public had stood on the sidelines up until this point. However, these events enraged them and challenged their sense of justice and of virtuous governance, changing the context of the movement for democracy in South Korea. Large numbers of office workers and others began to join the students, and a mass national movement developed.[203] On June 10, 1987, 240,000 people in twenty-two cities turned out in support of changes to the constitution. By June 18, one and a half million were in the streets in over sixteen cities as Korea's growing middle class offered their support.[204] The following month, 1.6 million people turned out for the funeral of Lee Han-yeol, the student fatally injured.[205]

With the Seoul Olympics to be held the following year, President Chun, worried about Korea's international image, backed down. He agreed to direct elections for the presidency, to changes in the constitution, and to the restoration of civil liberties. In this watershed for South Korea, democracy truly took root. The June 10 demonstrations brought an end to military rule and began a process of greater citizen engagement at every level of society through which the Korean people could continue to flourish. Because of the eventual broad-based character of the popular support, South Korea, in a very short time, established a stable democracy. Even though radical students, some of whom even supported North Korea's Juche ideology, were active in instigating early protests, their influence was subsequently diluted by the more active engagement of all South Korean citizens in the affairs of the nation.[206]

PEOPLE POWER, MORAL AUTHORITY, AND SOCIAL CHANGE

Like the events I described in Korea, similar dynamics ignited the Arab Spring. On December 17, 2010, Muhammad Bouazizi, a Tunisian street vendor, set fire to himself after officials confiscated his produce, allegedly because he did not have a vendors' permit. His action was the spark that ignited public protests against the twenty-three-year authoritarian rule of

President Zine El Abidine Ben Ali. The street vendor Bouazizi died from his burns on January 4, 2011. Ten days later, President Ben Ali resigned his office and the Arab Spring was under way. Before long, it had spread to Egypt and Yemen, where large public demonstrations drove Presidents Mubarak and Saleh, respectively, out of office. Protests in Libya grew into a civil war that ended with the killing of Muammar Gaddafi, who had ruled the country as a dictator for forty-two years. Civil war also followed protests in Syria and has yet to be resolved.

Bouazizi was supporting his mother, uncle, and younger siblings from the sale of fruit and vegetables from his vendor's cart. He even paid for one sister to attend university.[207] He was taking responsibility for his family and showing enterprise, yet he had been continually harassed by officials. It is not clear whether you even need a permit to sell from a cart in Tunisia, but it is clear that officials often harass market traders in search of bribes. On the day he burned himself, Bouazizi had gone into debt to buy his produce, which was then confiscated. He could not afford a bribe. Bouazizi's protest and death had a similar impact on the Tunisian people as did the death by torture of Park Jong-chul in Korea in 1987.[208] The public conscience was outraged by the injustice inflicted on Bouazizi, which was a reflection of the many other injustices that Tunisians suffered under Ben Ali's rule.[209]

Sometimes an act of injustice directly moves the conscience of large numbers of people. Sometimes a leader speaks and acts with moral authority that awakens the public conscience and inspires a popular movement. In either case, people recognize and respond to some fundamental principle of right and wrong and act together in pursuit of it.

One of the greatest examples of leadership based on moral authority in the last century is Mahatma Gandhi. As a young lawyer in South Africa before World War I, working for the Indian community there, he experienced discrimination firsthand. He was thrown out of the first-class compartment of a railroad train, even though he had paid for his ticket, and was then beaten by a stagecoach driver because he refused to give up his seat to a white person. These personal experiences sharpened his awareness of the systemic injustices vested upon the nonwhite population in Africa.

He lived in South Africa for twenty-one years, working to mobilize the Indian community and resist the efforts of the government to take away many of their civil rights, including the right to vote. In 1906, the Transvaal government passed a law requiring all Indians to register themselves with the authorities, a requirement that did not apply to whites. In response, Gandhi developed what became his signature philosophy and strategy: noncooperation with unjust laws combined with nonviolent acceptance of whatever punishments resulted.

Indian resistance lasted for seven years in the face of an intransigent government. Thousands of Indians were arrested, and hundreds went to jail for refusing to register or for burning their registration cards. Thousands of striking miners were arrested, beaten, and even shot. The resistance prompted international support and criticism of the South African government, which, finally, under pressure from the governments of Great Britain and India, agreed to some concessions.

In 1914, Gandhi returned to India and, from then until his assassination in 1948, worked for Indian independence using the approach he had pioneered in South Africa. As a strategy, this involved noncooperation and nonviolence, but behind it lay a spiritual philosophy that he called *satyagraha*. This idea is rooted in Hindu philosophy and means literally "truth force." Behind it lay the conviction that the power of truth, expressed peacefully, could expose the falsehoods and injustice of oppression.[210]

The most dramatic demonstration of his approach was the Salt March of 1930. Gandhi marched 250 miles to the sea at Dandi to make salt there as a protest against the British tax on salt, over which they held a monopoly. Thousands joined him on the march, which became one of the most famous examples of nonviolent direct action in history. Over 60,000 Indians were arrested as a result of the protest.

Gandhi's sense of justice was not limited to ending British colonial rule. He applied the principles and methods of *satyagraha* to improving the treatment of the lowest caste in India, the untouchables, by the higher castes. He even renamed them "Harijan" (Children of God).[211] Although he was a Hindu, Gandhi had a broad religious vision. After independence in 1947, when Pakistan was partitioned from India as a separate Muslim state, Gandhi continued to work to build bridges between Hindus and Muslims and to include Christians as well. His efforts led to his death, shot by a Hindu fundamentalist.

Gandhi was reviled during his lifetime, not only by the authorities in South Africa and India, but by quite a few Indians as well, and by both the Hindu and Muslim communities.[212] Yet, today he is recognized and revered for his vision and principled philosophy that touched and motivated millions of people and transformed India. He is universally known as "Mahatma," which means "great-souled one" in Sanskrit. He titled his autobiography *The Story of My Experiments with Truth*, seeing his life as an ongoing search for greater understanding. Although his focus was on achieving justice in India, he understood that the fundamental principles he lived by applied to all people. As he said, "When we come to think of it, the distinction between heterogeneous and homogeneous is discovered to be merely imaginary. We are all one family."[213]

He saw that a vision or dream rooted in truth generates a moral authority that naturally reaches out and touches growing numbers of people. He explains:

I want to find God, and because I want to find God, I have to find God along with other people. I don't believe I can find God alone. If I did, I would be running to the Himalayas to find God in some cave there. But since I believe that nobody can find God alone, I have to work with people. I have to take them with me.[214]

The moral power of a vision based on eternal ideals and truths resonates with the innate conscience of men and women everywhere. This impulse is far beyond politics and leaders, such as Gandhi, who touched upon these truths, moved large numbers of people, and brought about fundamental transformation in society.

Gandhi denied any interest in starting a new philosophy or religious movement. Rather, he said, "I have simply tried in my own way to apply the eternal truths to our daily life and problems."[215] In focusing on eternal truths and spiritual principles, he showed himself to be a spiritual leader, which is something different from a religious leader, a point I cannot emphasize enough. While Gandhi drew much wisdom from Hindu tradition, he understood that the truths he learned to live by are not exclusive to that tradition alone but are universal. That is how he could reach out to other faiths, especially to Muslims.

Religious leaders, in contrast, advocate only for their own faith tradition, seeking to expand its influence. Other traditions are viewed as competitors or even enemies, an outlook that produces confrontation among religions. Such an attitude fails to recognize that spiritual principles and fundamental truths are universal and come from God and are not exclusive to any one religion. Only through recognizing universal spiritual principles can we form the foundation of a world of peace where all human beings can dwell together as One Family under God. Unlike a religious leader who takes a sectarian approach, a spiritual leader has a vision that sees far beyond such religious barriers and can affect the course of human history, moving it closer to the original and eternal ideal.

I have continually emphasized the difference between spiritual and religious leaders in my interviews with the Korean media. My father, the Reverend Dr. Sun Myung Moon, was without question a spiritual leader whose vision stretched far beyond the boundaries of religions, including the organization with which he was associated. His vision is rooted in spiritual principles from God that transcend the divisions of religion, ethnicity, and nationality, and form the basis for a world of peace. I am committed through my life and work to honor and advance my father's legacy. One of my priorities in the work of the Global Peace Foundation is to promote cooperation among the world's faiths on the basis of universal spiritual aspirations, principles, and values. Without such cooperation, we can never achieve a world of peace.

Gandhi's spirituality rooted in universal truths and his approach of nonviolent social action had a major impact in other parts of the world. Nelson Mandela, the first black president of South Africa (1994–1999) and the first president elected in a vote of all South Africans, was strongly influenced by Gandhi's ideas.[216] When he died in 2013, he was acclaimed globally as a great and noble statesman who had acted on the basis of high ideals. In South Africa, he was celebrated as "father of the nation"[217] and often affectionately referred to as "Tata," the Xhosa word for father.[218] An article in *Newsweek* magazine described him as his country's "Washington and Lincoln rolled into one."[219] He was awarded the Nobel Peace Prize in 1993. According to his official biographer, Anthony Sampson, he was regarded internationally as a moral authority based on his concern for truth and justice for all.[220]

It was not always like that, however. In his younger years, Mandela was influenced by Marxism and ideas of armed conflict. He was long suspected of being a secret member of the South African Communist Party and, in 1961, cofounded Umkhonto we Sizwe (Spear of the Nation), the militant arm of the African National Congress. The group engaged in sabotage operations against South African infrastructure. Mandela was arrested for this in 1962, then convicted and sentenced to life imprisonment.

He spent twenty-seven years in prison, reflecting deeply on his life, and eventually changed to become the man who was revered and honored at his death. He understood that the Gandhian approach of noncooperation and nonviolence was far more likely to bring change in South Africa than armed conflict. But his realization in prison went deeper than that, touching on an understanding of fundamental truths and principles that were the basis of the moral authority he held when he emerged from prison in 1990.

As the apartheid system in South Africa crumbled and the country moved into a democratic transition, there was a real danger that blacks would take violent revenge on the white minority for the oppression that black South Africans had suffered. Mandela, with other powerful moral leaders such as Archbishop Desmond Tutu, preached reconciliation unreservedly. That Mandela could do this after his long imprisonment had great moral force and helped ensure a peaceful transition from the injustices of the apartheid system.

He described the transition he underwent in prison in his autobiography, *Long Walk to Freedom*. "It was during those long and lonely years that my hunger for the freedom of my own people became a hunger for the freedom of all people, white and black."[221] I came across a wonderful anecdote about Mandela from someone who heard it from a Bangladeshi diplomat. It captures the character of the man perfectly. On one occasion, during a visit to Bangladesh as president of South Africa, Mandela told a group of senior diplomats how important it is to make friends with one's enemies. It was remarkable for a sitting head of state, in this world of Realpolitik, to bring a spiritual dimension, yet one with practical consequences, into the political realm.

Mandela came to understand that certain fundamental principles are eternal and apply to all people. He told the Zionist Christian Conference in 1994: "We affirm it and we shall proclaim it from the mountaintops, that all people—be they black or white, be they brown or yellow, be they rich or poor, be they wise or fools—are created in the image of the Creator and are his children!"[222] When such a vision touches people's hearts, they are moved to action simply because it is right.

In his Nobel Prize acceptance speech, he said of those who had supported freedom in South Africa that they "had the nobility of spirit to stand in the path of tyranny and injustice, without seeking selfish gain. They recognized that an injury to one is an injury to all and therefore acted together in defense of justice and a common human decency."[223] As he told the people at his presidential inauguration celebration, "We must therefore act together as a united people, for national reconciliation, for nation building, for the birth of a new world."[224] That thought applies just as well to the Korean people today.

The U.S. civil rights movement in the 1950s and 1960s is another powerful example of moral authority based upon spiritual principles and values that inspired broad popular support to bring about fundamental social change. Its guiding vision rested upon a combination of Christian ideals, the founding principles of the United States as expressed in the Declaration of Independence, and Gandhian philosophy and practice. Ultimately, its appeal reached beyond the boundaries of both race and religion.

Despite Abraham Lincoln's Emancipation Proclamation in 1863 and the ratification of the Thirteenth Amendment in 1865, which freed blacks from slavery, black people in the southern states were still treated as second-class citizens. Under a system known as "Jim Crow," established in those states from 1876 on, public schools, public transport, and public facilities such as cinemas and restaurants were segregated. The right to vote, guaranteed in federal law, was in practice denied to blacks in the South through a variety of local regulations.

The first crack in this structure came in 1955 through a single incident that sparked a movement of moral resistance, much like the impact of the death of Park Jong-chul or Muhammad Bouazizi in Tunisia. On one of the segregated buses in Montgomery, Alabama, a forty-two-year-old African American woman, Rosa Parks, refused to give up her seat to a white person and move to the back of the bus. For this, she was arrested. Although she was already actively working for civil rights, she said in this instance she acted as a private citizen who was simply "tired of giving in."[225]

Her act was the spark that led to the Montgomery bus boycott, organized by a twenty-six-year-old pastor named Martin Luther King Jr. For over one year, the black people of Montgomery refused to ride the public buses until they were finally desegregated. In June 1956, a U.S. district court ruled the bus segregation laws unconstitutional, a decision upheld by the U.S. Supreme Court on December 17, 1956. The victory caused a violent reaction. Buses and African American riders were shot at, and churches and the homes of civil rights leaders Ralph Abernathy and King were bombed.

Yet, despite the violence, a pattern was established of direct but nonviolent action against unjust laws. It was inspired by Gandhi's ideas and practices and became the hallmark of the U.S. civil rights movement under King's leadership. Previously, he had believed that the Christian precept of "loving your enemy" only worked for conflict between individuals. At that time, he thought that when racial groups and nations were in conflict, a more realistic approach seemed necessary. However, from Gandhi, he learned that the power of truth, the power of principle, could be mobilized to fight injustice without resorting to hatred and violence. Reflecting this approach, in his famous "I Have a Dream" speech at the Lincoln Memorial in Washington, he stated, "Again and again, we must rise to the majestic heights of meeting physical force with soul force."[226]

The power of this approach moved the conscience of great numbers of Americans of all races and of many faiths and denominations. Civil rights workers registered black voters, held sit-ins in segregated facilities, and marched through southern cities. They were met with violence but did not respond in kind. When the American public saw black people, including women and children, knocked over by water from fire hoses and intimidated by attack dogs without retaliating, the tide of public opinion began to shift. In 1964, King won the Nobel Peace Prize for promoting racial equality through nonviolence. Consequently, by the time he was arrested in Selma, Alabama the next year for protesting segregation, the civil rights movement became international news, generating support worldwide.

The success of the civil rights movement came because it drew broad popular support far beyond the black population of the southern United States. This was possible because the movement had moral authority based on the fundamental spiritual principles that guided it, principles shared by all people of good conscience. In his "I Have a Dream" speech in 1963, King reminded Americans of the noble ideals their country aspired to as embodied in the founding principles expressed in the Declaration of Independence.

He declared, "I have a dream that one day this nation will rise up and live out the true meaning of its creed: 'We hold these truths to be self-evident, that all men are created equal.'" He stirred the conscience of Americans to realize that they could no longer ignore the injustices suffered by their black fellow citizens in the South. The inequality imposed on black people was a flagrant violation of the founding ideal that all men are "created equal and endowed by the Creator with certain unalienable rights."[227]

In 2012, I held our annual Global Peace Convention in Atlanta, Georgia, a hub of the civil rights movement. Rev. Bernice King, daughter of Dr. King, was one of the keynote speakers. She said that if her father were alive today, he would be a part of the Global Peace Foundation's work for peace. She also stressed that her father was a spiritual leader. She explained:

> I don't characterize my father as a civil rights leader. I characterize him first and foremost as a spiritual leader, as a man of God, as a moral leader who just happened to impact civil and human rights. And so everything that he did came out of his spiritual foundation. It didn't come from his political ideology.[228]

Moral authority and the power to move people to act for a noble cause always rise from a vision that transcends religion, politics, and ethnicity and are firmly grounded in universal spiritual truths. The accomplishments of Gandhi, Mandela, and King are a direct reflection of this insight. These great men, in their pursuit of truth, had to strip themselves of their own narrow perspectives, whether social standing, ethnicity, religion, or race. Had they not, they would not have developed the methods and messages that would stir the conscience of millions by exposing the injustice and hypocrisy of colonialism in India and the systems of segregation in South Africa and the United States, eventually changing the geopolitical landscape of the twentieth century. Most of all, their efforts have uplifted the notion of fundamental human rights and freedoms as absolute truths, although much work remains to be done to make it a living reality. As a result, it would be fair to say that true moral authority does not come from position, money, or power but from universally accepted spiritual truths that stir humanity's collective consciousness and, through it, can bring about tremendous social change.

MORAL AUTHORITY AND THE DOWNFALL OF COMMUNIST REGIMES

On November 9, 1989, East German citizens began to dismantle the Berlin Wall, the barrier that divided communist East Berlin from the West. They were joined by West German citizens in a mood of celebration as they took down the symbol of German division and that of Europe between the communist east and the democratic west. The people had finally risen up and cast off their oppressors. Just over a month earlier, Erich Honecker, the hard-line East German chancellor, had ordered the military to fire on rising numbers of demonstrators who were amassing in protest against his regime. However, the soldiers disobeyed those orders. Less than a year later, the two Germanys were united once more.

The wall was constructed to keep East Germans in, and the guards had shoot-to-kill orders. But the flow of information through West German TV and other media was an ever-present attraction, encouraging people to leave for a better, freer life. In 1989, thousands left through the newly democratized neighbor Hungary and later through Czechoslovakia until the East German regime closed the borders and isolated itself from all its neighbors. With all their exits shut off, growing numbers of East Germans joined demonstrations against the government.

Late in 1989, "Monday Demonstrations" in the city of Leipzig became a regular feature of the opposition. Once merely Monday prayer meetings in the 800-year-old Leipzig church, Nicolaikirche, these gatherings grew from a few dozen people meeting to pray and discuss ideas into peaceful rallies for democracy with 320,000 protestors in Leipzig alone. Other groups had organized similar protests in churches across the country. Fearful of this popular outpouring, the communist party—Sozialistische Einheitspartei Deutschlands (SED; the Socialist Unity Party)—forced Honecker to resign from power on October 18, 1989. The demonstrations crumbled the SED's will to resist. The SED authorized a demonstration in East Berlin that attracted over a million people and then simply lifted all travel restrictions to the West. Shortly afterward, the wall came down while the authorities stood by and watched.

Rapidly thereafter, the entire Cabinet resigned, the "leading role of the Party" language was removed from the Constitution, and a multiparty system was established, with free elections soon to follow. The SED abandoned Marxism-Leninism and renamed itself first the SED-PDS and then the Party of Democratic Socialism (PDS). As in other countries that made a peaceful transition from communism, important party leaders cooperated in the process. They got rid of the old die-hard element, abandoned the party's monopoly on power, and joined the new democratic political process.

This approach was infinitely preferable for them, because resistance to the last would have ended with their certain imprisonment and likely execution. This fate befell Romanian leader Nicolae Ceaușescu, who was shot, together with his wife, by his own forces after he made it clear that he intended to cling to power. As a result, the Romanian Communist Party is the only Eastern European party that did not continue in some form as a wave of new multiparty democracies emerged with the collapse of the Soviet Union.[229]

East Germany under Honecker had followed a very rigid, Soviet-style communism and suppressed dissent with a massive network of agents and informers operated by the Stasi, or security service. Honecker even banned certain Soviet publications after Soviet President Mikhail Gorbachev started to introduce reforms. As a result, some of the first expressions of opposition came from within the SED itself. Most notably, in 1977, the West German magazine *Der Spiegel* published a statement that claimed to be from the "League of Democratic Communists of Germany." The group was comprised of anonymous mid- and high-level SED officials who were proposing democratic reforms as a prelude to future reunification.

The key change that led to communist power crumbling in the face of popular opposition was the change in the Soviet Union. Gorbachev made it clear that the Soviet Union would no longer intervene militarily to support communist regimes in Eastern Europe. They were on their own. In addition, he urged the leaders of those countries to undertake their own reforms. He visited East Germany with this message just a few days before the wall came down. Honecker rejected it, and in less than two weeks, he was gone. One of Gorbachev's statements to the East German leadership was, "Life punishes those who come too late."[230]

The fall of the communist regimes in Eastern Europe had begun in Poland, where the freedom movement was associated with two men who represented religious and civil society. One was Pope John Paul II. The other was Lech Walesa, an electrician who organized the independent trade union Solidarity and later would win the Nobel Peace Prize.

John Paul II, the first Polish pope, is widely credited with playing a major role in the collapse of communist rule in Eastern Europe. It is not just supporters, such as Walesa or former U.S. president George H.W. Bush, who say so. Those on the other side—such as the military dictator of communist Poland (1981–1985), Wojciech Jaruzelski, who imposed the martial law in 1981 that shut down Solidarity, and former Soviet president Mikhail Gorbachev—agree. Gorbachev even said, "The collapse of the Iron Curtain would have been impossible without John Paul II."[231] When he introduced the pope to his wife at the Vatican in December 1989, Gorbachev said, "I have the honor to introduce the highest moral authority on earth."[232]

The pope's power lay solely in his moral authority, but his authority appealed not only to Poles and Catholics but to people everywhere. For those in Poland, he represented a standard of spiritual principles and values that was the antithesis of the communist system. John Paul II visited Poland in 1979, the year after he was inaugurated as pope. The communist authorities believed only a few hundred old ladies would turn out to hear him, but millions of Poles attended his events, inspired by the spirit of truth with which he spoke against the falsehoods of communist propaganda.

He repeatedly encouraged Poles with the admonition: "Do not be afraid." He reminded them of their history and great traditions, filled with moral lessons from which they could draw strength and that communism had tried to suppress. The Catholic Church was never completely controlled by the regime. The pope even warned the communist rulers that the papacy would be watching their actions and that they bore a heavy responsibility "before history and before your conscience."[233]

Washington Post columnist Anne Applebaum, who grew up in Poland, saw the pope as issuing a moral challenge to the communist worldview through the vision that he offered. "John Paul's particular way of expressing his faith—publicly, openly, and with many cultural and historical references—was explosive in countries whose regimes tried to control both culture and history, along with everything else," she wrote.[234]

British historian Timothy Garton Ash, who documented the 1989 revolutions against communist rule across Eastern Europe, summed up Pope John Paul II's role: "I would argue the historical case in three steps: without the Polish Pope, no Solidarity revolution in Poland in 1980; without Solidarity, no dramatic change in Soviet policy toward eastern Europe under Gorbachev; without that change, no Velvet Revolutions in 1989."[235]

The second pivotal figure in Poland's transformation was Lech Walesa. He believed that John Paul II inspired Poles with the hope and courage to change. The most important fruit of that inspiration was the establishment in 1980 of Solidarity, the first trade union in the Soviet empire that was not controlled by the government. It was created by ordinary working people who would no longer accept that the party state should dictate every aspect of their lives, including working conditions and what they could read and speak. Remarkably, the government signed the Gdansk Agreement accepting the existence of Solidarity.

The union quickly grew into a broad-based social movement attracting nearly ten million members, or one-third of the Polish working-age population. This movement was a challenge to the whole Soviet system, and Soviet leader Leonid Brezhnev told the Poles to suppress Solidarity or risk Soviet military action, as had happened in Czechoslovakia in

1968. The Polish leader, General Jaruzelski, then imposed martial law, "suspended" Solidarity, and jailed Walesa and other leaders.

But Solidarity continued to operate with support from the Catholic Church and international trade union organizations, providing an underground civil-society alternative to the ruling system. Despite the repression, Solidarity remained, and its influence spread until, in 1989, the government was forced to negotiate with it. The results were multiparty elections where Solidarity candidates swept every seat for which they were allowed to run. The elections led to a Solidarity-dominated government, and a little later, Walesa became the first democratically elected president of Poland since World War II.

Activity in Poland presaged the collapse of the Soviet Empire since it was the first time a noncommunist government had been installed with the cooperation of the existing communist elites. President Ceausescu of Romania called for joint Warsaw Pact military action to bring Poland back into the communist fold. But Gorbachev was not Brezhnev, and the Soviet leader made it clear that he would not use military force to intervene in the internal political affairs of Warsaw Pact countries. Change in Poland was then rapidly followed by change in Hungary, East Germany, Czechoslovakia, Bulgaria, and Romania.

All of these countries apart from Romania followed a similar pattern. The movements that brought change to the communist regimes used peaceful means based upon civil resistance and engaged a widening circle of people in the process. In the face of mounting pressure from this growing people power, the ruling communist elites capitulated, cooperating and participating in the democratic transition and thus securing their own survival. As a result, they did not face a humiliating trial, imprisonment, or execution. Most of the old leaders simply retired into obscurity, but the communist parties continued, giving up Marxism-Leninism and adapting to a multiparty democracy.

The liberation movements all used a wide variety of means to spread information and connect people, challenging the communist monopoly of news and public discussion through underground newspapers, faxes, and meetings in churches, theaters, and workplaces. Most of all, they united a broad coalition of people, ranging in many cases from reform communists to libertarians, on the basis of certain fundamental shared principles. Central to them were the ideas of human dignity and universal human rights rooted in the concept of eternal truths—in other words, in a principled vision. The leaders of the freedom movements challenged the lies of the communist regimes based on these truths. Vaclav Havel, leader of the Czechoslovak Civic Forum and the first democratically elected president of his country, called this "living in truth."[236]

LESSONS FROM MONGOLIA'S TRANSITION TO DEMOCRACY

The glasnost and perestroika reforms launched by Mikhail Gorbachev in the Soviet Union led not only to the downfall of communist governments in Europe. Mongolia, a Soviet satellite in Asia and, since 1924, the first communist state outside the Soviet Union, underwent an exemplary peaceful transition. During the communist period, Mongolia was a rigid, one-party state with a centrally planned economy and Marxist ideology imposed through the total control of education and news media.

During the 1930s, the country suffered fierce repression that coincided with Stalin's purges in the Soviet Union. Under Soviet pressure, many Mongolian nobles, intellectuals, military officers, and Buddhist monks were shot. Hundreds of monasteries were destroyed. Khorloogin Choibalsan, who was prime minister of the Mongolian People's Republic from 1930 until 1952, became known as Mongolia's Stalin. While reports on the actual number vary, the purges may have killed as many as 100,000 people.

At first sight, Mongolia in 1989–1990 might have seemed the least likely communist state ever to make such a transition. It had no tradition of parliamentary democracy and was one of the poorest socialist countries in the world, with a per capita income of less than 1,200 dollars a year.[237] In the mid-1980s, the government initiated some economic reforms along the lines of Gorbachev's perestroika in the Soviet Union, but several young people who became the leaders of the democracy movement wanted more. Among them was the current president, my friend Tsakhiagiin Elbegdorj, who had studied in Moscow and was impressed by the glasnost aspect of reform that allowed greater freedom of expression.

With the example of the dramatic changes in Eastern Europe before them, Elbegdorj and his colleagues announced the formation of the Mongolian Democratic Union (MDU) at the first demonstration in the country against one-party rule. They demanded a multiparty system of representation and the implementation of the Universal Declaration of Human Rights in the government and the party. They were committed to peaceful protest because they understood that this was the only way to successfully challenge a government that held a monopoly of force. Demonstrations in the capital, Ulaanbaatar, grew from a few thousand in January 1990 to 40,000 in April. When rumors spread that the government might use force on the demonstrators, greater numbers of Mongolians turned out to support them.

In the face of growing public pressure, the entire Politburo resigned and dissolved itself. The MDU entered into negotiations with the governing Mongolian People's Revolutionary Party (MPRP) and ultimately agreed on the end of the one-party system. On July 29, 1990, Mongolia held its first free, multiparty elections, and the MPRP won. Nevertheless, they observed democratic principles, saw a new constitution passed in 1992, and moved into opposition peacefully when they were defeated in the 1996 general election. Since the end of communism, Mongolia has experienced seven general and six presidential elections, each time with a peaceful transition in power. There have even been coalition governments between the MPRP and other parties.

Mongolia is a striking example of a successful transition from a poor country under totalitarian communist rule to a functioning democracy committed to human rights and freedoms. It now has a growing market economy and has opened up the potential to tap the great wealth of natural resources it possesses. Its path was not easy. Mongolia suffered extreme economic hardship after Soviet subsidies ended, even having to provide food rations at one point in the early 1990s. Yet, Mongolians persevered throughout this difficult period, with their commitment to a society built upon human rights and freedoms for which they had overturned communist rule.

President Elbegdorj stressed the principles upon which Mongolia stood when he spoke in Pyongyang at Kim Il-sung University in 2013, a visit I described in Chapter 3. Calling the desire for freedom an "eternal power," he declared, "Mongolia is a country respecting human rights and freedoms, upholding rule of law and pursuing open policies. Mongolia holds dear the fundamental human rights: freedom of expression, right to assembly, and the right to live by his or her own choice."[238]

Mongolia offers many lessons for North Korea. Mongolia's rise from a poor totalitarian regime with no history of popular government to what it represents today shows what could be possible in the North. Mongolia, in a short twenty-five years, went from being a defunct communist state to a vibrant young democracy with a booming economy at the heart of the Asian continent. This transition unleashed the potential and enterprise of the Mongolian people and helped lead the economy out of its doldrums and on the path to prosperity. Despite being surrounded by two vast, nuclear-armed, authoritarian powers in Russia and China, Mongolia to this day does not seek to reinforce its own security through nuclear weapons. President Elbegdorj also underlined these lessons in his visit to Pyongyang.

With the regime increasingly unstable and the future uncertain, the North Korean elite and the party cadre face some serious challenges. Mongolia's example offers them the prospect of a peaceful move out of totalitarianism, as the Mongolian Communist Party and most of the communist parties of Eastern Europe did in their respective countries to ensure their survival during the inevitable transition to democracy and a free market system. The only regime that did not survive was that of Romania, as mentioned above. This lesson should not be lost on Pyongyang's leadership.

The parallels between Eastern Europe in 1989 and North Korea today are striking. Change came in Eastern Europe because the Soviet Union could and would no longer militarily back their satellite regimes. After the USSR dissolved, China became the North's main backer. Today, however, China is making it clear that its support for the North Korean regime is not unconditional. Beijing would like to see a leadership that aligns more closely with China's interests of economic development and regional stability.

Finally, North Korean leaders must realize that the hold the regime has on its people is weakening daily. Hearkening back to the "good old days" under Kim Il-sung and promoting a so-called neo-Juche ideology will not change that reality. As described in Chapter 3, breakdown in the food distribution system and the impact of changes in access to information make preservation of the status quo untenable.

North Korean citizens and the rest of the world know much more now about the reality of North Korea. As a result of these developments and his own actions, Kim Jong-un does not command the respect that his grandfather or even his father did. He is no longer the trusted leader North Koreans were indoctrinated to look toward but is seen as inexperienced and morally corrupt.

For the North's leadership, as well as the bureaucrats who run the country, this is a moment of truth. Change is inevitable and almost certainly will come sooner rather than later. The lessons of recent history lie before them, and the North Korean reality is becoming ever clearer as it emerges from the fog of past propaganda. The North's regime eventually will have to decide what to do when the metaphoric North Korean ship starts to sink. Will they drown with the sinking ship, remaining hardliners to the end, or will they reconcile to ensure their survival in the next chapters of Korea's story as a unified nation, poised to lead the world?

TECHNOLOGY BOOSTS PEOPLE POWER

In the Velvet Revolutions of 1989 in Eastern Europe, activists used photocopiers to spread information and announce demonstrations. In China that same year, the students in Tiananmen Square used fax machines to tell the world what was happening. This situation was revolutionary compared with the technology available to opposition groups in the past.

However, these methods were soon to be eclipsed through the revolution of the internet, the advent of smartphones, and the rise of social media.

When Muhammad Bouazizi set fire to himself, he sparked the Jasmine Revolution in Tunisia that became the Arab Spring across the Middle East because of social media. Bystanders captured his action on their mobile phones and posted it to Facebook. Tunisia has a young population, like most of the Arab world, who are highly educated.[239] It is one of the most connected countries in the region apart from the Gulf States, with nearly 40 percent of the population online.[240] News of Bouazizi's action spread rapidly through the country and then across the Arab world, particularly Egypt. The mass protests that followed his funeral were similarly captured on video and spread.

Tunisia's regime had a strong system of internet censorship, and Egypt blocked YouTube for a month during the protests. But young Tunisian activists with strong IT skills set up paths around the roadblocks so that information and images continued to flow. Interest and engagement gathered momentum as social media mobilized people power. A significant shift was observed in the postings from social to political topics. On January 14, 2011, President Ben Ali was gone.

The experience of Tunisia quickly spread to Egypt. Less than a month after Ben Ali's departure in Tunisia, Hosni Mubarak, dictatorial president of Egypt for almost thirty years, was gone also. The catalyst for the eighteen days of demonstrations that led to his resignation was one more incident of official injustice and one individual who took it upon himself to publicize the abuse of power through social media. A young businessman, Khaled Said, was beaten to death by Egyptian police. Such events were not uncommon, and the police rarely suffered any consequences.

On this occasion, however, someone took photos of Said's battered body in the morgue on a mobile phone. The images came into the hands of Wael Ghonim, a Google executive working in Egypt, who decided he could not remain silent in the face of such injustices with no one held accountable. He brought the Khaled Said story into the light of day by creating a Facebook page titled "We Are All Khaled Said" where he posted the photos. The page rapidly attracted a quarter of a million members in three months and was a key tool in organizing the first of the massive public demonstrations in Cairo's Tahrir Square that led to Mubarak's ouster.

Throughout the protests, social media played a key role both in disseminating information, within Egypt and globally, and in coordinating the protests. As one activist, Fawaz Rashed, tweeted at the time, "We use Facebook to schedule the protests, Twitter to coordinate, and YouTube to tell the world." Even though the government tried to block Facebook and Twitter and limit internet access, young techies, this time with international support, created new information pathways.

Egypt has a youthful population, half of them younger than twenty-five. Among them are four million Facebook users (5 percent of the population), including most of those ready to protest for change when the circumstances were ripe. Videos of the protests went viral worldwide and Twitter comments about Egypt rose from 2,300 to 230,000 per day in the final week of protests.[241]

Burma is another example of the difference that social media can make to public protests and the strength it can add to people power. In 1988, tens of thousands of Buddhist monks, students, and ordinary citizens poured onto the streets of Rangoon to demand human rights and democracy from the dictatorial military junta. Their protests were brutally suppressed by soldiers with orders to fire directly into the crowds. News of this atrocity reached the world through the traditional international media channels. These reports were relatively slow, appearing after the event, and necessarily came from a small handful of sources.

In 2007, the scenario repeated itself, except that this time many of the demonstrators had mobile phones that could take video and transmit it via the internet almost instantaneously. Only 1 percent of Burmese had home access to the internet at the time, and even then, it was tightly controlled by the government, far more stringently than in Tunisia and Egypt.[242] Nevertheless, enterprising and courageous Burmese citizens found ways to get the news out to the world in real time via blogs, email, and mobile phone photos and videos. The news that emerged from Burma generated a response online through petitions, support groups, and public pressure on governments to take a stand. During ten days in September, the Facebook support group for the Burma protesters grew to 110,000 members and has grown since then.[243] This type of phenomenon does not guarantee the capitulation of repressive authorities, but it puts added pressure on them, knowing that the eyes of the world are scrutinizing their every action.

The internet and social media, together with mobile technology, have made it possible to revolutionize the structure of media and communications and the way information is disseminated. They have opened up previously unimagined possibilities for exposing injustice and for bringing social transformation. Media in the nineteenth and most of the twentieth centuries transmitted information to the public through mass market channels, such as newspapers and magazines, and then radio and TV. The selection and reporting of news was in the hands of a few gatekeepers. In democracies, these gatekeepers were media corporations, but in authoritarian states, it was the government, which exercised monopolistic control of information and pushed out propaganda that their people had no independent way to verify.

The advent of social media has changed all that. Ordinary men and women armed with a mobile phone can now become independent news sources, sending videos, photos, and reports to a global audience across the web. This is how the story of Muhammad Bouazizi spread across the Arab world. Together with vivid images of him burning, an issue of social injustice was captured in an intense and personal image that moved people. Individuals had captured that image and spread it with Bouazizi's story.

The new technology has also enabled people to receive information directly from a multitude of sources all across the globe. They can bypass the gatekeepers of the traditional media, whether Western media companies or state-run news agencies that disseminate propaganda. In a world of instant news and communication, the old media paradigm instantly became obsolete because of social networking platforms such as Facebook, Twitter, YouTube, and blogs.

For traditional media in the West, this development has been a blow to their business model. In the United States, even a respected national newspaper like the *Washington Post* felt forced to sell to Jeff Bezos, founder of Amazon, in the hope that he could revive its fortunes with some digital magic.

For dictatorships everywhere, the impact has been revolutionary. Totalitarian regimes rely on their monopoly control of information to feed their people their own version of reality in the form of propaganda. This was the case in Eastern Europe, where the regimes' monopoly power over information was gradually undermined through a variety of means, ranging from a pope's messages to West German TV to photocopied leaflets. Dictators want to isolate their people from news of the outside world, from unmonitored communication with each other, and from the truth about the regimes' own abuse of power. Social media and mobile technology undermine all these intentions, breaking down and bypassing the monopoly of information.

For this reason, Wael Ghonim launched the Facebook site for Khaled Said. He said, "We [wanted] to expose the bad practices of the Egyptian police because the last thing a dictator wants is that you expose his bad practices to his people."[244] It was the same in Burma in 2007. The government could not control news and images of how the military was mistreating demonstrators, and information reached the outside world, where it generated great support for the opposition cause.

Once a repressive regime loses its monopoly over information, it has lost one of the pillars on which its power rests, and it becomes vulnerable to forces and ideas that it can no longer control. The regime becomes increasingly fearful of what information is reaching its people but finds it ever more difficult to regulate. Repressive governments face a dilemma: Should they accept social media as an important technology for a modernizing economy and risk all the new ideas it might put into circulation? Or should the regime reject social media and be left behind economically?

Tunisia and Egypt are two of the most wired countries in the Arab world. Their governments tried but failed to block social media when the sites were used to expose government injustice. There were too many young, idealistic, and tech-savvy people who knew how to get past the barriers. The governments' efforts to block the free flow of information actually damaged their economies and operations. In a wired world, the social infrastructure—business, finance, and government—is interconnected and relies on social media. When a government tries to suppress voices on social media, it disrupts the whole system, as happened in Egypt. When the internet is blocked, it damages business, leading to protests from businesspeople, and even hampers government operations.

NORTH KOREA AND THE COMMUNICATION REVOLUTION

North Korea has tried to get the benefits of new technology while attempting to avoid the dangers that free communication represents to its hold on power. Back in 2004, the government tried to ban mobile phones.[245] Yet, in 2008, North Korea officially established a mobile phone network known as Koryolink, set up by the Egyptian company Orascom. By 2013, it was reported to have two million subscribers, but it has no international access.[246] North Korea also has its own intranet that links approved individuals, usually officials and scholars, but does not connect to the world wide web.

The regime is acutely aware of its vulnerability to the inflow of information, as its futile attempt to ban cellphones demonstrates. News of the Arab Spring caused North Korea's leadership extreme nervousness. There was a crackdown on illegal cell phones coming across the Chinese border. Universities were closed for ten months beginning in June 2011, and students were sent out to farms and factories. The official reason was to prepare for Kim Il-sung's birth centenary the following year, but most observers believe it was to avoid the possibility of students discussing the Arab Spring.

North Korea and other repressive regimes fear the power of free information. Ultimately, they fear the power of truth. As Vaclav Havel and other leaders of the 1989 Velvet Revolution observed, the power of totalitarianism is built upon lies.[247] For such regimes today, the power of the new information technologies is like a flood. If it does not sweep away the foundations of their fortresses immediately, it will erode them over time. Social media and mobile technology are the most effective ways ever devised of spreading information and connecting people.

As a result, technology has the power to expose injustices and to highlight the truth in a way that makes these larger issues immediate and personal. By giving injustice a human face, as we saw in the examples of the Arab Spring and Burma, technology connects and involves individuals everywhere. Social media today has the potential to channel a great vision or an idea based on spiritual principles and eternal truths to millions of people through the internet and to touch them personally. The original visionary spark can then rapidly become a powerful force of committed individuals joining together to catalyze tremendous social transformation.

In South Korea, the issue of unification has slowly receded as a relevant issue to many people as generations have lived with the reality of division. Nevertheless, with these new advances in communication technology, this situation can change overnight if the reason for unification could be made relevant to average South Koreans. In this book, I have stressed the importance of our history because it personalizes the Korean narrative to the story of our own parents, grandparents, and ancestors, as well as our collective quest as a united people to realize our unique identity and providential destiny. Each one of us can then understand ourselves as part of Korea's greater story, a story whose next, but not last, chapter will be our unification as one Korean people. The power of social media will help spread that story and make it a substantial reality.

South Korea is one of the most wired societies on the planet, so we are perfectly positioned to exploit the power of social media for this cause.[248] Today, every person who is connected online is the active center of his or her own universe of information, social relationships, and engagement. From this position, any motivated individual who has a vision and message to convey is in a position to influence and move society.

Jody Williams is a striking example of what is possible. She founded the International Campaign to Ban Landmines in 1992, which she ran by herself from her home in Vermont. Through the use of the internet, she worked with the United Nations, national governments, and the International Red Cross, establishing a network that started with six NGOs and grew to over 1,000 in over sixty countries in five years under her leadership. In 1997, an international Mine Ban Treaty was signed in Oslo, and she and her organization were awarded the Nobel Peace Prize.

Examples like this can be repeated in South Korea, not once, but thousands of times surrounding the issue of unification. Activists can personalize the issue through social media, connecting the issue to family histories, to the experience of our fellow Koreans in the North, and to the broad flow of Korea's history that has brought us to the present. Through such initiatives, an ever-widening circle of Korean citizens can become engaged and form a nationwide consensus on our purpose and direction as a Korean people.

North Korea may have isolated itself from the internet, but isolating itself from the flow of information both into and out of the country has become impossible. The regime is in an untenable situation, as the following anecdote illustrates. A group of students at Kim Chaek University of Technology in Pyongyang organized a soccer club using their Koryolink cellphones, according to a report sponsored by the US-Korea Institute at SAIS, "Cell Phones in North Korea." The authorities then introduced a more restrictive regional cellphone service, a decision thought to be related to this incident. If cellphones can be used to organize soccer, what else might they be used to organize?[249] The story illustrates the level of insecurity of the state and the impossibility of it damming the tide of communication with all the possibilities it opens.

In Chapter 2, I described some of the difficulties faced by North Korean defectors adjusting to life in Seoul. But a core of defectors is actively engaged in efforts to open up the society they escaped from. Using a variety of media, they are bringing information out of North Korea and also feeding it back to the people there. Some twenty organizations based in Seoul have secret informants in the North reporting on many aspects of life there. They use illegal Chinese cellphones that are widely sold in the border region with China where they can pick up an international signal.[250] Among them are farmers, factory workers, teachers, and even some mid-level party officials.

Daily NK is probably the largest of these groups, with a website in Korean, Chinese, Japanese, and English. The others include the Buddhist Good Friends organization through its publication *North Korea Today*, and the Osaka-based *Rimjin-gang* magazine published by Asia Press International.[251] Their reporting gives a remarkably clear and detailed picture of life in North Korea for a worldwide audience. It removes the mask from the Hermit Kingdom, covering issues like the food supply, the state of the markets and government action toward them, currency, and energy—all told through personal stories.

Much of this information is then pushed back into North Korea, particularly through radio. Melanie Kirkpatrick, in her book, *Escape from North Korea*, describes Chinese traders in the North selling small, easily concealed radios that can receive foreign broadcasts for about three dollars. North Koreans can listen to Seoul-based radio run by defectors, such as Free North Korea Radio, Open Radio North Korea, and Radio Free Chosun, as well as Voice of America and Radio Free Asia.[252] An InterMedia Institute survey in 2008 estimated that 57 percent of North Koreans owned a radio.[253] Fewer own DVD players, but the markets seem to do a brisk trade in DVDs of South Korean soap operas pirated and copied by traders in Northeast China and sold in North Korea.[254]

North Korean Intellectuals Solidarity is a group of defectors with college degrees or professional qualifications.[255] They formed the group in 2008 to reach out to their peers in North Korea through a number of clandestine methods. They establish contact with government officials, scholars, and professionals to inform them both of life outside North Korea and the realities inside of which they might not be aware. According to Melanie Kirkpatrick, this information includes "the history of revolutions and grassroots movements that gave birth to them. It discusses the institutions that sustain democracies, such as an impartial judicial system."[256]

The people receiving this information are the potential opinion leaders who would play a key role when change comes to North Korea. The reality facing the Kim regime is that the flow and reach of information into the North cannot be stopped. It will only extend its reach and influence as access and communication technologies improve.

This bodes impending doom for Kim Jong-un's regime. However, it does not ensure the peaceful end of that regime nor a peaceful transition to the formation of a new nation true to our founding aspirations. Thus, we as the Korean people all need to be vigilant and feel a deep sense of urgency and ownership over the process of unification, with a clear vision of the final objective in mind. That is why we all need to own the Korean Dream. It is the only path forward for our people, the peninsula, and the world.

You Can Make a Difference

The transformational changes that took place in Eastern Europe, South Africa, Mongolia, and the southern United States occurred because people joined together and demanded a new way of life, even in the face of tremendous opposition. What gave these movements their power was not just numbers but a guiding vision that moved the collective consciousness of the masses to fight injustices and correct wrongs based upon eternal truths and enduring spiritual principles. In other words, the numbers were the by-product of the message and cause, and not the other way around. People power came from the moral authority of the purpose or reason for transformation rather than the processes or just for the sake of change. That is why a unifying dream is so important. In my mind, that is the Korean Dream, since it is rooted in our history and provides a clear path forward toward unification and Korea's place in the world community.

Throughout this chapter, we have seen the examples of how acts of injustice prompted grassroots social action, such as the pro-democracy movement in Korea, the Arab Spring, and the Velvet Revolution in Eastern Europe. However, we have also seen how charismatic individuals articulated a vision and message of moral authority by upholding fundamental spiritual truths that moved the conscience of humanity. This was the position of Mahatma Gandhi, Nelson Mandela, Martin Luther King Jr., and Pope John Paul II. All were spiritual leaders who reached far beyond the frontiers of their own faith traditions and limited agendas to appeal to a universal human consciousness that resonated with certain universal spiritual principles and shared values.

Korea today faces a moment of historic transformational change at least as great as any of the momentous shifts I have just described. Such a change cannot be undertaken by governments alone but needs the full collective will and support of the Korean people. This should be our priority task since it involves our identity as Koreans, our history that has brought us to this point, and our destiny to live out the ideals of Hongik Ingan, which stand as our legacy and birthright. However, this can only be realized when all Koreans, whether North or South or those living in the diaspora, take personal ownership over the vision that should animate our people at this pivotal moment for our collective destiny. Without this broad support and interest of the whole Korean people, the ideals of our founding are but a dream and can never become a reality.

However, with the wide-spread support of our people, then as sure as day follows night, we will realize the Korean Dream of creating a new united nation that is something greater than the sum of its two parts. I envision a nation that reflects our original ideals and our unique character and identity as a people. Such a nation is destined to be an example to the world.

With the communication revolution, we have the necessary tools that can personalize our ownership of the Korean Dream and, at the same time, connect it to a larger network of like-minded individuals anywhere in the world, making the impact of our social action that much more powerful. As I have mentioned above, these advances in technology are already making inroads in North Korea, setting the stage for impending change. Transformation of the peninsula will come, but the question is how and to what effect? Will it be a peaceful process centered upon the unified goals of the North and South, or will it be confrontational? Will it remain in the realm of ideas or, far worse, be brought about by force? As I stated clearly in Chapter 1, we have to think of unification with the end in mind, and we have to develop a vision that all Korean people can fully endorse and support, superseding our differences. Only then will we find a peaceful solution for our national unity.

That is why I undertook the task of articulating the Korean Dream as a national vision of a new Korea. Yet, it should not be the hopes of one, a few, or half of the Korean people, but rather all of us—North and South. It should spark the hopes of our collective dreams, as our ancestors tried to realize throughout our history. The dream should not lie with anyone else—not the government, nor the international community—but with each individual Korean. In this age of a communications revolution, we must be the driving spiritual and moral force in this endeavor with firm commitment and ownership and act as proud contributors in building a noble future for our people.

As this chapter's opening quote so aptly implies, although we might not be able to change the world alone, we definitely can "create a ripple" in the waters of change that collectively can become a tsunami of transformation, sweeping the current state away in its wake and revealing the promise of a new future. Yet, it all starts with us, the Korean people. What are we willing to do about it? What are we going to do about it? Today, there are many possibilities for social engagement, which I explore in the next chapter.

CHAPTER 6

Engagement Beyond Government: The Role of Civil Society and NGOs

"At the head of any new undertaking, where in France you would find the government or in England some territorial magnate, in the United States you are sure to find an association [...] I have often admired the extreme skill they show in proposing a common object for the exertions of very many and in inducing them voluntarily to pursue it."
—ALEXIS DE TOCQUEVILLE

Great social transformation requires the engagement of a broad public united in pursuit of a common cause. The previous chapter described several dramatic historic examples of such engagement and also explained the importance of a clear vision, alignment with fundamental principles, and the power of moral authority. The unification of our divided peninsula will undoubtedly be a moment of great historic significance. It will remove the last vestige of the Cold War, enabling Korea to finally move beyond the legacy of colonialism in Asia. Through unification, the Korean people will become one again, thus able to pursue unhindered our destiny to become a model nation rooted in our time-honored ideals.

The unification process cannot remain solely in the sphere of politics and government negotiations. Recent experience has reminded us how easily intergovernmental dealings can be stalled or diverted from their original intent. The Sunshine Policy was launched with high hopes of inducing North Korea to change gradually. But as we saw, the government of Kim Jong-il extracted revenue from the South while, in return, nothing changed. Unification will be the coming together of a separated people, and so, in addition to the political and economic issues to be addressed, a vast social and cultural transformation will have to take place. Koreans from the North and South will need to engage with one another on many different levels.

Unification must be a movement with broad popular involvement if it is to succeed. I have explained that Koreans are now faced with a historic opportunity. We can seize the moment and determine our own future, free of the controlling influence of outside forces. To do this, we must take that responsibility upon ourselves as a people and act with firm conviction, united in a common goal. Every Korean can become engaged and act to make a difference. The Korean people must work together in partnership with their government to successfully achieve unification.

Civic organizations and NGOs provide the perfect means for such partnerships. Groups from all types of backgrounds, including religious and professional associations, are growing in number. They represent a broad spectrum of Korean society and are engaged in a wide variety of issues related to North Korea that include humanitarian aid focusing on food, healthcare, education, and human rights. These groups offer a natural channel for the energy of all Koreans who decide they want to make a difference on the unification issue. The answer to the question

"What can I do?" is clear. Work with one of these groups that can use your skills and expertise, or even start a new one to tackle an unaddressed issue.

The private nonprofit sector also offers a natural path for the government to work together with the people in public-private partnerships. This sort of broad alliance geared toward practical action on a wide social front is a necessary foundation in preparation for unification, which will probably come much sooner than many expect. The partnership between the government and civic organizations is not simply a matter of mobilizing public support for government policy. The government needs the active engagement of the nonprofit sector to address the wider social and cultural aspects of unification and ultimately to expand people-to-people connections as opportunities widen.

The governments in Seoul and Pyongyang are constrained by having to deal within the framework of the ideological division that arose out of the Cold War. Civic organizations can bypass this constraint and operate outside of the political context. A feature of a growing number of these groups in South Korea is that they are committed to a nonpolitical approach to unification. For them, it is not a matter of reconciling two political systems but of recognizing the common humanity and heritage of the people in the North and working to support them.

In order to achieve this, civic associations in the South must work in cooperation with the government but, more importantly, with one another. We must not repeat the mistakes of the past when my father's meeting with Kim Il-sung opened the doors of engagement with the North, but there was no guiding vision nor organizing strategy to coordinate the efforts of the government and private-sector players in dealing with the North. Everyone pursued their own separate interests while government efforts ultimately came to naught with the bankruptcy of the Sunshine Policy.[257]

What was missing was an overarching national vision to unite the many private initiatives while working in cooperation with a clear governmental strategy. I believe that vision can be found in the Korean Dream. At the same time, there needs to be a vehicle to coordinate the various private-sector efforts for unification so that they are mutually supportive and interface naturally with the government. That is why I initiated Action for Korea United[258] as the umbrella organization of civil society for all the disparate actors on the unification issue. By uniting behind it, Korea can avoid repeating the same mistake.

RISE OF CIVIC ASSOCIATIONS AND THE IMPORTANCE OF FAITH

Civil society groups are not merely a useful addition to the work of government. They form the backbone of every healthy and vibrant democracy. They are the instruments through which the energy of a people is harnessed and directed toward important social goals. Civil society groups are the means for citizens to be responsible for and actively engaged in the life of their community, society, and nation. Through them, principles are put into practice.

The modern term NGO (nongovernmental organization) that is used for many of these groups is a relatively recent designation, only appearing after the establishment of the United Nations.[259] But the importance of civil society, expressed through civic associations, has long been understood as an essential component of a free society. Alexis de Tocqueville, the French aristocrat who wrote the classic and still-influential *Democracy in America*, understood this well.[260] In studying the success of America's experiment in popular government, he observed that voluntary associations were a widespread feature of American life and an important foundation for citizen engagement and social stability as well as promoting a general culture of service. He concluded that these ingredients were all essential in creating a well-functioning free market democratic state.

Tocqueville underscored the importance of such associations in his study of the French Revolution. He examined the period prior to the revolution, looking for the activity of civic associations. He found that whenever there were attempts to establish them, they were invariably stifled or suppressed. Hence, when the revolution came, there were no mediating and moderating social institutions. As a result, the revolution rapidly took a violent turn with the Terror and the establishment of all the despotic features of the old regime but taken to new extremes. He concluded that voluntary associations were an essential feature of a stable, just, and dynamic democracy.[261]

These associations are almost always established by people who have an earnest will to help all of humanity. Often their motivation springs from their faith or fundamental moral principles that inspire them to fight injustices or fulfill certain unmet social needs. These civic associations have been a feature of life in free societies, especially in modern times.[262] In Britain in the nineteenth century, for example, civic associations sprang up like mushrooms to meet the many serious challenges brought about by industrialization.

The Industrial Revolution rode on the back of a population explosion that brought hundreds of thousands into the great, new, hastily constructed industrial cities. Conditions for the poor in these places were desperate. Sanitation was primitive or nonexistent, epidemics of typhoid and cholera were common, and crime was widespread. In response, many groups, both secular and faith-based, were formed to address the needs of this new urban proletariat, in order to bring their plight to the public's attention. Many of these associations were founded by Christians motivated by the gospel message to "Love thy neighbor." One example is the Salvation Army, founded in 1865 in London by a onetime Methodist minister and evangelist, William Booth, and his wife, Catherine, which has become a global presence that is still active today.[263]

The dramatic social transformations brought about by the examples of people power described in the previous chapter relied on various forms of civic associations to channel popular support toward realizing a common goal. Churches and religious groups were especially prominent among such associations. They played a central role in the U.S. civil rights movement, in Poland, and in East Germany.

In America, many of the civil rights leaders were African American ministers, and their churches were the natural focus of the black community and the context within which they planned future activities and supported one another. Strikingly, although churches played such a central role, the movement served a universal cause that transcended denominationalism. The civil rights movement appealed to broad moral and spiritual principles that ultimately became the source of its power.

The same was true in Eastern Europe. Lutheran pastors and church communities played a central role in opposing the communist state in East Germany. They worked in common cause with many other groups and people with a wide spectrum of religious and political views. The same was true in Poland where the Roman Catholic Church played an important role.[264] The church did not actively campaign against the state, but it represented a realm of civil society that the government tried to constrain but could never completely control.[265] As a result, Catholic churches provided a space for dissident groups to meet, discuss, and plan, even if the priest was not directly involved.

The church provided moral support and an alternative vision to the ruling communist ideology, thus nurturing other forms of civic association. In Chapter 5, I described the role of Solidarity, the independent Polish trade union movement. Its significance was huge precisely because it was organized outside the hitherto monopolistic sphere of communist state power. Poles then had the opportunity to act in the public sphere without communist control. The appeal was immense, and millions joined Solidarity in a matter of weeks.

In Czechoslovakia, the opposition to communist rule simply labeled itself the Civic Forum. It did not identify itself with any political ideology. Rather, it stood for the restoration of civil society, beyond the realm of politics,[266] and was based upon fundamental human rights and freedoms rooted in universal moral principles, which is what the state had systematically sought to suppress.[267] Where the Poles used churches to meet, the Czechs and Slovaks found their meeting spaces in the theaters of the arts and entertainment world, another sphere where the government did not have total control.

In many of these examples, people of faith provided drive and inspiration, which is understandable as faith offers the principles and values that motivate a person to want to live for the sake of others. Many people from the Korean diaspora who work in China with North Korean refugees in the Underground Railroad are motivated by their faith. The refugees they deal with are confused and overwhelmed by the care they receive from people whom they have never met. The refugees have never experienced anything like it in their lives. The power of selfless love motivates us to reach out to fellow human beings in need, for no other reason than that we are members of One Family under God.

While faith often provides the impetus for action, what inspires people to work together for a noble cause is a shared aspiration or common vision that is not exclusive to any particular faith tradition or philosophy. The leaders I described in Chapter 5 on people power—Gandhi, King, and Mandela—held great moral authority because of the fundamental principles and values they upheld. They stepped beyond sectarian limitations and spoke to humanity's universal aspirations.

Among the many NGOs and civic associations in South Korea that perform work related to North Korea, there are Buddhist, Catholic, and Protestant groups. Faith-based organizations are destined to play a major role in outreach to the North, but they must do so in partnership. The challenge is to bring all these groups to work together. I have been actively promoting such partnerships through the work of GPF; cooperation among faiths based on a common vision is an essential element of principled social transformation, and it will be a powerful force in achieving Korean unification.

One example is an inter-faith trip to North Korea in 2011 organized by the Jogye Buddhist sect, which undertakes active humanitarian projects in North Korea. After the North attacked the South, the relationship between the two Koreas became especially hostile. However, on the occasion of the thousand-year anniversary of Palman Daejanggyeong (Tripitaka Koreana), both governments granted the Jogye Buddhists permission to make a pilgrimage to their holy site in North Korea. The Jogye Buddhists used that opportunity to call other faiths to come together in a demonstration of inter-faith solidarity, and I was invited to join as part of the delegation.

This was the first visit after the North Korean attack, and it became a high-interest story for the media.[268]

The role of faith in initiating and participating in all major principled social and cultural transformations in human history is undisputable, yet people of secular views who dominate the intellectual and media elites in the Western world think of religion as outmoded and belittle or ignore it. However, the vast majority of the world's people hold deep religious or spiritual beliefs. Secularists are the minority. According to December 2012 Pew Forum research:

> Worldwide, more than eight in ten people identify with a religious group. A comprehensive demographic study of more than 230 countries and territories conducted by the Pew Research Center's Forum on Religion & Public Life estimates that there are 5.8 billion religiously affiliated adults and children around the globe, representing 84% of the 2010 world population of 6.9 billion.[269]

While religious differences sometimes fuel conflicts, faith is also the source of meaning, value, and ethical standards for billions of people. Most of the great movements for social and cultural change have been driven by faith-inspired people. Imagine the possibilities if faith traditions were able to work together, instead of looking at the others as competitors or rivals, to bring about fundamental social transformation reflective of widely held, universal principles and values. The majority of humanity would be well-served as vast reserves of people, funding, and assets across national and regional lines could be mobilized to tackle the most pressing global challenges, such as identity-based conflicts. That is why true interfaith work rooted in common aspirations, principles, and values is so important. The purpose of engagement is clearly not just to gain acceptance and understanding of one's faith tradition but to work together to solve the real problems of the world while remaining true to one's convictions.

MODERNIZATION, GLOBALIZATION, AND CIVIC ORGANIZATIONS

One of the most striking phenomena of recent times is the rise of a global civil society involving a vast and ever-growing number of people willing to reach out to distant lands to help their fellow humans in need. This was made possible by the great leap forward in information and communication technology (ICT). As we saw in the previous chapter, the advent of the internet, social media, and smartphones was an essential component that fueled the Arab Spring. However, ICT also personalizes these events by enabling someone sitting at a breakfast table in Seoul or New York to learn about a disaster thousands of miles away through images that are both vivid and intimate.

As a result, the response today to natural and manmade disasters is global in scope. The 2004 tsunami in the Indian Ocean that claimed over 225,000 lives, the 2010 Haiti earthquake, the 2011 tsunami that hit Japan and caused the Fukushima nuclear power plant crisis, Typhoon Yolanda-Haiyan in late 2013 that devastated the Philippines, the famine in South Sudan or the Sahel ... all have generated a massive international response that has not been limited to inter-governmental assistance. The main thrust of support in terms of charitable giving and volunteerism came from the private sector through a myriad of international and domestic NGOs and civic organizations.

In fact, as Don Eberly pointed out in his book *The Rise of Global Civil Society*, the substantial amount of aid contributed by the U.S. government in the wake of the Indian Ocean tsunami was outstripped by the amount raised and sent overseas by private organizations and individuals.[270] These disasters mobilized a global network of private aid organizations, such as the International Red Cross, Oxfam, and World Vision, who worked in partnership with governments to coordinate relief efforts. In addition, thousands of smaller NGOs contributed to the overall effort in their particular fields of specialization, as did millions of individual volunteers and donors.

Eberly, who subtitled his book *Building Communities and Nations from the Bottom Up*, sees this spread and greater engagement of civic associations as a phenomenon that has emerged in recent decades but is exercising increasing influence. His book suggests that civil society partnerships in the twenty-first century may overtake the traditional role of governments in providing aid and services in far more responsive and innovative ways.[271]

Apart from disaster relief, NGOs tackle a wide range of issues on an ongoing basis. Food, housing, health, poverty, education, the environment, conflict resolution, and a combination of development issues are all within the range of problems being addressed. There are currently an estimated 20,000 recognized international NGOs that tend to be sizeable and well-established.[272] But the number of NGOs that operate domestically within countries are huge by comparison. The United States alone has 1.5 million NGOs,[273] while India estimates there are 3.3 million in the country;[274] even Russia, whose current government is no friend to private citizen initiatives,[275] has over half a million.[276]

The majority of local civic associations involve just a few citizens who want to make a difference on an issue that concerns them. Many work in places and on issues where the government has neither the reach nor the resources to make any impact. The most successful of them involve the community they work with in their projects, generating local ownership that leads to real and sustainable development. Even where the immediate geographic impact is limited, good projects offer models that can then be implemented more widely.

Furthermore, while governments are very active in providing relief in the wake of major disasters, their long-term involvement in humanitarian efforts is often dictated by national interests and domestic political considerations. NGOs, on the other hand, are issues-based organizations that focus on their particular cause. They do not face the same political constraints as governments. As a result, they are much better placed to develop consistent policies and practices over the longer term toward the type of humanitarian and moral issues with which they typically deal.

Some NGOs pioneer social innovations that governments are usually too inflexible to even imagine. One outstanding example is the Grameen Bank founded by Muhammad Yunus, an initiative for which he and the bank won the Nobel Peace Prize in 2006.[277] As an economics professor in Bangladesh in the early 1980s, Yunus realized that what he was teaching his students seemed to be irrelevant to life in the poor rural villages that surrounded his university. He believed that poor people had great untapped potential for growth that could be released with very small amounts of credit.

He had his students research ways to deliver credit to rural villages, which gave birth to the concept of microcredits or microfinance. The concept is now used throughout the developing world as a means to jump-start the entrepreneurial abilities of the rural poor. Yunus combined the loans, which required no collateral, with a community development approach. Grameen Bank does not lend to individuals but to small groups that provide support for each other with developing their project and making their repayments.[278]

Civic associations and NGOs are having a transformative effect on the way people get involved and make a difference on any number of public and social issues. Like the ICT revolution, this has happened in the course of only two to three decades. In the words of Don Eberly, "Civil society ... takes isolated individuals and weaves them into the larger social fabric, linking them to purposes beyond narrow private or parochial interests."[279] He might also have added that it can operate in a realm beyond the capacity of effective government action.

In Korea, such groups are increasingly affecting the lives of ordinary Koreans. These groups will be essential for the unification process, allowing citizens to involve themselves in practical and substantial ways. The government cannot do without them and the citizen energy that they mobilize. However, civic associations are still young in Korea, and much can still be done to develop them. I realized long ago that civic associations and NGOs would play an increasingly important role globally and pioneered their development in Korea. Early in 2001, I established

Service for Peace (SFP) in order to promote peace through voluntary service by giving young people, particularly from the developed world, the opportunity to serve in local communities, as well as communities across the developing world.

Volunteerism was a relatively recent arrival in Korea. Once the government became committed to supporting and publicizing it, SFP played a pioneering role in helping to promote and shape the public's understanding of the value of volunteerism. It was one of the original members of the National Volunteer Organizations Council that helped NGOs work effectively and generated public support for them.[280] SFP made it easy for students to get involved by having them engage in fun activities with blind and handicapped children. They also engaged parents in the process since the initial reaction from many was that their son or daughter should be studying rather than volunteering. Working with companies, SFP promoted the value of service and corporate social responsibility.

Civil society will be a critical partner to the governments of North Korea and South Korea in the unification process, acting as a neutral intermediary since civil society's purpose is usually nonpartisan or ideological but mission specific. Civil society will also fill in the gaps for real social and cultural needs that the two governments are not equipped to address, as well as weave concerned individuals into the larger social fabric of a united Korea. In other words, unlike what Tocqueville observed in the French Revolution, civil society's presence will offer the social stability necessary to make the transition to unification peaceful. Most important, the faith and humanitarian orientation of such groups will also highlight the common humanity and, more specifically, the common identity of our people, beyond the political and ideological divide—thus making the goal of unity a matter of our collective destiny.

INTERNATIONAL PROJECTS OF GPF: ALL-LIGHTS VILLAGE AND CHARACTER AND CREATIVITY INITIATIVE

I founded the Global Peace Foundation (GPF) in 2009. GPF promotes an innovative, values-based approach to peacebuilding, guided by the vision of "One Family under God." GPF's purpose is to apply this vision to critical challenges facing the human family to develop practical models that translate the vision into concrete and transformative action. Two of GPF's signature projects deserve mention: the All-Lights Village project and the Character and Creativity Initiative.

All-Lights Village (ALV) supplies solar-powered lanterns to light the homes and streets of rural villages in Asia and Africa that are off the electrical grid. There are lanterns for home use and for street lighting. Solar lights provide several hours of light each day and, unlike kerosene lamps, do not burn expensive fuels and emit unhealthy fumes.

More important, however, the lamps open up the night and transform the possibilities of village life. Villagers become more productive: children can study longer in the evenings, while money saved on kerosene can be used to buy books and school supplies, creating more opportunities for education and possibilities to break out of the inter-generational cycle of poverty. The young can develop new skills they can then apply to benefit the whole community.

In Molo District, Kenya, the solar street lighting had a big impact on security.[281] Crime at night dropped, and people felt safer to move around. One result was greater interaction among community members, who began to cooperate on new projects that they themselves created. Another result was new community infrastructure appearing where there was none before, producing greater social stability.[282]

In the Philippines, the test launch for the project with more than twenty All-Lights Villages, the lanterns are combined with other forms of appropriate technology, including cheap and simple water filtration systems and clean-burning cookstoves. Simple revenue-generating initiatives are developed in cooperation with local residents who manage and run them once they are launched. Villagers experience a sense of pride, hope, and empowerment as they become a self-supporting community, operating on a traditional cooperative family model, yet starting to learn developed-world practices.

While the solar lamps illuminate the night, the light switched on in the villagers' minds is most significant—the change in mind-set that occurs as they realize the new possibilities available to them. ALV has learned from the Saemaul Undong model. The key to Saemaul Undong's success was promoting a change of attitude among rural communities through helping them engage with and be responsible for their own growth. The ownership that each villager exercised over a new project was always more important than the materials they received.

Wherever I travel and speak in the emerging world, I emphasize the lessons that many developing countries can learn from the Korean experience of development, since we shared their predicament only a little more than a half century ago. Among the developed nations in the world, Korea stands as a shining example of how a country can pull itself from dire poverty to first-world status. Of course, it was due to the hard work of our people, but significant lessons can also be learned about fighting the dehumanizing effects of poverty. Most importantly, the change in the South began with changing the mind-set of poverty by encouraging self-reliance, hard work, and ownership, thereby uplifting one's sense of self-worth and dignity, which naturally fuels one's desire to excel.

ALV operates in Asian countries such as the Philippines, Indonesia, and Nepal, as well as Africa and South America. A number of organizations have recognized its effectiveness as a model for socially transforming poor rural communities. In 2013, ALV was chosen as an example of best practices in the field of appropriate technology and the improvement of rural village life by both Engineers Without Borders and the Advanced Institute of Convergence Technology.

In February 2013, GPF-Korea was one of only seven civic groups to receive a national merit award from the Republic of Korea, recognizing its contribution to the unification movement in Korea. International acclaim came for the All-Lights Village project as well. "The extent of social volunteer work is unprecedented for a civil society organization. It has made notable contributions to developing Korea's national standing," said Minister for Special Affairs Ko Heung-kil.[283] The experience of social transformation at the village level can be applied directly to rural North Korea in the future. In fact, discussions are already under way to start an ALV pilot project in Chongju, in North Pyonganbuk-do.

The ALV village projects also offer a tremendous opportunity for international volunteer service. A growing number of Korean companies are sponsoring the purchase and delivery of solar lanterns and then encouraging employees to volunteer to go to the villages where they will be installed. There they work together with the villagers on a much-needed community project, such as constructing a multipurpose village hall. Korean students also take part in these and other projects through the "Global Poomashi" movement, working in the Philippines, Nepal, Mongolia, and Kenya.[284] Over 1,000 volunteers have participated since the project began. As a result, Koreans are increasingly becoming connected to the wider world and its communities.

Villagers and volunteers both benefit from this exchange. The villagers gain not only the lights and a useful new building but also the opportunity to change their current status through increased productivity, security, and education, as well as having the sense that they are not isolated in the world. They understand now that people out there know about them and want to help them as if they were part of one family. The volunteers experience a new culture and a much simpler and humbler way of life. Their vision of humanity is extended beyond their Korean experience to touch other people and parts of the world. They develop a moral perspective that encourages all of us to be responsible for each other as part of a global family.

Lifting up poor and isolated rural communities through opportunities to take greater control of their lives is one essential element in transforming an emerging nation. Another essential issue for the developing world is its young people's future. Most have populations that are very young. Through my travels, I recognize that many of these nations would not be able to produce enough traditional jobs to employ all their young people. Population growth has outstripped job creation.

This situation is unfortunate since these young people are the key to the developing world's future. The values that guide them, the quality of their characters, and the level of social responsibility they feel for their communities, as well as the skills they have, will be critically important in determining their and their countries' futures. Many nations have received aid from the West for decades, often with secular and progressive values tied conditionally to that support. Many traditional societies that happen to be deeply religious are finding the cost of aid too high for them because the secular progressive values undermine the most cherished traditions of their culture. In addition, the financial crisis and global recession in the developed world beginning in 2007, stemming from the moral decay of greedy Wall Street financiers, has led many to question the previously dominant Western model of development. Developing nations are open to new approaches, especially ones that do not replace traditional cultural values with rampant self-interested individualism.

Nevertheless, recognition is growing that economic development is the tip of the iceberg in terms of the total development picture. Being successful must depend on a foundation of social and political stability, which is difficult to achieve with a large population of uneducated and alienated youth. Consequently, developing the moral character and integrity of young people, together with their enterprise and leadership abilities, will be an essential component in the successful transformation of emerging nations.

With these considerations in mind, I launched a project to address these issues. The Character and Creativity Initiative (CCI) was pioneered in Kenya in the wake of inter-tribal violence following the 2007 presidential elections. Over 1,200 people were killed and about a quarter million displaced from their homes. The main perpetrators of the violence were gangs of young men, instigated, and often paid, by unscrupulous and demagogic politicians.[285]

I held a Global Peace Festival in Nairobi in 2008, right after the worst of the violence, to promote the message of One Family under God as the foundation for peace and unity. One of the candidates in the election, Prime Minister Odinga, spoke at the rally, calling Kenyans to live up to their better principles and traditions. CCI developed as a long-term initiative to change the culture and attitudes of Kenya's young people.[286]

CCI works in partnership with the Ministry of Education, Brand Kenya, and educational groups such as the National Association of High School Principals. The CCI program is unique in its approach. It is not another item on the curriculum menu, as Kenyan schools did not have any space in the school day to add a new class.

The fundamental understanding of the program is that character and creativity are both rooted in a certain type of culture that is an expression of relationships within a community. Just as relationships within a family express certain principles and moral values and create a family culture, so, too, do the relationships within a school community. With this in mind, CCI has shifted the focus away from classroom interaction and the transfer of intellectual knowledge alone to the life of the school community as a whole in all its aspects.

Each CCI school establishes a council that includes the principal, an administrator, representative teachers and students, and sports coaches from within the school. From outside the school, CCI recruits representative parents as well as community leaders, businesspeople, and faith leaders. The council then devises ways to bring the practice of certain values, such as honesty, integrity, and public-mindedness, into the school's daily life. Community representatives help the school see itself as part of a wider community and help set up local service projects in which students can be involved.

This approach gives responsibility and initiative to the members of the school and community. The experience has released a great deal of imaginative and creative energy. One example is a girls' high school that started to assign each new student a "mother" from the next-oldest grade whose job was to mentor and guide her "daughter" through her school life. Of course, the "mother" had her own "mother" in the year above her, creating a lineage across the different school years. The focus again is on relationships, based on a family model, as the human framework in which moral character is formed.

A landmark study by the Kenya Institute for Public Policy Research and Analysis (KIPPRA), an independent think tank, in August 2013 confirmed the success of this approach.[287] The study looked at the performance of six of the CCI pilot schools over a two-year period, comparing them with six control schools. The report showed improvements in a number of areas over the time of the study compared with the control schools. Disciplinary problems, such as violence, bullying, and substance abuse, decreased. Academic performance improved, even though that was not a primary goal of the program.[288]

The impact on the school culture was tangible, measured by student and teacher survey responses. Teachers reported greater job satisfaction, and students experienced more self-confidence. Teachers' and school staff's engagement with and support provided to students increased.

The report concluded that to prepare students for success in life, the school community needed to work together toward a shared vision of ethics and excellence through successful collaboration between students, administrators, teachers, parents, and the surrounding community. The report went on to recommend the integration of national values into the school curriculum as a pillar for building a transformative culture on a foundation of moral principles. "This will help articulate who we are, what we stand for, and the value of our contribution to life both in Kenya and in the global village," the report stated. The final conclusion was that the CCI program should be extended throughout the whole country.[289]

Plans for this are already under way in cooperation with the Ministry of Education and the many other partners who make up the National Character and Creativity Council. The community and relationship model CCI has followed lends itself well to expansion. CCI pilot schools will act as a hub for other local schools and mentor them in establishing CCI. Once the program is in place, these schools will mentor other schools.

Universities, too, are becoming involved through their students becoming mentors to pupils in their local high schools.

The success of this approach has altered the way in which Kenya assesses its schools' performances. Now an assessment of nonacademic factors is taken into account as part of the education of the "total child." At a program announcing the KIPPRA report, the secretary of the Ministry of Education, Science, and Technology, Professor Jacob Kaimenyi, said that schools "will not only be ranked on the basis of academic excellence but will include other parameters such as talent development, cultivation of creativity, and good character formation toward nurturing all-round students."[290]

The United Nations has also recognized the significance of this work by awarding GPF-Kenya a Certificate of Commendation in October 2013 for its "outstanding efforts to promote a culture of service among youth in Kenya."[291] The award cited CCI as well as the All-Lights Village work in the country.[292] Inspired by the impact of CCI in Kenya, Nigeria and Uganda have both adopted the project. CCI has also been launched in Indonesia, Malaysia, Mongolia, Nepal, and the Philippines in Asia, and in Paraguay and Brazil in South America.[293]

I started ALV and CCI as pioneering experiments in two forms of social development in emerging countries. One addressed the issue of rural communities trapped in poverty, the other formation of youth as engaged and responsible citizens in emerging countries. Their track record is proving them successful. Both are necessary components in successfully transforming a nation out of poverty and dysfunction and into modern practices.

No one silver bullet is available for any country's development. Many elements have to work together. I am a person of faith with a unique spiritual legacy, and my firm conviction is that any harmonious and prosperous human community needs a solid foundation built upon the spiritual principles and moral values espoused by all the great faith traditions throughout history. These principles and values are then given practical expression through human relationships in families and communities and in social and political institutions.

ALV and CCI are social initiatives that put principles and values into practice, demonstrating that they are not simply abstract ideas and can have real social impact. In fact, principles and values are the essential foundation for material development, by raising citizens with the integrity, initiative, and responsibility necessary to sustain that development within a free and technologically advanced society. All of these ideas and experiences related to social transformation have come together in my work with Paraguay, which has brought transformation on a national level.

THE SOCIAL FOUNDATIONS FOR NATIONAL TRANSFORMATION: THE PARAGUAY EXAMPLE

The destinies of Korea and Paraguay are intertwined, an assertion that may seem surprising to many Koreans today, so let me explain. In June 2014, Korea's Il Sung Construction Company broke ground on a roadbuilding project in Paraguay.[294] It won the contract as the sole international bidder, competing against Paraguayan firms.[295] The Il Sung project is significant in that it is a major step in ongoing cooperation between the two nations. It is also the first case of a foreign company winning a bid for an infrastructure project in Paraguay, thereby bringing higher international standards into the process.

During that same time, our institute and GPF-Paraguay organized a Korea-Paraguay Symposium and brought together a group of Korean bankers and former minister-level officials in the fields of transportation and infrastructure to meet with Paraguay's minister of planning, the president of the central bank, and several business leaders. They presented and discussed plans for the comprehensive development of Paraguay's infrastructure.[296]

I also urged the major Korean economic and financial media (*Maeil Business Daily*, *Korean Economic Daily*, and *JoongAng Sunday Magazine*), to examine the emerging partnership between Korea and Paraguay and to learn its significance for both countries. I explained to them that the real story is not just the meetings and agreements taking place at the symposium, but the contribution our work has made to Paraguay's advancement in just a few years from being widely viewed as a backward country plagued with corruption and a fragile democracy, where no serious foreign investors would dream of risking their money.[297]

Ever since I first visited Paraguay in 2008, I have felt a deep bond with the nation and its people. It is positioned at the heart of South America, directly opposite Korea on the globe. Oddly enough, it is even shaped like Korea. I view Paraguay as the womb of South America with potential not only to achieve national transformation but to be a regional hub and the center of rebirth for the whole region.

Paraguay is an emerging democracy that is still a blank slate in many respects.[298] Its political institutions and social practices are still taking shape and, if they are grounded upon the right principles and values, will support a well-functioning democracy that operates to the benefit of all its people and supports an enterprising free market society. Its people have strong traditional values. Also, in this modern era, Paraguay is striking a balance in finding ways to live with its indigenous heritage. Significantly, the native tongue, Guarani, is an official language of the country, spoken by 90 percent of the people.[299]

None of this seemed possible, however, when I first visited Paraguay in 2008. In 1989, Paraguay emerged from thirty-five years under the repressive government of General Alfred Stroessner and elected its first civilian president—my friend, Juan Carlos Wasmosy—in 1992. A democracy in name only, it ranked near the bottom in all international indexes of corruption perception, global competitiveness, and independence of the judiciary.[300]

As in most of Latin America, a small group of oligarchs have controlled most of the wealth. The income gap between the wealthy and the rest of the population, who are poor and ill-educated, is still huge. The oligarchs have run the political system for their own benefit rather than that of the nation as a whole; as a result, there is little confidence in the rule of law.[301]

Corruption was rampant, and the economic life of the nation was in the hands of a few, with no discernable middle class.[302]

This was the context of my 2008 visit. At the time, the U.S. State Department had issued an advisory against travel to Paraguay by any U.S. citizen. A violent radical group in collusion with criminal cartels had been illegally squatting and invading properties connected to our work, and some government officials were supporting their cause.[303] What's more, the president of one of the companies managing the land at the time was even kidnapped at gunpoint and held for ransom for two weeks. Under these circumstances, and with my father's strong urging, I went to Paraguay for the first time to find a solution to a seemingly unsolvable problem. There, I met with then-president Nicanor Duarte Frutos, who was being urged by a combination of radicals, corrupt politicians, and businessmen to overturn property rights and expropriate the land for their own benefit.[304] In essence, it was a scheme to steal foreigners' private property.

To President Nicanor Duarte, this no doubt seemed the politically expedient course of action because of the overwhelming internal pressures. Issues of principle never entered into consideration. I argued the matter with the president for almost two hours. I told him that expropriating land in this way would do great damage to Paraguay's future. First, taking the land and simply giving it to the rural poor would not solve the problem of poverty as the people would have no connection to the national or international economy. Consequently, they would have no prospects for opportunities to break out of their lives, if they so choose, as subsistence farmers and strive for something better. What they needed was jobs in a growing economy.[305]

Second, to ignore property rights and seize land would send the wrong message to the international community. Paraguay needs jobs to address its poverty, and jobs require direct foreign investment.[306] But no foreigners would invest in the country if they expected that private property rights would not be respected. I emphasized to the president that his Realpolitik approach that justified the corrupt short-term gains of a cynical land grab would have damaging long-term national and international consequences for the country. Paraguay would end up isolated from the global economy.

I explained to him that well-functioning democracies stand on a foundation of principles and values. These spiritual principles and values are not derived from any human institution but are endowed by our Creator. These are not just abstract ideals but have real-world implications. I told the president that ignoring them would come at a cost to the country. Embracing these ideals would open the way to a better future for Paraguay and all its people.

Finally, President Nicanor Duarte accepted the logic of this position and stepped back. He then said, "I must admit that you have made me change my mind about a number of things." Neil Bush, whose older brother, George W. Bush, was the U.S. president at the time, was with me in that meeting. As we left, he told me that he had never seen anything like the discussion that had just taken place. Seeing how President Nicanor Duarte had been led to a new understanding, Bush called me a "true transformer."

For Paraguay to realize the potential I knew was possible, a foundation of political and social stability was necessary. From my experience around the world, I can see clearly that such transformation requires grounding in universal human aspirations, principles, and values. I determined to advocate their importance. As a result, during that same visit, I spoke to legislators and government officials in Paraguay's Congress, emphasizing why we must acknowledge God as the sole source of human rights and freedoms and not any human power or institution. Not recognizing God's sovereignty creates a vacuum that despotic rulers and institutions then fill. They then start to determine what rights and freedoms citizens will be granted. The inalienable rights that are our eternal, spiritual heritage are suddenly made to appear changeable at the will of a ruler.

I pointed out that the very different paths of development followed by Latin American countries and the United States were not the result of blind chance. Many who made the long voyage across the Atlantic came with hopes of a new beginning, filled with opportunities in these new lands. Yet, over the course of several centuries, the stories of North America and South America unfolded very differently with real qualitative and quantitative consequences for their people, although they were all of primarily Christian and European descent.

The fundamental difference lay in their heritage. North America was shaped by the British legacy, which paved the way for a constitutional government and the recognition of the "fundamental rights" of all Englishmen.[307] On the other hand, Central America and South America were largely influenced by the more feudal political-religious traditions of the Iberian Peninsula, which remained a bastion and champion of old Europe.

The impulses for fundamental reform and changes that the Renaissance and Reformation brought to Great Britain did not materialize in Spain and Portugal. Naturally, this had a great impact on the relative development and history of Central America and South America and on their respective national revolutions for independence from their European progenitors.

So, although the South American revolutions in the nineteenth century strove to establish regional political blocs similar to those in North America, they were unable to do so. Latin America fragmented into many independent autonomous nation-states that were still heavily influenced by the old systems and traditions of the Iberian Peninsula.[308]

Even today, Latin America struggles with this legacy, since relatively small elites control the political, social, religious, and economic lives of their nations, thus creating the circumstances of discontent in which radical ideals such as communism and liberation theology have emerged and taken root.[309] Whereas many developing democracies around the world have dealt with the inequities of feudal societies, Latin America still faces that challenge.

I repeated this message during subsequent visits in meetings with government, business, and social leaders. I have met with every sitting president of the country since 2008, telling them that Paraguay had to align itself with the universal principles and values that allow a democratic society to function for the well-being of all its citizens and to offer them the widest range of opportunities for their enterprise in a free market system, which is what the U.S. example teaches.

In 2010, I called for the establishment of Instituto Patria Soñada (IDPPS), a top-level think tank, to develop a long-term road map for the country's future direction. This move was a significant first step toward a better future for Paraguay. Many Latin American countries lack consistency in government. In Paraguay, policies and even projects would change unpredictably from one administration to the next.[310] Politicians typically take the short-term view, but in countries with no tradition of policy consensus, this approach creates political uncertainty that in turn increases nation risk.[311]

This was Paraguay's situation. The IDPPS provides a long-term view of Paraguay's development, free of the shifting winds of political change. It offers consistency in policy from one administration to the next, creating a new level of political stability that is a necessary foundation for national transformation. The members of the institute needed to be very experienced and highly respected. Led by the honorable former Supreme Court Justice Dr. Jose Altamirano, the IDPPS includes former government ministers, members of Congress, ambassadors, retired military leaders, professors, spiritual leaders, businesspeople, and others. All of them are known for their integrity in a country where public corruption is endemic. They are committed to transforming Paraguay on the basis of the principles and values I promote.

In 2009, a national chapter of GPF was established in Paraguay. Where IDPPS has been improving the country's political stability by providing consistency in policy planning,[312] GPF-Paraguay is tackling many of the issues that affect its social stability. Paraguay faces many social challenges, such as corruption, crime, and poor education for the majority,[313] which it must resolve in order to become a well-functioning democracy.

GPF-Paraguay runs programs to educate the country's political and social leadership regarding the essential elements needed for good governance. These programs explain the importance of fundamental principles and values that are the basis for human rights and freedoms endowed by God and are vital for uplifting and transforming a nation. GPF has also been running a number of social initiatives in the NGO sphere that put these principles into practice. They include character education, youth initiatives, and social services, as well as an energetic and enterprising women's division that does pioneering work with families and children.

The character education program, which includes the Character and Creativity Initiative, is run nationally in cooperation with the Ministry of Education. The ministry was so impressed by its impact that it has encouraged teachers, professors, education directors, and ministry staff, as well as the students, to experience the program. Through the program, a national standard of ethical responsibility and a culture of social engagement are being spread among young Paraguayans, enhancing the nation's social stability.[314]

Through their activities, IDPPS and GPF are improving the political and social stability of Paraguay, constructing a launchpad for national transformation. The two organizations jointly sponsored an international conference in Asuncion in 2010 that assembled leaders from all sectors of Paraguayan society, as well as several former Latin American presidents. The conference produced the Asuncion Declaration, a clear statement of the principles and values that should guide Paraguay and its future development.

The former presidents with other heads of state in the region, now some twenty in number, formed the Latin American Presidential Mission in 2012. They are applying their great experience to help guide the development of Paraguay and other Latin American countries on the basis of those principles and values. With the help of such leaders, the model emerging in Paraguay can become an example for the region. The model can change the course of the Latin American experience politically and socially and bridge the gap between the two halves of the Western hemisphere.[315]

Corruption is rife throughout the developing world—the biggest obstacle to establishing stable and sustainable democracies and free markets.[316] Paraguay has been no exception.[317] The poorest and most neglected part of the country is the Chaco region, west of the Paraguay River, and particularly the state of Alto Paraguay, the largest but least-populated and poorest in the country.[318]

Alto Paraguay was run by politicians[319] and businessmen. Local officials siphoned off the funds that came from the national government in Asuncion and spread them among their cronies.[320] As a result, the state was a basket case of underdevelopment with no infrastructure. It was politically and socially unstable, lacking jobs, paved highways, electricity, piped water, and sewage disposal.[321] Not surprisingly, violent radical groups sprang up in response.[322]

IDPPS produced a plan for the development of the Chaco region, and Alto Paraguay in particular. From 2009, GPF began active social service work among the population in the town of Puerto Casado.[323] It began with basic assistance in health, education, and housing, then expanded to help local people establish sustainable projects including a fish farm, communal vegetable farm, and bakery. Residents of the town thus got jobs in rotation and a basic income and began to develop an entrepreneurial mind-set. As these problems were addressed, the radical forces started to lose their influence in the town.

IDPPS helped local officials in Puerto Casado,[324] the main town, establish an efficient and accountable administration that directed the support received from the national government to the benefit of the community,[325] where before it had disappeared into the pockets of corrupt local politicians and businessmen. The impact of these local reforms was then projected to the state level in 2012, when, to everyone's surprise, Marlene Ocampos, GPF's former social director in Alto Paraguay, ran for governor.[326]

Marlene is native to the region. She had been coordinating GPF's social projects in the state for several years[327] and is widely known and respected in Alto Paraguay. Nobody thought she could win against the entrenched and corrupt political system. Everyone presumed that her opponent would buy the election and continue to line his own pockets with the region's money.[328] He was probably the most shocked of all when Marlene actually won.[329]

Her election marked a small revolution in people power. She overcame the power of money through popular support based on what she had done for local people. Everyone in the state knew her because of her hands-on involvement with their communities. She had visited every family in the state, and they had all experienced her commitment to help them better their lives.

As governor, she continues in the same manner.[330] When a devastating flood struck, she lobbied actively for more relief assistance from the national government and received it.[331] She even spent her own money on emergency relief. Although she had no experience running a state administration, she has been able to draw upon the great depth of knowledge in IDPPS for advice and support.[332] Members of the institute helped her set up efficient and transparent operational procedures that would expose the corrupt dealings that had been hidden in the shadows.[333]

This was a radical departure from the status quo for Paraguay and created shockwaves throughout the country. The Paraguayan media covered the story of the Chaco extensively and what it might mean for Paraguay's future. At the groundbreaking ceremony for the Il Sung Construction project, another state governor came up to me and said that he wanted GPF's help to do in his state what Governor Ocampos had done in Alto Paraguay.

What happened in Alto Paraguay can set the precedent for a new type of leadership that can transform the nation. Then President Horacio Cartes took Governor Ocampos under his wing and made clear that he supports her style of leadership. She is always on the scene when a problem or disaster occurs, making sure that her people get the help they need. The president uses her example to push the other governors to adopt the same with-the-people style of leadership.

IDPPS has been instrumental in helping Governor Ocampos secure her success and operate effectively on the state level. When I met with the board in June 2014, we discussed the way forward. One of the board members, Dr. Bernardino Cano Radil,[334] a political scientist, told me that in Alto Paraguay the steps we had taken had caused a "crack" in how things have worked in Paraguayan politics. However, there would be a political reaction, and to secure the change, we would need strong support from the country's elite.

Some of Paraguay's elite, particularly business leaders, did not understand what I was doing or why it was important for Paraguay. They complained that I spoke of Paraguay's great potential but had not invested in the country. In my June 2014 visit to Paraguay, I had been invited to a private dinner, hosted by my dear friend former President Juan Carlos Wasmosy with many of Paraguay's top business leaders. I used that opportunity to clarify my vision for Paraguay that has motivated my purpose and activities there since 2008. Every year, so much work has been carried out through organizations such as IDPPS and GPF to help build the social and political stability that this nation needs to attract direct foreign investment. Though I am not a Paraguayan citizen, I have been making such investments for the nation, and I challenged the leaders that they as the leading families of Paraguay should set the right precedent in investing in their own nation's development.

I explained that the many projects I had sponsored helped to mitigate national risk through a new approach based on aspirations, principles, and values, combined with well-targeted social activities. IDPPS has been dealing with political uncertainty through a long-term plan for the prosperity of the nation, providing consistency and predictability. GPF has been addressing a range of shorter-term social needs that have helped to improve the country's social stability. In particular, GPF and IDPPS initiatives in Alto Paraguay and the election of Marlene Ocampos have struck a blow against the pervasive and deep-rooted problem of corruption.

If the level of political and social risk were mitigated as a result of these initiatives, then Paraguay's level of national risk would decrease as well and definitely help Paraguay's investment profile. But given its small domestic market and primarily agriculture-based industries, those developments alone could not justify large-scale investment. I explained, however, that if Paraguay was to become a hub for large-scale direct foreign investment to access the entire regional market of Latin America, capitalizing on its natural advantages, then the value proposition of the nation would change exponentially. Given its central geography, Paraguay could become the Singapore, Switzerland, or Dubai of Latin America. As I concluded my presentation, former president Wasmosy and the business leaders were impressed and excited at the possibilities.

I continued by explaining to them that the key to such a strategy would be investor confidence. Although Paraguay's political and social stability had improved and it was in good shape fiscally,[335] it is still below investment grade for foreign investment.[336] I proposed creating a private equity fund to build up Paraguay's infrastructure so that it could support a modern economy.[337] I challenged those business leaders to support the fund, asking how they could expect foreign investors to show confidence in the country's prospects if they themselves, the Paraguayan business elite, were not ready to risk their money. Their commitment to the country's future would send a powerful signal to potential foreign investors.

A private equity fund for national development projects was a new concept for them.[338] The fund means greater personal individual risk but has the potential for far greater returns since it will enlarge the pie of national prosperity. My dinner partners were all hardheaded pragmatists. They understood that these ideas would work. Once investor confidence is achieved, foreign direct investment will open the door to a hub strategy where Paraguay grows as a pivotal nation at the heart of Latin America.

South America has a population of about 400 million people, similar to North America. Businesses deciding where to locate in North America consider the advantages offered by the United States and Canada and their various states and provinces. Businesses will take the same approach in South America, and Paraguay offers many advantages. In addition to its traditional industries in the agricultural sector, plenty of opportunities will be available in other sectors, such as manufacturing, distribution, and services, if the hub strategy is implemented.

For manufacturing, Paraguay has low-cost labor, with plenty of young people anxious for jobs. It also has low energy costs, being rich in hydroelectric power, and is a leading global exporter of electricity. Location makes the country attractive as a distribution hub once transportation infrastructure is in place, which is why creating that infrastructure is a priority and the purpose for my bringing Korean infrastructure experts to Paraguay and launching the private equity fund. The Bi-Oceanic Highway, a regional project connecting the Atlantic and Pacific coasts, will run through Paraguay, enhancing its suitability as a distribution hub.

Paraguay has trading partners throughout the region, and as Latin American economies become more integrated, greater demand for financial and legal services will arise. Paraguay has the lowest corporate and personal income tax rates in the region, as well as favorable laws and regulations for foreign entities that want to do business in manufacturing, agriculture, and other industries. Paraguay's national transformation would have powerful repercussions throughout Latin America, and not only economically. Many countries are being drawn to the statist form of socialism that Hugo Chavez established in Venezuela and promoted regionwide. Even Argentina is flirting with restricting democratic freedoms. Paraguay has a strong tradition of political independence. It was the only country within the Mercosur bloc to stand up to President Chavez. A nation that upholds human rights and freedoms based on fundamental principles and values in a democratic constitution and creates a prosperous free market society will act as a powerful antidote to negative regional trends.

To execute a hub strategy, Paraguay needs a partner. It will have to expand beyond agriculture, which currently sets the horizon for many of its political and business leaders, and become a model industrialized state. Korea's experience of growth from a poor, feudal agricultural society to an advanced high-tech economy in less than a century makes it an ideal model for Paraguay—or any emerging nation—to emulate.

A natural synergy exists between Paraguay and South Korea, which is why I have been promoting connections or an alliance between them.[339] Korea needs new markets, as its domestic market is limited, and it faces fierce competition from China and Japan in Asia. Paraguay offers a unique access point to the Latin American market. In particular, the Korean infrastructure industry is world-class, with great capacity that remains underused in Korea today. The South needs new projects while Paraguay needs new infrastructure as the foundation for its hub strategy. Also, Korea is resource-poor whereas Paraguay is resource-rich.

Korea has all the experience in development that Paraguay needs, from launching whole new industrial sectors from scratch to the Saemaul Undong community development movement that engaged villagers actively in the process of national growth. As Paraguay grows and increases its trade with the rest of South America through the hub strategy, those Korean companies invested in its economy will reap the benefits of an expanding continental market.

Most important, South Korea has a particular interest in helping to lift a country into economic development and prosperity. The experience that Korean institutions, both public and private, gain in Paraguay will prove invaluable in developing North Korea in the future. The lessons learned in Paraguay will help ensure that the unification process in Korea has better results than that in Germany. Paraguay was considered one of the most troubled nations in South America,[340] a place that businesses avoided. North Korea is a basket case, perhaps the worst in the world politically, socially, and economically.[341] All the sectors addressed in Paraguay to create the social and political stability necessary for growth will also have to be part of North Korea's revival. All need to be integrated in a total effort to develop North Korea after unification.

Paraguay has come a long way in the years since I had that first meeting with President Nicanor Duarte Frutos. At the time, the country was at a crossroads. The nation faced a historic choice. Fortunately, Paraguay today is on the right trajectory and is poised to emerge as a modern democracy rooted in the proper principles and values as a thriving regional economy.

KOREA'S CIVIC ASSOCIATIONS AND NGOS

In Korea, President Park marked the beginning of a new perspective on unification that highlights the economic opportunities it can offer. The investment community was inspired by her Dresden Declaration laying out a strategy for peaceful unification and her 2014 New Year's speech in which she declared that unification would bring an economic "jackpot." Money has been flowing into two unification-related equity funds, according to a *Financial Times* report.[342]

In April and May 2014, these funds attracted $35 million (Won 35 billion). This may not seem like a lot, but it happened during a period when $35 billion (Won 35 trillion) was being pulled out of other South Korean equity funds. The main beneficiary has been a fund run by Shinyoung Asset Management, which invests in companies in fields likely to benefit from unification, such as construction, agriculture, and utilities. The fund has recorded a 6.8 percent return on investment since it opened in March 2013, almost double the return at comparable domestic equity funds, according to the *Financial Times*. Shinyoung's chief investment officer, Huh Nam-kwon, said, "Many rich individual investors now seem to agree that unification is needed for both countries."[343]

The funds are significant as an indicator that the idea of unification is gaining acceptance in South Korea. No longer is it something to be put off into the distant future. The funds reflect shifting South Korean attitudes, but they will not be the key to change in North Korea even if their assets are counted in the billions rather than millions. In fact, the return on such funds in the future could be far higher if they were part of a post-unification strategy that integrates all sectors: political, social, and economic.[344]

This was the lesson of Paraguay. Investment was the final, not the first, piece of the picture. Economic development, to be successful, had to stand on a foundation of social and political stability. The work that we did in these areas, through the IDPPS think tank, GPF social initiatives, and programs like CCI, created the framework within which a well-functioning free market democracy could emerge.

The NGOs and civic associations of South Korea and the Korean diaspora will have to be at the heart of a similar enterprise for North Korea. They are already making an important contribution, although there is much room to expand. Direct contact with the North by South Korean NGOs began during the famine of the mid-1990s. Although subject to shifts in government relations between Seoul and Pyongyang, these contacts have endured at some level through groups such as the Korea Sharing Movement and Good Friends South Korea.[345]

Even when the two governments were not speaking, the NGOs enabled some minimal level of unofficial contact to be maintained. They have also opened direct channels to some of the North Korean people, gained years of experience working with North Korean officials, and learned a great deal of direct information about life, work, and social conditions in North Korea.

South Korean NGOs have already added an important dimension to North-South relations[346] that would not have been possible through government-to-government contact alone. This observation is endorsed in an Asia Foundation paper titled "From Charity to Partnership: South Korean NGO Engagement with North Korea." It summarizes the role and future potential of NGOs in the move toward unification:

> NGO engagement represents the first steps toward people-to-people reconciliation between South and North Korea. Given the vast economic gap between the two sides, NGO engagement will continue to have an essential role to play, not only in addressing humanitarian and development needs in the North, but more importantly, in creating the multiple strands of human contact on which reconciliation and unification must be built.[347]

The author also proposes that the South Korean government treat the NGOs as an essential partner in engaging with the North and not just as another tool of government policy. Critical for the NGOs to play this role is effective cooperation among them. They should not be divided by politics or self-interest but must work guided by the common vision of the Korean Dream, based on fundamental principles and values.[348]

That is the reason I initiated the Action for Korea United coalition, as I described in Chapter 3. AKU was designed to provide a framework for coordinating the efforts of many different groups. As I mentioned, AKU unites civic associations, business organizations, faith groups, and academic institutions, all of which will have important parts to play in the unification process. They represent a wide spectrum of views, yet work together under the shared vision of the Korean Dream.

In fact, one feature of the civic groups working for unification today is that they operate outside of politics. They engage with the people of the North as fellow Koreans in need, not in pursuit of any political agenda. This is in marked contrast to the Roh Moo-hyun era, when South Korean civic groups pushing for unification were often highly politicized. Observing this change, the president of the University of North Korean Studies—formerly known as the Graduate School for North Korean Studies, Kyungnam University—Choi Wan-kyu, said in the *Weekly Chosun* in April 2014, "Insisting on the old framework of conservative-liberal in the discussion of unification is an outdated perspective that goes against the current of the time."[349]

While NGOs have been engaged with North Korea for some time, there is now growing interest in unification from Korean citizens in a wide variety of professional fields. Unification is in the air, and more Koreans are feeling the need to prepare for it. A class at the University of North Korean Studies, described in the *Weekly Chosun*, drew students from the legal profession, finance, media, medicine, the civil service, and corporate economic research.

Professor Ko Yu-hwan of Dongguk University, which also has a North Korean Studies Department, told the *Weekly Chosun*, "There is now a general feeling that preparation for unification should not be decided from administration to administration but be consistently developed through the private sector including universities."[350]

This is a very important insight. Academia, comprising universities, and think tanks can play the role in Korea that the IDPPS think tank played in Paraguay. They can provide a long-term road map for the post-unification development of the North that is not subject to shifting political moods. With this in mind, GPF-Korea set up the Korean Peninsula Future Strategy Research Institute to develop ideas for fresh approaches to unification from scholars and policy experts.

Advancing the Korean Dream in a practical way means, first, inspiring a broad movement of South Korean citizens to support a process of unification based upon a vision that arises from our Korean heritage. Next, it means engaging with people in the North. The Global Peace Foundation in Korea has been active in both areas. We have been bringing the issue of unification to the Korean public through initiatives such as the Unification Donation Pledge, the Unification Idea Contest, and the Miracle of 1000 Won campaign that supports the distribution of bread to orphans in the North. Once people's interest has been awakened, they can join their efforts to those of an NGO or civic association.

The Service for Peace project I described in Chapter 2 is a model example of what an NGO can accomplish engaging with North Koreans on a local level. It provided briquette-burning boilers for home heating and cooking in the Kumgang Mountain area of North Korea. The boilers met an urgent need for heating throughout provincial North Korea, where every winter people die from the cold. The boilers also addressed indirectly the problem of deforestation and the resulting soil erosion as people stripped the land of trees for fuel.

Over 700 volunteers from South Korea worked together with North Korean residents during the life of the project, sharing work, meals, and cultural performances. In this way, the images each group had of the other were changed, replaced by personal experience of heart-to-heart contact working for a common purpose. The project also provided employment; the boiler parts, which came from the South, were assembled in a local factory by North Korean labor.

In 2007, SFP proposed to North Korean officials that once the volunteer programs had operated for a period, then reciprocal projects could be established that brought North Korean volunteers to the South. The suggestion was accepted in principle by North Korean officials but was never implemented because of changes in the political environment. Nevertheless, the experience shows an openness to such ideas among certain sectors of North Korean officialdom.

In the South, GPF-Korea works with North Korean defectors in Seoul to help them adjust to life in that fast-paced metropolis. One project we are pioneering is to connect each defector with a South Korean family to give them moral and practical support. This pilot project is being assessed as the basis for a future plan that would connect each family in the North with two families in the South in order to make the unification process a matter of personal involvement for people in the South.

PURSUING THE KOREAN DREAM THROUGH PRINCIPLED CIVIC ACTION

All over the world, civic associations and NGOs are springing up, a new phenomenon that is allowing individual citizens to channel their united energies for a greater purpose. They enable us to live and act effectively for the sake of others.

Today, civic groups are sometimes even referred to as the "Fifth Estate," indicating their growing impact on public life.[351] In the past, the media was often referred to as the "Fourth Estate," with an informal but essential role complementing the three constitutional branches of democratic government: the legislative, executive, and judicial. Through the power of social media, much of the influence that traditional media once wielded is passing into the hands of a much broader public network of people. Social media has also enabled people to form new types of civic groupings involved in specific issues and causes.

The many NGOs affect various areas of society, but their outputs when taken in aggregate have a broad social impact. This has been our experience working in Paraguay, where the various initiatives pursued by GPF, IDPPS, and our partners each formed part of a broader plan for national transformation. Through these projects, influential political, business, and social leaders began to see that talk of principles and values was not simply idealism disconnected from reality but could be put into practice. Things they thought impossible were shown to be possible. A state such as Alto Paraguay was not destined to remain backward and riddled with corruption forever. With the right choices, based upon the right principles and values, it could become a place with transparent and effective government that served its people.

The lessons learned from the Paraguay experience can provide a playbook for dealing with the challenges of bringing a future transformation to North Korea. The many member groups of Action for Korea United are engaged in a wide variety of projects in all the fields that will be important in the North's future. The organization's breadth makes it a natural partner for the government in a public-private cooperation since AKU will be able to operate in all those areas that are outside the government sphere.

AKU is also the natural instrument to build consensus within South Korean society since it embraces the whole political and social spectrum. Member organizations include political associations of both right and left, religious groups from the different faiths, civic groups, and NGOs that include those focused on humanitarian aid as well as those campaigning for human rights, business associations, and many others.

These NGOs and civic associations, working in harmony, will have an indispensable role in the transformation needed in North Korea. Alexis de Tocqueville understood the great power of civic associations almost 200 years ago when he saw the energy they generated bring about social transformation in the young American republic. This was in marked contrast to the absence of such associations that he observed in France prior to the French Revolution. That same energy will be urgently needed to construct a unified Korea.

Through these organizations cooperating together, the Korean people can unite around a clear common goal and work to achieve it. That goal is not just to unite the two halves of the peninsula but to do so based upon our unique Korean heritage and identity. The movement for unification must take its inspiration from the spiritual principles and ethical practices that we find in the Hongik Ingan ideal that we have inherited from our founding. This is the essence of the Korean Dream.

That dream is not just to achieve national unification. It is to fulfill the Hongik Ingan ideal of bringing benefit to all humanity. Korea's destiny is to promote this ideal on the world stage. The next chapter looks at Korea's global role and her providential responsibility to advance the vision of One Family under God.

CHAPTER 7

From the Korean Dream to One Family under God

*"More powerful than an invading army
is an idea whose time has come."*
–VICTOR HUGO

The twentieth century has torn and frayed the fabric of our history, and we must mend it with a vision that can weave together the tapestry of our people's story as we create our new future. For the Korean people to begin anew, removed from the imposed circumstances of the last century, we have to be the masters of our own destiny. But what is that destiny? As I stated in the first chapter, the answers to our future lie in our past.

History has never really been part of the discussion on unification until the writing of this book. This is truly a sad commentary on the state of our people and the circumstances on the peninsula. We are like a ship adrift without a rudder or a compass on a wide-open sea. How can we know where we are going if we don't remember from where we came? Why did we make this journey in the first place? How did we get to where we are now? Where do we go from here? That is why, to me, the answer to "Why is unification necessary?" started with rediscovering our past.

We have a unique history for an ancient civilization that spans five millennia. While most other ancient civilizations sought to extend their borders and wealth through conquest and subjugation, Korea aspired to uphold high ideals that resonate with our modern sensibilities but were completely foreign to the ancient world. This is what made our people special in the course of human history, and if we rediscover and manifest those ideals, it will make us special again.

The Hongik Ingan ideals were truly revolutionary for the time and show their enduring affinity even to this day.[352] In these ideals, we unlock the purpose and destiny of our people: to reclaim our homeland and to become a shining example to the world. Independence activist Kim Gu wrote in 1947, during the inter-war years when Koreans were fiercely debating the future of their homeland, "I wish my nation would be a nation that doesn't just imitate others, but rather it be a nation that is the source of a new and higher culture, that it can become the goal and an example [for others]."

This sentiment is captured in what I have coined the Korean Dream. It is a vision for a new Korean homeland defined by our founding ideals yet made relevant to the modern world. It takes the best of the East and West and weaves it into our unique cultural heritage, connecting our past, present, and future into one seamless fabric. This dream makes it clear that national unification is a step to something greater still: the fulfillment of the Hongik Ingan ideal "to broadly benefit all humanity."

Thus, the purpose of this chapter is to explore the destiny of the Korean people. I want to explain how we have been prepared not only for a significant role far beyond the dynamics on the Korean peninsula and Northeast Asia but also for addressing the most critical issues facing our entire world in the twenty-first century. How much do we understand the roots of our Korean identity that have made us a unique people with a special destiny? This understanding will be essential for the successful creation of a new unified nation and for Korea to emerge as a global leader.

KOREANS FACE AN IDENTITY CRISIS

I will not speak of North Korea since its society is desperately dysfunctional and its people have little control over their own destiny, but what about South Korea? The country is admired worldwide for its amazing growth from poverty to become one of the world's leading economies in a little more than half a century. However, the "Miracle on the Han River" was achieved at a tremendous cost. Beneath the veneer of success, our true Korean identity, which made that success possible, has been eroding. Important traditions were being lost in the rush to modernity with little regard for its social, cultural, political, and economic consequences.

The cultural impact of development, and the Western cultural norms it brought with it, has hit the Korean extended family particularly hard. I examined what is being lost in depth in Chapter 4. The many relationships within the extended family network nurtured the unique Korean qualities of *han* and *jeong seong*. Out of them grew an *uri* (we) outlook of living for the greater good of the whole. Nuclear families, the pursuit of educational and career success, and concern for material security have undermined this spirit. It is being replaced by a more self-centered individualism.

The sinking of the *Sewol* ferry on April 16, 2014, with the loss of 304 lives, 250 of them high school students, served as a harsh wakeup call to South Koreans. It created national outrage over the causes of the accident and the ensuing inadequate rescue efforts. Even more than that, the *Sewol* incident forced South Koreans to see a true reflection of themselves in the mirror of national and world opinion.[353] They did not like what they saw.

What followed was an extended period of national self-questioning. People saw that the Korean soul was becoming shallow and bankrupt, and they were forced to wrestle with fundamental issues that they had hitherto neglected: Who are we as a people, and what have we become? How great a nation can we be when people act like this? Is the price we are paying for modernization too great in spiritual terms? All these questions led to one final big question: Are we losing our soul and our humanity?

The loss of life when the ferry capsized was so tragic because it was avoidable. This incident exposed Koreans at their worst, behaving with no regard for the life of others.[354] The ship should never have capsized in the first place, and once it had, most of the passengers could have been rescued. The captain and crew never told the passengers to abandon the ship. In fact, they ordered them to stay in their cabins, particularly the Danwon High School students. Of the 325 students on board, only seventy-five survived. When rescue boats started to arrive, the captain and crew were the first to leave the ship, except for three brave crew members who stayed and gave their lives trying to help passengers. When the captain left, the passengers had still received no orders to evacuate.

Though the ROK Coast Guard and Navy ships were dispatched, fishing boats and commercial vessels in the area were actually first to the scene and started rescuing passengers. The inadequate response roused public discontent, as did official statements early on that seemed more concerned about justifying government actions and avoiding criticism than about the loss of life. So great was the outcry that Prime Minister Jung Hong-won was forced to resign and President Park disbanded the Coast Guard.

Yet, it was the actions of the Chonghaejin Marine shipping company that operated the ferry and its owner, Yoo Byung-eun, that opened the eyes of South Koreans to the cost of the pursuit of material success. The ferry had been modified by the company to carry more passengers by adding cabins on the upper levels. This made the ship more unstable, although the Korean Register of Shipping gave it a safety certificate with the specification that it should carry more ballast and a limited amount of cargo.

These requirements were routinely ignored by the company since it made most of its profit from the *Sewol* on the cargo it carried. The ship was often loaded with two or three times the permitted weight of cargo. In order to accommodate the extra cargo, some of the required ballast would be pumped out. The result was that the ship became unstable and dangerous. These were deliberate actions taken by the company that put the lives of its passengers at risk for the sake of profit. This was the shock that continued to reverberate throughout the nation long after the event as South Koreans asked themselves what sort of people they had become.

South Korea's unprecedented growth is a testament to the spirit of the generation that built up the nation out of the devastation of war. In many ways, South Koreans today have lost touch with the culture of sacrifice for a greater purpose that drove our parents' generation. Worse than that, they are losing their connection to the vision that has guided our history and shaped our Korean identity.[355]

Now is the time to reflect deeply on these issues since many people, including myself, are advocating a greater leadership role for Korea in the world. We have to ask urgently: What will it take to prepare for such a role? What will it take to prepare for unification? This is not a matter of politics and economics but of the spirit and character of the Korean people. In order to find the way forward and meet these new challenges, Korea must look to its past. In our rich spiritual heritage, we can rediscover the Korean identity that was forged through our long-suffering history and understand clearly the providential destiny of our people.

By reconnecting with our past, we will come to recognize the present as a defining and pivotal moment in our history that will determine Korea's course for the future. We can finally realize the dreams of our ancestors and create a new nation that is true to the Hongik Ingan ideals, or we will deteriorate into a shallow, material society that lost its soul in the abyss of self-indulgent consumer comforts. If we, as a nation, walk the former path, we will initiate a series of events that will alter the course of our history, the region, and the world in line with our founding vision. If, however, we choose to walk the latter path, which reflects our current trajectory, we will see whatever accomplishments we believe that we earned wither before a litany of security, economic, and social problems that will surely face the South.

I have laid out a vision for the future of the Korean people that can guide the nation at this moment of historical decision. That vision is the Korean Dream, and it is the remedy to the identity crisis that Koreans are suffering today. It can become the catalyst that ignites a noble future, bringing not only unification but also Korea's emergence as a global moral leader and advocate of the vision of One Family under God.

A CASE FOR THE KOREAN DREAM

In the course of this book, I have tried to draw a clear picture of where we Koreans stand as a people. I have outlined the great opportunity presented to us but also the challenges that we must face in order to seize it. I have put forward the Korean Dream as the key to our future and articulated it throughout the book.

In the opening chapter, I described the power of a vision to transform the world with historical examples from Korea, the American founding, and the Mongol Empire of Genghis Khan. I then introduced the vision of the Korean Dream and gave an overview of all the book's major themes. The roots of national transformation lie in a vision, principles, and values. That is why I looked to the origins of our nation and people in the spirit of Dangun to explain what shaped our identity. The Korean Dream draws upon the spirit of our founding, expressed in the Hongik Ingan ideal with its remarkable exhortation that the Korean nation and people should live for the "benefit of all humanity."

The Korean Dream was then forged through the historical experiences of the Korean people. A history of suffering—and the struggle to digest it guided by Hongik Ingan—produced in our people a deep spiritual consciousness that then informed every aspect of practical life. The Hongik Ingan ideals and our spiritual consciousness found their deepest, yet most practical, expression in the relationships cultivated within the Korean extended family. Here, principles and values were given heartfelt expression and passed on to each new generation through the example of their elders.

These are the elements of the Korean Dream. The founding ideal of Hongik Ingan, the unique spiritual consciousness forged through the experience of a suffering history, and the culture of the extended family that nurtured deep bonds of heart and the habit of living for others together formed the Korean identity. This model has been the basis for raising virtuous individuals, building virtuous families, and keeping a virtuous nation throughout our history. It has produced remarkable moral leaders among us with visionary aspirations for the nation and beyond.

The Korean Dream is not limited to achieving unification of the Korean peninsula. Rooted as it is in the ideal of living for the benefit of humanity, its vision reaches out from the nation to the world. I concluded the opening chapter of this book by urging that Korea, standing upon its Hongik Ingan ideal, should become the global advocate for the vision of One Family under God.

In Chapter 2, I described the suffering that Korea underwent during the twentieth century in its struggle to become an independent and united nation. I highlighted the tremendous human cost imposed first by Japanese colonialism and then by the ideological division of the peninsula and the Korean War. The human cost continues to this day in terms of divided families and the suffering of Korean people in the North. My own family experience is inter-woven with this history, as members of my extended family still live there.

My father's life and work were intimately tied to the unification of the peninsula and the creation of a new nation. He was imprisoned in the Hungnam labor camp in North Korea before the war and was freed during the war by UN forces. He later pioneered a historic opening with the North through his meeting with Kim Il-sung in 1991. That has been an important part of my father's legacy for as long as I can remember. Today, it is part of my legacy as I carry forward my father's unfinished work toward the realization of our people's destiny.

Living in America, I am part of the Korean diaspora who remains connected to our homeland and committed to its future destiny. I have challenged the apathy of so many South Koreans, especially the young.

Unification is not simply a matter of politics and economics to be left in the hands of governments. Continued division imposes terrible suffering on the people of the North. They are not a foreign nation but our separated kinfolk who share the same culture and heritage. The resolution of their plight is a moral imperative for South Koreans and the diaspora that can only be resolved through realizing the Korean Dream.

In Chapter 3, I laid out the geopolitical, security, and economic challenges to unification. Digging below the surface, I showed that behind every challenge there lay significant opportunities. In particular, the geopolitical context has changed dramatically.

With the collapse of the Soviet Union, the geopolitical structures of the Cold War era that produced the division of the Korean peninsula disintegrated. Consequently, it no longer makes any sense to view the division of North and South within that context. The time is ripe for new thinking and new approaches. Once North Korea lost its major economic and military supporter, it was no longer viable as a nation. As North Korea was unwilling to open up and reform, its economy and society began to deteriorate.

Kim Jong-il developed a nuclear weapon as an insurance policy for regime survival. Although China stepped in to replace some of the support that North Korea had previously received from the Soviet Union, China's involvement is no longer within the Cold War framework. China's national interest lies in economic growth and regional stability as it vies for global leadership. In spite of its reliance on China's economic support, North Korea has pursued policies that have set it at odds with its sponsor. Like his father, Kim Jong-un has continued to develop nuclear weapons despite Chinese opposition, and he has failed to implement meaningful economic reforms despite Chinese encouragement.

North Korea has become a barrier to the economic development of the region and a source of frustration to China.[356] In fact, China's interests in the economic as well as security spheres converge much more closely with those of South Korea than with the North. China has become South Korea's largest trade and investment partner. Meanwhile, Chinese president

Xi Jinping had held five bilateral meetings with President Park Geun-hye as of July 2014 before having a single meeting with Kim Jong-un.

These events make it clear that Pyongyang can no longer count on unconditional support from China.[357] The playing field in Northeast Asia has changed dramatically, and new opportunities are opening up. Unification is becoming a real possibility, seriously considered, and no longer a distant dream for future generations. In fact, it is becoming a necessity, an opportunity that we cannot allow to pass because of the ever-present and growing risks from an increasingly unstable and unpredictable regime in the North.

Through its nuclear weapons program, North Korea has become a security threat to the whole Northeast Asia region and, through the risk of proliferation, to the world. Moreover, these weapons are in the hands of a young and inexperienced leader who is isolated internationally. He has shown himself to be violent and ruthless, and in this respect, his leadership standard marks a decline from his father, Kim Jong-il, who, in turn, was worse than his father, Kim Il-sung. This deterioration in North Korean leadership and growing dysfunction of the country has produced an unstable and unpredictable situation in the region. The growing consensus is that unification is the only viable solution to all the problems the North Korean regime poses.

Chapter 3 also highlighted the economic opportunities that unification could produce, arguing that the benefits in the long term will outweigh the costs, which have been given too much negative attention. North Korea has abundant labor and mineral resources that the South lacks. North Korea would also offer a larger domestic market at a time when South Korea is facing some market constraints. The potential synergy between North and South can drive significant growth that will push the new Korean economy to a whole new level, as high as eighth in the world according to a Goldman Sachs report. At the same time, the regional economy would receive a boost once North Korea is no longer an obstacle to trade, transport, and investment.

To take advantage of these emerging opportunities, the Korean people must act on the foundation of aspirations, principles, and values that are true to their founding ideals and reflect their Korean identity. Chapter 4 explained the key elements of that identity and of the Korean Dream. A separation of sixty-five years is nothing for the Korean people compared with our 5,000-year shared history. The problem is that Koreans are losing their connection to that history. In the North, totalitarianism and Juche ideology, and in the South, the rampant materialism of a consumer culture have eroded the Korean identity. That is why it is important to understand what has made us a unique people.

I already touched upon the importance of our founding and history in recalling the opening chapter. The Hongik Ingan ideal, present from our people's ancient origin, is something unique in our history that marks Korea as a special nation. This chapter shows how its presence throughout Korean history as a touchstone of principles and values shaped the spiritual consciousness of our people and guided the way they responded to their tribulations and historical circumstances. It is expressed in the way that we Koreans have embraced great faith and ethical traditions such as Buddhism, Confucianism, and Christianity, yet adapted them through our own unique experience.

Korea was never just an imitator but infused the traditions and teachings it received with its own perspective. This was true in the realm of politics and social virtues, as well as religion. Koreans accepted the insights of other philosophies and cultures and then adapted them to their own unique cultural heritage. That is how, in the example that I used, the Joseon dynasty could develop a form of quasi-constitutional monarchy with an early form of separation of powers that limited the power of the monarch and guaranteed a certain level of rights and freedoms to its subjects. Out of the Donghak movement in the nineteenth century came the original concept of In Nae Chon, the unique idea that humanity is the equivalent of heaven. This profound spiritual insight has great social and political implications.

Hongik Ingan remained a powerful force in Korean history well into the twentieth century, guiding the way that Koreans grappled with challenges and painful experiences. The thirty-three signatories of the Korean Declaration of Independence that launched the March 1, 1919 movement held it as an ideal. As I have mentioned, those early independence campaigners took Hongik Ingan as the foundational principle of their efforts and, as a result, aspired to create a nation that was not only independent but also a light to the world.

These aspirations lived on among the founders of the Republic of Korea. They envisaged a unified nation guided by the Hongik Ingan ideal. They even made those ideals the basis for the curriculum in Korean schools that the Ministry of Education published. These examples make clear that Hongik Ingan has been a thread running through Korean history that our people have looked to at moments of great decision. The patriots of the March First Independence Movement turned to our founding for the principles to guide a unified nation. Now that the dream of unification is once again a real possibility, Koreans today also need to turn to that source and revive the spiritual consciousness and connection with history that will resurrect our Korean identity.

How is the virtue of living for the sake of others, which is the expression of Hongik Ingan, learned and passed down from generation to generation? That is role of the Korean extended family, a unique cultural institution unparalleled anywhere in the world, even among cultures with traditional family structures. In the Korean family, every relationship has its own distinct value with a unique corresponding form of address for even the in-laws and distant relatives. Each position in the ever-growing network of relationships has its own distinctive role and responsibilities. This extended family structure was addressed in Chapter 4.

In such a family, a child grows up supported within a rich web of relationships embraced by grandparents, parents, aunts, uncles, cousins, and others. In that environment, children learn the moral virtues and responsibilities of every type of relationship from the people who love them most. This is the foundation of an ethical society through which virtue is nurtured and passed on through the generations. The family is the place where moral education to raise future citizens takes place, and it does so at a level of intimacy that develops the most deeply rooted moral qualities.

The Hongik Ingan ideal applied to historical circumstances and the virtues nurtured within the traditional extended family are at the core of the Korean Dream. That dream will become a reality as it is owned by all the Korean people, and especially as it is cultivated within families, from where it can expand throughout society to ultimately bring national transformation. As I have made clear, this task is for the Korean people as a whole, not just politicians, officials, financiers, and business leaders.

The Korean Dream speaks to our origins as a people and to our common identity. In so doing, it transcends the ideological division of the past sixty-five years. We will not unite as political systems but as a separated people finally coming home together as one family on the basis of our shared culture and heritage.

That is why I gave so many examples in Chapter 5 of people power bringing about dramatic social and political change. Dictatorial regimes that seemed to hold all power collapsed in the face of determined popular movements—in the Arab Spring, in the peaceful revolutions against communist rule in Eastern Europe, and in overturning apartheid in South Africa, among others. These are examples of what popular movements can achieve.

None of these popular movements were simply angry mobs. They were comprised of people with a purpose, protesting injustices on a foundation of spiritual principles and moral values that upheld human rights and freedoms. As a result, the movements wielded moral authority that proved more powerful in the end than the state's security apparatus. Sometimes that moral authority was focused in a charismatic leader such as Gandhi, Dr. Martin Luther King Jr., or Nelson Mandela. Sometimes it was more widely spread among a group of like-minded moral leaders, as was the case in much of Eastern Europe. But the key common feature was that the moral authority stemmed from upholding universal principles and values that appealed to people of all backgrounds and transcended political and religious differences.

The other feature of popular activism I referred to was the revolution in information and communication technology and its ability to multiply the power of these movements. Social media allows people to report and share information instantly. The power of journalism now lies in the hands of anyone with a smartphone and an internet connection. News can flow from anywhere to anywhere in the world, bypassing the old monopoly control of information that dictatorships used to enjoy. The world is opening up in unprecedented ways, enabling people to mobilize globally in support of a just and noble cause.

I wanted to show how the mobilization of popular energies for a principled purpose can bring social and political change. That is why in Chapter 6 I featured the role that civic associations and NGOs can play in mobilizing and bringing focus to citizens' concerns. Civic associations are the heart of a thriving democracy. They are the medium through which citizens contribute to and build the life of the national community.

In the process of unification, the Korean people, North and South, will have to engage with one another, not just their governments. Civic associations and NGOs are the perfect means to do this. They can work on issues and in local areas that are beyond the government's scope and competence. That is why public-private partnerships between civic associations and the government will be crucially important.

Civic associations are active in every kind of issue imaginable. When their efforts in different fields are combined—along with a common vision, principles, and values—then a foundation can be created for a new nation. That is why the initiatives I started in Paraguay are so important. They demonstrate how all the factors I have described in this book come together in practice to bring about national transformation.

I began with the importance of foundational principles and values that originate from God and protect human rights and freedoms. I challenged the country's political, social, and business leadership to recognize that principles and values make a profound difference to the culture and hence the possibilities of a nation, as the widely divergent courses of North America and South America demonstrate. Principles and values are the foundation of well-functioning free market democracy.

I then set up organizations such as the IDPPS think tank and GPF-Paraguay to enhance the political and social stability of the country by putting into practice the principles and values I spoke of—creating a national road map and undertaking a wide range of social activities. GPF-Paraguay clearly demonstrated the ability of NGOs to effect significant social change, providing leadership programs, character education, and community development initiatives that addressed the roots of the corruption culture that was stifling progress. The possibility of international investment to address the economic piece of the puzzle came last. It was the fruit of all the earlier work on principles and values, on a national plan, and in social activities in key areas. This created a foundation of political and social stability upon which major economic development could happen that ultimately will link Paraguay to the global economy.

I have been building connections between Korea and Paraguay for three reasons. One is that, through being actively engaged in helping Paraguay emerge from underdevelopment to join the modern global economy, Korean institutions—public and private—will learn a great deal about every aspect of national transformation. These lessons can then be applied to the resurrection of North Korean society and, ultimately, its economy.

The second is that in helping Paraguay to grow, Korea will begin to step forward to play a global leadership role, particularly in the development and future direction of emerging nations. The last reason is that Korea will access the Latin American market and the rich resources of the region, both of which it needs given its current strategic trade situation.

All of this work is preparing a foundation for the transformation of North Korea and showing the way forward. If Koreans embrace the Korean Dream and unite to implement it, we can build a new nation on the Korean peninsula. As a unified nation, Korea can exercise global leadership—not only economically, as the nascent interaction with Latin

America makes clear, but more important, morally. The new Korea will stand in a position to be the true advocate of the vision of One Family under God.

THE HISTORICAL CHALLENGE OF THE TWENTY-FIRST CENTURY

Every age in history has faced challenges. Humanity had to confront and overcome them in order to progress to a higher level of development. Civilizations that fail to meet their challenges begin to disintegrate and finally collapse. The twentieth century was the bloodiest and most violent on record, largely as a result of the worldwide struggles between colonial powers and of free societies against totalitarianism, in the form of fascism and then communism.

When the Soviet Union collapsed, ending the Cold War, there was tremendous hope that the experiences of the twentieth century would never be repeated. People anticipated that the new millennium would turn a page in history and produce a new global order that guaranteed prosperity and lasting peace. We soon learned that peace is not achieved so easily. The twenty-first century launched itself on a trajectory that brought a new type of challenge, one perhaps more difficult to resolve even than that of the twentieth century.

When Islamist radicals flew two planes into the World Trade Center in New York on September 11, 2001, it sent the new millennium in a very different direction from what people had hoped. The attack produced the global war on terror in response, bringing with it the very real danger of a global religious conflict between Muslims and Christians. Samuel Huntington, in his book *The Clash of Civilizations*, predicted a world of cultural spheres, each identified with a major faith tradition and in competition, at times violently, with one another.[358]

The global war on terror, most notably U.S. military intervention in Afghanistan and Iraq, has not ended the terror threat or brought greater stability to those regions, although a tremendous amount of blood and treasure had to be paid for more than a decade. At the time, it created war weariness among the American public[359] that led the Obama administration to pull the United States back from its traditional global role, even though it is the world's sole remaining superpower. In the resulting power vacuum, regional powers have felt less constrained.[360] Russia's President Putin pursued his adventurism, annexing Crimea and destabilizing his neighbor Ukraine because of its flirtation with the West.[361] The players in the Middle East make their calculations with less concern about what the United States might do, while in East Asia the risk of regional militarization[362] is growing due to the threat of North Korea, stirring up old historical tensions.

Western economic leadership is also in question after the 2007–2008 financial crisis, precipitated by Western financial institutions and causing a global recession. The economies of the United States and Europe still have not fully recovered, experiencing stagnation or slow growth, and carrying a large debt burden, $17.5 trillion in 2014 in the case of the United States, according to the U.S. Department of the Treasury.[363] The high debt level together with their aging populations will make the extensive social welfare programs of most Western nations more and more difficult to maintain.

At the same time, changing cultural patterns, due to the progressive social revolution of the 1960s, have intensified family disintegration on a wide scale, especially in the inner cities, exacerbating social, racial, ethnic, and religious tensions in the West.[364] These negative trends, economically and socially, are shifting the balance of power in the world. The emerging world no longer sees the West as the paradigm of development, and the unquestioned patina of Western excellence is fading because of its own inner struggles and shortcomings.

The nations of the Southern Hemisphere have been impacted less by these challenges than the developed world. Most of them also have large youth populations, in marked contrast to the aging populations in the West. Given that most of the conflagrations after the Cold War are taking place in the developing world, the potential of these nations to impact global stability is enormous if they can get their act together politically, economically, and socially. The good news is that many countries of the Global South are ready to chart new courses, albeit independent of Western models. The Global South holds the key to the world's future peace and prosperity, and those who can lead them will have an enduring effect on the twenty-first century.

The global order that emerged after the Cold War is dramatically different from what it used to be. The confrontation between communism and democracy pitted two superpowers, the United States and the Soviet Union, against each other, and the rest of the world was sucked up into the orbit around their conflicting ideological poles. Nevertheless, their rivalry imposed a certain level of geopolitical order on the world stage and constrained the actions of lesser nations and non-state actors.

Once that order ended, the geopolitical and ideological constraints of the Cold War disappeared. In that vacuum, new interests and factions arose in its wake, fragmenting humanity against itself ever since. There are no longer overarching ideological systems or geographically based groupings to provide order to the world. In addition to these developments, the fast-paced progress of modern transportation and communication technology means that conflicts may no longer be constricted by locality, space, or time. The threat of violence or terror is global: 24/7/365. New terror groups such as ISIS can be a threat not only to communities in Syria and Iraq but to Western cities as well, due to technological advances.

One's national identity is only one of several organizing groupings today. Fragmentation is occurring along ethnic and, especially, religious lines and is now transcending national boundaries, as is happening in Iraq and Syria. Muslim extremists from all over the world, including Western countries, have been motivated to leave home and fight in Bosnia, Chechnya, Afghanistan, Syria, and Iraq. As people identify themselves by their religion or ethnicity more than their nationality, identity-based conflicts proliferate like brushfires burning out of control, threatening our entire globe. These conflicts are the historic challenge of the twenty-first century, where the future peace of the world will be decided.

Ethnic and religious conflicts that often appeared to be long buried have resurfaced with a vengeance. Yugoslavia, for example, was a country of diverse ethnic and religious groups that seemed to live together harmoniously under a restrictive communist rule. Yet, once that rule ended, not only did the country split into different nations, but a bloody and genocidal war broke out between the various ethnic groups. The fighting among Serbs, Croats, Bosnians, and Kosovo Albanians devolved into ethnic cleansings and the massacre of civilians on a massive, calculated scale. As is often the case, ethnic and cultural identities were reinforced by differing religious identities that added fuel to an already passionate conflict, heightening its intensity.

This latter trend of using faith as a justification for violence is the most concerning trend of all. Religious groups with an extreme political agenda can become the focus of a distorted identity that lends itself to fanaticism, making the danger of a global conflagration based upon a narrow conception of religion very real. The situation is particularly volatile in the Middle East, which has become a tinderbox. In 2014, Syria and Iraq disintegrated into violent conflict fueled by sectarian differences. Militant Islamist groups active in Syria and ISIS, the most extreme of them, took control of territory in Iraq. ISIS was intent on dissolving national borders and establishing a caliphate in Iraq and greater Syria that would be a region ruled by an extreme interpretation of Islamic law.[365]

ISIS and a resurgent al-Qaeda have also recruited young Muslims from Europe and the United States to fight in the region for their cause. They are trained in weaponry and explosives, have experienced combat, and eventually return to their homes in the West with ideas of establishing an Islamic caliphate and the conviction that the use of violence to achieve it is divinely sanctioned.[366] Thus, the events unfolding in the Middle East have not remained there but have eventually found their way back to the West's doorstep. With advancements in transportation and communications technology, the next 9/11 could happen far sooner than we might want to think and accept in the developed world.[367]

Even within Islam, Sunni-Shia clashes are already occurring in Syria and Iraq. The danger is that they could escalate into a regional conflict with Iran leading the Shia against the Sunni monarchies of Saudi Arabia and the Gulf States[368] and the Sunni militants in Syria and Iraq. The Sunni monarchies and the military rulers of Egypt have faced broad-based popular opposition from the Muslim Brotherhood and other similar groups. Meanwhile, the predominantly Jewish state of Israel has faced the hostility of most of the surrounding Arab Muslim population and the very real threat that Iran will obtain a nuclear weapon.

North Korea is an ever-present threat in Northeast Asia but also in the Middle East because of the North's nuclear program and its willingness to share its military technology with the highest bidder. It has cooperated with both Iran and Syria on ballistic missile technology in the past[369] and helped Syria with the technology to build the Al-Kibar nuclear facility that was destroyed by the Israeli Air Force in September 2007.[370] The possibility of proliferation of nuclear materials from North Korea to a state like Iran or even to a non-state actor only adds to the region's instability.

Thus, identity-based conflict[371] threatens the safety of the human race and poses the greatest challenge of the twenty-first century. It affects every corner of our globe. It recognizes no boundaries and festers like a cancer in every region, pitting one group against another. As it grows, it prompts further fragmentation and a reciprocating response in violence as one group avenges the wrong done by another, feeding itself on cycles of hatred and vengeance.

Although tribal, ethnic, and religious identities seem to pose the most pressing problems throughout the world, tribal and ethnic identities are primarily local in scope, with the possibility that ethnic struggles can be elevated to a national conflict, as was the case in former Yugoslavia. Religious identity, however, is already fueling a regional war in the Middle East with the potential to engulf the world in its wake with a scale and intensity not experienced in our modern history, since it will be fueled by fanaticism grounded in a distorted understanding of faith. That is why radicalization of religion poses the greatest threat to our humanity.

Under such circumstances, the only way to break the cycle of violence is through a spiritual vision and message rooted in universal truths. Although the twentieth century was a period of ceaseless struggle, it set the bar in terms of movements for social and political change on a national and international level. As we saw in Chapter 5, the last century also marked the rise of a global consciousness that recognized such ideas as fundamental human rights and freedoms. These ideals were championed by leaders who were able to transcend their narrow agendas and provide a universal vision that led to the end of segregation in the United States, the end of apartheid in South Africa, the end of colonialism, and the rise of nationalism in India and the rest of the world.

Such leaders are needed today to counter the negative effects of identity-based conflicts that are tearing apart the human family. This type of leadership should start from within faith traditions themselves, challenging religious leaders to move beyond the furthering of only the narrow interests of their adherents and to seek what is good for the entire human family. In this way, the power of faith can be harnessed to inspire, guide, and motivate people to heal divisions, resolve conflicts, and build ethical societies.

I call this spiritual leadership that can bring together people of different faiths and backgrounds through a common platform of shared aspirations, principles, and values and, thus, can be a mitigating force against the alarming trend of radicalization and the subsequent politicization of faith.

Spiritual versus Religious Leadership: Transcending the Sectarian and Religious Divide

The radicalization of religion through a distorted and politicized understanding of its doctrine is a direct challenge to all the world's great faith traditions. This type of identity-based conflict is causing chaos in the Middle East, raises the possibility of radicalizing other religions in response to persecution and terror, threatens the peace and stability of Western societies, and heightens the terrifying prospect of nuclear materials falling into the hands of an extremist group or nation-state. Violent radicalism that seeks to justify its actions through an appeal to religion must be countered by faith leaders who demonstrate the falsehood of that appeal.

They have to show that violence runs counter to the original spirit and the fundamental guiding principles and values of all spiritual traditions.

To do so, religious leaders themselves have to step outside their traditional boxes of representing their own particular faith community and aspire to represent the well-being of all mankind. This is the only way to counter radical elements distorting their traditions that seek to hijack the faithful for political rather than spiritual ends. In contrast to the intentions of the radicals, people of faith should aspire to embody universal principles and put into practice the values taught by their founders and shared by all the great faith traditions in order to be the true peacemakers of this age. This is what I mean by being a spiritual leader versus a religious one. It is someone willing to transcend the traditional roles of religious leadership in order to attend our one Creator, God, by serving our common humanity.

In addressing people power in Chapter 5, I described some of the great social and political transformations in the twentieth century that were brought about by popular movements inspired by such aspirations, principles, and values. That inspiration often came from spiritual leaders with great moral authority: Gandhi in India, Dr. Martin Luther King Jr. in the United States, and Nelson Mandela in South Africa. Each of these men aspired to universal spiritual truths that piqued the collective conscience of our humanity and, in turn, stirred a global community to action that brought tremendous social change. It gave India its independence, secured civil rights for black people in the United States, and ended apartheid in South Africa.

Each of these leaders had to overcome their own narrow identities and objectives, be they racial, religious, or political. Gandhi had to transcend his Hinduism, which he did at the cost of his life, since he was killed by a Hindu nationalist. Dr. King had to aspire to speak on behalf of a greater community than that of a black American or a Baptist preacher. Nelson Mandela had to reach beyond his early radical political views and grow to embrace all people, white as well as black.

By moving beyond their own racial, ethnic, and religious backgrounds, they marshaled a moral authority that amplified the universal truths that they were committed to realize. As a result, their message resonated in the conscience of all people, regardless of their diverse backgrounds. In other words, they talked to and for all of us and not just a particular group or interest. These are the types of figures that the world needs today: men and women who are willing to strip themselves of all pretentions—ethnic, religious, or racial—and be the advocates and peacemakers of an undying truth that we are all One Family under God.

When Dr. King's daughter, Bernice, spoke at our Global Peace Convention in Atlanta in 2012, she described her father as first and foremost a spiritual leader, before he was a civil rights leader. She noted that his message reached far beyond racial politics or the Baptist denomination to which he belonged. Likewise, Gandhi had no interest in founding a new philosophy or religious movement, despite the urgings of some of his supporters. He saw his life and teaching as an effort "to apply the eternal truths to our daily life and problems." To him, creating a new religious movement would distract from that effort and add to the divisiveness in society that he was working to overcome.

King and Gandhi are examples of spiritual leadership and highlight how different that is from religious leadership. Religious leaders work within the confines of their own sectarian or denominational tradition. Their primary goal is the promotion and preservation of that tradition and its institutions. This goal can sometimes lead to a compromised moral perspective in which institutional survival becomes more important than spiritual truth and values. Such an outlook is what led the Roman Catholic Church to deny and cover up the actions of pedophile priests for decades.[372]

Religious leaders and institutions often claim that their particular doctrine and tradition has an exclusive access to truth and salvation. However, as a student of religion, I've always felt that most of these doctrines and traditions came after the death of the founder, usually by disciples who sought to build an institutional legacy. An examination of the actual teachings of the founders themselves reveals that much of the content resonates across all the great monotheistic and spiritual faith traditions.

In fact, no single faith has a monopoly on truth. Truth is universal and, by its very nature, found in all the great traditions that sought to embody it. These statements are not meant to diminish the unique contributions and relevance of different religions but to point out that the purpose of faith is to align the faithful to our spiritual rather than earthly goals. In terms of the spiritual goals, my assessment is that all the world's religions, outside of their doctrines and creeds, share common aspirations, principles, and values. Furthermore, the confusion of "truth" with "belief" in a set of doctrines shifts focus away from the practice of living for the sake of others, which is how we can grow to resemble God and establish a world of true peace and harmony.

Therefore, I believe that many fail to see that God is not confined to any one religion since God was the inspiration behind the founding and development of all the great faith traditions. Maybe this way of thinking is due to my unique heritage since my father deeply respected all faiths and believed that each had a providential purpose. He taught that the differences in these traditions reflected the historic cultural patterns of the region from which they arose, yet God was the inspiration behind their founding. My father, in his autobiography, explains how all religions strive for an ideal world of peace, using a metaphoric image of a flowing river. He wrote:

> The river does not reject any of the streams that flow into it. It accepts them all. It embraces all the streams and forms a single flow as it continues toward the ocean. People in the world today do not understand this simple truth. The streams that seek out the river and flow into it are the numerous religions and denominations of today. Each stream traces its origin to a different spring, but they are all going to the same destination. They are seeking the ideal

world overflowing with peace. Peace will never come to this earth unless we first tear down the walls between religions.[373]

Due to his deeply held convictions, my father led many efforts and initiatives to harmonize and unite religions in a common cause for peace. In his speech titled "The Path to World Peace in Light of God's Will," which he gave on October 20, 2001, shortly after the 9/11 events, he clearly stated his view of the role of religions in promoting world peace. He began with a thesis that "world peace is the original ideal of God." Yet, he recognized that "we cannot expect world peace unless religious people reconcile and cooperate." My father saw the true role of religious leaders as "guides who lead people to peace." In other words, they should be spiritual leaders. He continued:

If religions only emphasize narrow-minded denominationalism and fail to teach true love for God and the universe, we will never free humankind from the horrors of war. In the face of this global crisis, religious leaders have to practice true love, humbly following God's Will, walking hand in hand beyond the boundaries of their own religion.[374]

He recognized the ability of faith in transforming the individual, society, nations, and the world through the "inner power of religion" since it "touches our hearts and can re-create us as people of peace." In addition, "It can cultivate our ability to practice self-control from within. It can overcome historical hatreds and resentments among us. This is the root from which arises true peace and stability." Therefore, he concluded, "If religions demonstrate love for each other, cooperate with each other, and serve each other, putting the higher ideal of peace ahead of particular doctrines, rituals and cultural backgrounds, the world will change dramatically."[375]

I know that my father was truly a spiritual leader transcending the confines of religion. Although he is most often thought of as a religious founder, his intention and primary purpose were actually encapsulated in the title of his autobiography: "peace-loving global citizen." He made it clear to his members on many occasions that he was willing to sacrifice his church organization for the sake of humanity; although he remained true to his spiritual calling throughout his life, many leaders in his organizations focused on building institutions and assets. I witnessed firsthand how the spiritual message and vision of the founder as expressed in his teachings can be sidetracked by leaders' intent on building earthly foundations, failing to see that true spiritual strength comes from the moral authority in representing eternal truths rather than political power, assets, and money.

I believe my experiences and observations in this regard are indicative of the struggles in all denominations and faith traditions where competing tensions exist between those who want to stay true to the vision and those who seek to protect the institutional legacy of their religion. In today's world of identity-based conflicts threatening the very existence of our humanity, people of faith have a moral imperative to rise above their narrow self-interests and become the noble peacemakers of tomorrow by staying true to their founders' teachings.

As people of faith, we need to recognize that God has worked through all faith traditions and respect the deep convictions of others. In addition, we should be asking ourselves how we can all come together to realize a peaceful ideal world rather than ripping our human family apart in an effort to impose our particular system of beliefs on others. Although we live in trying times, it is also an opportunity for people of faith to become the true peacemakers of this century and lead humanity away from falling into the abyss of identity-based conflicts.

As I have explained above, the great challenge of the twenty-first century of identity-based conflict requires a powerful vision that calls forth our common humanity. That vision is "One Family under God." I created the Global Peace Foundation with the important mission to advocate for this vision throughout the world with a threefold platform of inter-faith, family, and service. As an international peace NGO with a uniquely spiritual vision, GPF has been on the forefront of creating a new inter-faith paradigm that challenges the old inter-faith models. Our goal is not just to engender dialogue and understanding but to create a common platform of universal aspirations, principles, and values that then becomes the framework through which people of diverse faith backgrounds can work together for a world of peace and co-prosperity.

GPF has found that this approach, focused on spiritual leadership, has had tremendous appeal in those regions of the world where identity-based conflicts have been tearing up communities, societies, and nations. Many faith leaders there realize the futility of arguing over their different doctrines when they see people murdered and terrorized on a daily basis. Circumstances dictate action. They choose to act and become the spiritual leaders who can lead their people to peace.

In short, the outlook of narrow religious leadership divides humanity along religious lines. It sets religions against each other—in competition or conflict. In an age when the major challenge is identity-based conflicts and where the most extreme conflict arises from religious identity, religious pretensions become part of the problem and not the solution. Spiritual leadership, in contrast, reaches beyond these divisions through its appeal to universal truths. The great social transformations of the twentieth century came about through spiritual leaders who expressed spiritual truths that awakened the human conscience. The solution to the challenge of the twenty-first century, identity-based conflict, will arise in the same way.

Our fragmenting world of religious and ethnic tribalism has an urgent need for an overarching spiritual vision. One Family under God offers such a vision. It is true to the realization that universal spiritual truths, taken to heart by men and women who leave behind their narrow beliefs, can bring about tremendous social transformation and build a world of everlasting peace. In the end, as the twentieth-century examples I gave illustrate, true peace cannot be established solely through political, social, or diplomatic means. At its core, the establishment of peace is a spiritual and moral issue that must stand upon universal principles and values that become reflected in how we live.

THE KOREAN DREAM FULFILLED IN ONE FAMILY UNDER GOD

The nation of Korea, based upon its history and culture, is uniquely positioned to play a spiritual leadership role in the twenty-first century if the Korean people reclaim their identity and destiny. I have already described how Koreans developed a deep spiritual consciousness to digest the great tribulations of their history through their unique culture of *han*. That consciousness today must be directed toward rebuilding our families, the creation of a new nation, and promoting a vision that can build a world of lasting peace. That is where our founding ideals naturally lead us.

The Hongik Ingan ideal has been continually pointing our people to serve the greater humanity. This was evidenced in the vision that inspired the independence movement after World War II. Their desire was to establish an ideal nation, not just for its own sake, but as a model for the world to emulate. In the words of Kim Gu, "And thus true world peace could come from our nation. I wish peace would be achieved in our nation and from there to the world. I believe that that is the Hongik Ingan ideal of our national ancestor Dangun."[376]

The Korean experience resonates with the developing world since it faced and endured many similar challenges and is still tackling such challenges today. Within the span of a century, Korea had to deal with the humiliation and violation of colonialism and the loss of its national identity, as well as endure the unnatural division of our people and homeland. Yet, through it all, if we have the internal resources to overcome these trials and create something better, we will have the moral authority to inspire others through our example.

The Korean War brought conflict and devastation to the country on an unprecedented scale, with most of its infrastructure and institutions utterly destroyed. Nevertheless, the "Miracle on the Han" sixty-plus years later is a testament to what is possible. Today, the developing world is a hotbed of local rivalries, civil conflict, and regional wars, making the Korean story and experience relevant to their development. In other words, our history has uniquely prepared us to understand the real challenges of the developing world, unlike many nations in the West. If Korea takes the next step of unification and creates a new nation, it will offer a powerful model of principled national transformation to the world.

In terms of raw industrial and economic development, South Korea sets a new bar in what is possible if there is a comprehensive plan of public and private partnership for economic growth. To my knowledge, its track record and span of development have been unprecedented in the modern world. Per capita GDP in 1954, the year after the Korean War ended, was $70, making the country one of the poorest in the world. Many countries that were better off than Korea back then stagnated for decades and are only recently starting to develop. On the other hand, during that same time period, South Korea attained a per capita GDP of $24,329 by 2013,[377] an increase of 348-fold, making it one of the world's fastest-growing economies.

This astonishing achievement, of course, is due to the hard work of the postwar generation of Koreans who were willing to put up with the necessary sacrifices to make their country the envy of the developing world. This level of dedication and self-sacrifice should not be lost to this generation that has inherited the fruits of their forefathers' labors. With its lengthy list of achievements, South Korea stands as an inspiration to the emerging world, in terms of both economic policy and social transformation through education and community development initiatives such as Saemaul Undong. Whatever socioeconomic challenges many of these countries are likely to meet, our people have already faced and overcome them. To play the role of global leadership, however, Korea must consciously connect to emerging economies around the world.

Culturally, the emerging world is much closer to Korea than to the West. The traditional extended family structure has been the foundation of these societies just like the Korean family. These societies are now recognizing that models of Western industrialization and modernization come at a high cost to traditional cultures. Social and cultural practices undermine their most sacred traditions and relationships. The dissolution of extended families and the support network they once provided are replaced with government welfare programs that negatively impact the character of their citizens, as well as those in need, in addition to creating unsustainable debt, leading to socioeconomic instability and major social upheavals.

Faced with this sobering assessment, nations in the emerging world are looking for other models of development that can increase prosperity without destroying the network of traditional social relationships and deeply held cultural values. These nations will have a much closer affinity to Korea than to the West, if our people can reclaim our identity and destiny. The Korean extended family nurtures relationships that are the foundation of a stable and ethical society in raising virtuous citizens. That is why I stressed the importance of Korea's unique family culture. We must not succumb to the pressures of Western culture as an inevitable outcome of modernization but be willing to pioneer our own unique paradigm, as Kim Gu hoped. I firmly believe that we can, if we look to our past.

I believe that Korea's unique spiritual history has been preparing us for the great providential mission rooted in the vision of One Family under God. This vision cuts to the heart of identity-based conflicts with universal spiritual truths that originate in God's purpose for humanity. As I have noted throughout this book, recognition of all fundamental "inalienable" rights and freedoms, which are the bedrock of all free societies, comes from the realization that they originate in a Creator and not any human power. This powerful insight allows one to transcend the divisiveness of identity-based conflicts and opens a door to a new understanding of our humanity.

It is an insight that has allowed our people, throughout their 5,000-year history, to develop an open-minded attitude toward religions in uncovering the world's truths and adapting them into our own unique culture. Likewise, it has guided the United States to champion human rights and freedoms, especially freedom of religion, by recognizing the importance of individual conscience in building a nation upon universal spiritual principles and values. Most of all, it allows humanity to recognize the fundamental truth that humans share a common heritage in one

Creator and, with the help of divine enlightenment, are meant to live as One Family under God.

In short, the Korean Dream prompts us to look beyond just the unification of the peninsula and aspire to be global leaders who can bring enduring peace to a troubled world. I think it is clear that Korean leadership in the world today can be a powerful force for peace since our history and identity uniquely qualify us to implement the vision of One Family under God globally. The Korean nation today aspires to be a global leader and particularly to make a significant contribution to the developing world. I have encouraged and advanced this goal through the many national and international initiatives. What is it that will enable Korea to exercise this sort of leadership?

That is what I want to achieve through bringing Korean expertise and enterprise to Paraguay. This activity will do more than open the door to new markets for Korea in Paraguay and, through the hub strategy I am proposing, in the Latin American region. It will place Korea in a key leadership role in bringing about economic development and the necessary social and political transformation for the sustainable development of Paraguay and the wider region.

This pattern of national and regional transformation can be repeated in many different parts of the world. There are countries in major regions where, through GPF and other initiatives, I have been laying foundations for political and social stability as in Paraguay. Kenya in East Africa, Nigeria in West Africa, and Malaysia, Indonesia, and the Philippines in Southeast Asia can all become the focus for national and regional transformation and the development of a hub strategy in the same manner that I outlined for Paraguay and Latin America. Most of all, of course, a unified Korea would become an especially potent force for transformation in the Northeast Asia region.

National transformation does not begin with economic development. It ends there, as I made clear in the example of Paraguay. Transformation takes place on a foundation of political and social stability that, in turn, rests upon the adherence to and practice of fundamental principles and values. To build a foundation of stability, those principles and values have to be implemented through practical projects that tackle major challenges. In Paraguay, for example, as we saw, GPF made inroads into one of the biggest issues: the endemic corruption in government and business.

GPF is addressing the great global challenge of identity-based conflicts in several regions of the world through projects based on the vision of One Family under God. In Kenya, One Family under God became a powerful call to rise above the tribal violence that broke out after the 2007 presidential election and uphold national unity. GPF worked with groups in the Rift Valley to establish inter-tribal cooperation to prevent future violence. In Mindanao, in the south of the Philippines, GPF worked with Muslim and Christian communities to build bridges in a region filled with years of religion-based conflict.

Nigeria has been suffering a violent insurgency from the radical Muslim terror group Boko Haram. They want to impose a strict interpretation of Sharia law on the country by force. Although they have attacked many communities and public targets, they have singled out Christians in particular. In the first six months of 2014, seventy-five Christian communities were attacked and over 1,600 Christians killed. Nigeria's population is almost evenly divided between Muslim and Christian, and the destabilizing impact of widespread religious conflict would be disastrous.

In November 2013, GPF held a Global Peace Leadership Conference in Abuja, Nigeria that addressed these issues. In his message to the conference, President Goodluck Jonathan said, "The theme of this conference, One Family under God, is not only apt but could not have come at a more auspicious time, when many parts of the global community have come under the threat of sectarian violence, oftentimes waged in the name of God by extremist elements."

After the conference, leading Christian ministers of different denominations, Muslim imams, and traditional rulers worked together to resolve religious conflict. When they first heard the vision of One Family under God, many of them said, "This is what our country needs." They saw that it was the key to overcoming religious division and launched a One Family under God grassroots campaign to take the message of Christian-Muslim cooperation to local communities.[378]

The message of One Family under God has a power that resonates in the hearts of people whose consciences are attuned to universal principles and values. H. E. Hajiya Amina Sambo, the wife of Nigeria's vice president, is a Muslim and very active in social projects to assist women and youth. She is the patron of the Global Peace Foundation's Nigeria chapter. At the Global Peace Convention 2013 in Malaysia, she told me that the vision of One Family under God was a message sent by God and that I should be proud to be God's messenger. Others have felt the same. Bishop Manuel Ferreira, lifetime president of CONAMAD, the Association of the Assemblies of God Churches headquartered in Brazil, has also expressed to me that this vision is a mission from God that I must protect and advance. Also, our GPF conferences have inspired leaders from nations such as Uganda, Guatemala, and Cambodia to initiate activities guided by the vision of One Family under God, even before formal GPF chapters were established in their nations.

While the scope of the vision of One Family under God is global, it should manifest itself first within the family, the smallest social unit and a microcosm of the larger society. Within a family, this vision is substantiated in practical living until it becomes a part of familial culture as natural as breathing. There is no better place for such a culture to grow and blossom through the passage of generations and its ever-widening web of extended family networks than in traditional families rooted in sacrificial love. Korean history and society are full of examples of just such families.

Today, model families can become a powerful transformative social tool in substantiating our ideals, setting real precedents for others to follow. The Korean family culture is perfectly suited to embody the vision of One Family under God since it resonates with our founding ideals of benefiting all humanity as well as in the unique manner we adopted the Confucian ideals through *han* and *jeong seong*. This legacy gives the Korean people a special appreciation of the power of the familial social unit and the culture it manifests, extending into the larger society, the nation, and the world. If the vision of One Family under God is the antidote for identity-based conflicts that are consuming our human family in an endless cycle of war, then our destiny as a people is interwoven with that vision, for that is how we can truly benefit all mankind to eventually build a world of peace.

In short, the unification of the peninsula will not only make the Korean people whole again, as well as provide a unified national framework, but it will also give credence to the notion that peace and reconciliation are possible in even the most impossible of circumstances. With unification under these circumstances, the Korean people will have a unique moral authority to tackle the issue of identity-based conflicts as we overcome our own ideological, social, political, and economic divide and, in the process, bring closure to the legacy of colonialism and the Cold War in Asia and the world. As I mentioned in Chapter 1 and throughout this section, undertaking such a venture will endear Korea to all the developing nations of the world since it will have pioneered a path that all of them with similar experiences and challenges could follow. Our nation and the collective story of our people will then be the inspiration to the emerging world and, in turn, will affect the course of human history into the twenty-first century.

CONCLUSION: THE CHALLENGE BEFORE US

Korea stands at a crossroads, facing a historic choice. At stake is the future of the Korean people for generations to come. We can accept the current state of a divided peninsula with the ever-present possibility of civil conflict, or we can determine a new path driven by the conscious pursuit of our destiny to create a unified homeland and to "broadly benefit all humanity." If you are Korean or someone interested in helping Korea, I hope that this book has already helped you make up your mind. The answer to this choice is clear to me, and it should be clear for you.

The only true path going forward is to accept our destiny and forge a new nation steeped in Hongik Ingan ideals. The other path is not even an option. Given today's changing world dynamics, our people have a golden opportunity to realize the elusive dream of an independent sovereign state, true to our founding, that animated the hopes of our patriotic ancestors throughout the course of the twentieth century, yet was unfulfilled. It will bring closure to the tragic history of colonialism and the Cold War, turning a new page in a new chapter of the Northeast Asian region. Those pages should be marked by Korean leadership in creating a new nation and ushering in a world of peace through the vision of One Family under God.

The center of gravity in the world today is shifting from the West and the Atlantic region toward Asia and the Pacific Rim.[379] Korea has a 5,000-year history and an ancient culture married with a highly developed and technologically advanced economy. Rooted in the very origins of our culture is the universal ideal of Hongik Ingan, which valued humanity in a way that only found its full modern expression a little over two centuries ago in the U.S. Declaration of Independence, which upheld human rights and freedoms as coming from God. Thus, Korea can be a natural intermediary between East and West, especially between China and the United States, since it historically was a partner to China before Western involvement in Asia and, due to its founding ideals, has a unique relationship with the United States.

As the world completes the shift from the Atlantic era to that of the Pacific Rim, a new world order will have to emerge. To many, especially in the developing world, the Western development model is lacking, and they are looking for new, alternative models of development. Korea, upon unification, will be well-positioned to be a leader in this changing landscape. The Korean development model will be the most relevant since its track record and affinity to the experiences in the emerging world will be unrivaled by any other developed nation. It will offer a path to national transformation that balances economic development on the foundation of sound political and social change that will complement the cultural heritage of that nation.

The emerging world will be at the heart of what unfolds going forward. There, the greatest global challenges lie, but also the greatest opportunities. For that reason, leadership among these nations is so important. Today, however, they are ablaze with a multitude of brushfires ranging from widespread poverty and pervasive corruption to identity-based conflicts. How does one deal with those issues?

The answer is clear. The first issues of poverty and corruption can be addressed in the model of national transformation currently being developed in Paraguay. Upon unification, that model should be further fine-tuned with the assimilation of North Korea into a new national paradigm. Paramount to that framework of development is the creation of political and social stability through the advocacy and implementation of universal aspirations, principles, and values. Only then can economic development begin and prosperity, rooted in the rule of law, materialize, tackling the issue of poverty and corruption.

Identity-based conflicts are, as I have mentioned above, the greatest global threat in the twenty-first century. I have already explained how this challenge could be met. True peace can never be built upon economic, political, and diplomatic effort alone. Its solution must rest upon spiritual truths—rooted in common aspirations, principles, and values—that move humanity's collective conscience to seek forgiveness, reconciliation, and peace. The vision that has the power to do this is One Family under God.

We face a moment of decision. We stand at an inflection point in history where all factors are converging to accentuate the destiny of our people. Unlike during the twentieth century, the future of our peninsula, the region, and the world lies in our hands. We hold all the cards, if only we are bold enough to seize this moment and shape what is to come. The Korean Dream is our pathway forward, and the vision of One Family under God represents our global mission in building a world of everlasting peace. It is up to you to take that idea and run with it.

The natural advocates for One Family under God are the Korean people, since they have been prepared with Hongik Ingan ideals, tempered by a challenging history to develop a deep spiritual consciousness, and forged through our unique extended family culture of *han* and *jeong seong*. Our destiny is to create an ideal nation that is true to our founding and then "to broadly benefit all humanity." Victor Hugo said that "more powerful than an invading army is an idea whose time has come."[380] That time is now, and the idea is the Korean Dream manifested globally in the vision of One Family under God.

CHAPTER 8

Realizing the Dream

"It always seems impossible until it's done."
−NELSON MANDELA

At the writing of this centennial edition, the situation on the Korean peninsula is again increasingly unstable. The opportunities for a dramatic breakthrough toward peaceful reunification at the beginning of 2018 have slipped away into the all-too-familiar détente between the two Koreas that has plagued the peninsula for the past seventy-four years. South Korea continues an opportunistic engagement policy reminiscent of past efforts without any strategic vision or coordination with its allies, and North Korea has resumed its military missile program and continues its pattern of hot-cold diplomacy, oscillating between threats and negotiations. In the face of such entrenched positions, how can we move forward, let alone speak of unification?

Yet, I also know that we have made significant progress, especially in 2019, the centenary of the March First Korean Independence Movement.

Throughout the year, member organizations of Action for Korea United (AKU) have worked diligently to connect Koreans to the spirit of the 1919 Independence Movement. I recall many encounters throughout the year with dedicated activists who are sincerely pursuing the fulfillment of the vision that ignited the hearts of our ancestors.

This vision—the Korean Dream—is our enduring aspiration, our destiny as the Korean people. It is a vision that is in our DNA, pushing us to continually seek to better ourselves, guiding us through the hardest times in our history. Today, it is what will light the way out of the darkness of this hour.

I wrote *Korean Dream: A Vision for a Unified Korea* as a reminder to all Koreans that we are a people called to fulfill a providential mission to bring benefit to the world. It is a textbook that clearly articulates the vision of the Korean Dream, rooted in our ancient philosophy of Hongik Ingan. It inspires and catalogs the initiatives needed to empower a global, Korean-led citizen movement that owns this vision and takes action.

This Centennial Edition has been prepared not only to honor the past and the courage of our forefathers. It is a call to action, a call to view the future with fresh eyes and to take on the ideals and principles embodied in the Korean Dream: to build a new, unified nation on the peninsula that finally reflects the long-delayed aspirations expressed in the Korean Independence Movement.

This chapter begins with a geopolitical analysis of developments on the Korean peninsula since 2017 and their implications and then summarizes how the Korean Dream approach is being applied with great impact in Korea and around the world.

NAVIGATING AN UNCERTAIN FUTURE

Events on and around the Korean peninsula over the past two years have grown increasingly volatile and unpredictable, making our work all the more urgent. Many in Korea have been in denial that a hot war is possible. Most on the peninsula are accustomed to the vicious cycle of "threat-crisis-talks-concessions" that Pyongyang employed in the past. The events of 2017 changed all that.

Kim Jong-un's nuclear and missile tests united the world against him in a strong-sanctions regime. Under the Trump administration, Korea became the top international priority for the U.S. It imposed biting sanctions and galvanized global support to enforce those sanctions, even getting North Korea's traditional allies, China and Russia, to follow suit. That was a break, for the first time and however briefly, from the Cold War framework which has dominated Korean peninsula dynamics since the end of World War II. At the same time, sanctions were backed up by a credible U.S. military threat to the North, underscored by the example of U.S. airstrikes in Syria. This aggressive American response, with the full support of the international community, especially the North's former allies, isolated Kim Jong-un and forced him into a corner.

This was a "perfect storm" that could trigger major change on the Korean peninsula and, with the right strategic vision, could lead to the peaceful resolution of the division. At the close of 2017 at the International Forum for One Korea in Seoul, I warned against short-sighted policies and offered a "Third Way" to bringing lasting peace to the peninsula—the peaceful reunification of Korea led by a grassroots citizen movement and inspired by the founding ideals of the Korean people. I urged the ROK and international players to recalibrate their approach to support this goal.

Yet, this brief window of opportunity was squandered and quickly closed. When Kim sought reprieve from his perilous situation, he found a willing partner in South Korea's president, Moon Jae-in. Representing the legacy of Kim Dae-jung and Roh Moo-hyun, Moon naturally saw the North's overture as an opportunity to pursue a "Sunshine Policy 2.0." This would build his and his party's political capital domestically and win him international prestige as a peace broker.

Though Moon's "peace initiative" facilitated an unprecedented summit between the North Korean leader and the U.S. president, it broke with the long-established diplomatic precedent of firm U.S. support of the South in relation to the North. Both the U.S. and the ROK took independent tracks of engaging with the DPRK, leading to strains on the fragile tripartite alliance between South Korea, the United States, and Japan. The overall effect was to dissipate the critical pressure on Kim, who exploited the opportunity by mending relations with China and renewing relations with Russia.

Given these circumstances, I called for an urgent international forum on Korean reunification in Washington, D.C. at the end of 2018 to address the surprising and often chaotic events of the past year and a half. This forum brought together policy experts, scholars, and former officials from East Asia, the U.S., and Europe. I offered my analysis of existing U.S. strategy, cautioning against a narrow focus on denuclearization that would end up creating more problems than it solves.[381]

THE PROBLEM WITH CVID

The problem with the Singapore Summit and the evolving U.S.-DPRK relations was the naive assumption that the U.S. could narrowly negotiate North Korea's "complete, verifiable and irreversible denuclearization" (CVID), leaving out both its South Korean ally and the many other issues that plague relations with the North. In return for a promise to dismantle its nuclear program, the United States was prepared to aid the North's flagging economy and thus ensure the protection and survivability of the Kim regime. By doing so, it would be supporting the most despotic dictatorship in the world today and, more importantly, it would be assenting to the permanent division of the peninsula.

Although the North agreed, in broad and undefined language, to these terms, most Koreans believed that Kim Jong-un had no intention of honoring this agreement. The U.S. failed to see that the North's nuclear program is more than its insurance policy against Western aggression. It is Kim's crowning achievement in the face of a hostile world. It is a source of personal and national pride as well as evidence of his intrepid independence from foreign influence. Even many North Korean defectors confess they felt pride that the DPRK was a nuclear state.

Unlike the South, the North has no accomplishment other than its nuclear program that it developed at an enormous cost to national resources and strained diplomatic relations with the larger global community. For Koreans, whose fate was determined by foreign powers throughout the twentieth century, the need for independent self-determination is a powerful force and, therefore, admired even when exhibited by a dictator like Kim.

Nevertheless, shortly after the summit, the North made several concessions, such as the closing of an obsolete nuclear test site, the return of American service members' remains, and the cessation of missile tests and other acts of provocation. These concessions were hailed by voices in the West as great achievements in U.S. relations with the North. The Trump administration saw them as the "goodwill" developed between the U.S. president and Kim and continued to believe that negotiations would lead to denuclearization. They assured the public that sanctions were still effective and there was no reason to ease them unless the North complied with the agreement.[382]

LACK OF STRATEGIC VISION AND EROSION OF REGIONAL COOPERATION

Even before the Singapore Summit, U.S. actions in the Northeast Asian region set off a series of events that caused the sanctions regime to unravel. After the summit was announced, China's president, Xi Jin Ping, invited Kim Jong-un to China for the first time since Kim took power. Ironically, the summit became the catalyst to mend the then-souring relations between North Korea and China. Similarly, Russia followed suit by sending Foreign Minister Sergey Lavrov to Pyongyang.

We can deduce the contents of both meetings from subsequent evidence that both China and Russia violated previous agreements to impose sanctions on North Korea. In effect, U.S. willingness to enter into bilateral talks with the DPRK had the net effect of breaking down the pressure that brought it to the negotiation table in the first place. If the U.S. was taking the lead by itself in dealing with North Korea, then China and Russia were certain to keep a close eye on what was happening and do so with an adversarial frame of mind.

Moon Jae-in had facilitated Trump's meeting with Kim and was no doubt satisfied with the initial results as it cleared a path for his own policy ambitions. Moon quickly followed the announcement of the Singapore Summit with a focus on global sanctions relief on behalf of North Korea. During the UN General Assembly on Sept 26, 2018, he stated that "now is the time that the international community should give something in return for the new choice and efforts that North Korea has made." On October 19 that same year, in a gathering with heads of European nations, he called on them to relax sanctions on the North, even trying to set up meetings on behalf of Kim Jong-un with prominent leaders like Pope Francis.

President Moon's approach was running on its own separate track, just like U.S. policy. There was no deep coordination between them and certainly no overall guiding strategy that united the regional allies. These separate tracks created deep fissures in the delicate alliance of South Korea, U.S., and Japan that was formed out of necessity with the end of the Second World War and the beginning of the Cold War. Without the impending threat of global communism or North Korean aggression due to the peace initiatives, all three parties pursued their own perceived national interests at the expense of this alliance. All this played into Kim Jong-un's hands.

For South Korea, what followed was an evolving policy of greater cooperation with the North. The Moon administration focused on the "relaxation of sanctions" and the "declaration of the end to war" between the two Koreas and the United States, to the chagrin of the U.S. and Japan. In September 2018, in his speech at Rungrado Stadium on his visit to Pyongyang, Moon stated that he and Kim Jong-un pledged "to hasten a future of common prosperity and reunification on our own terms." This statement was made under "the principle of autonomy for our people, whereby we ourselves determine our own fate," meaning the two Koreas with no interference from other nations. This may sound like an admirable expression of national self-determination, but North Korea's long-standing geopolitical aim is to isolate South Korea from its American and Japanese allies.

We need to clearly understand that Kim Jong-un and the North Korean ruling elite are an inter-generational dictatorship that has not abandoned the dream of Kim's grandfather, "Eternal President" Kim Il-Sung, of a united peninsula dominated by the North and its ideology. One might scoff at the idea that this could become a reality, but we must remember that it was Kim Jong-un's grandfather who instigated the Korean War. Unification has always been the stated goal of both Koreas and something the North has been preparing for decades with its ties to South Korean labor unions and elements of the ideological left.[383]

The North has a larger strategic view of a unified Korea that can reap the benefits of the South Korean economy with the might of their own nuclear weapons capability. And what they can no longer achieve by force they will seek to achieve by geopolitical maneuvers and exploiting the polarized ideological divides within South Korea. When we look at the wider context of the most recent North Korean nuclear crisis during the years of 2017 to 2019, a fuller picture of the North's unification ambitions becomes apparent in what should be alarming to the entire global community.

As we have already seen, the DPRK has sought the official end of the Korean War, so that the U.S. would be pressured to remove its military presence from the peninsula, something that the Moon Jae-in administration is working for at this very moment. The North will appeal to the anti-American and anti-Japanese elements of the progressive left in South Korea under the pretense of Korean self-determination to erode the tenuous alliance in Northeast Asia between the ROK, the U.S., and Japan and, in doing so, seize the opportunity to build a new nation in its image.

That these remain North Korea's goals was further evidenced when satellite imagery revealed that the North was continuing to develop its nuclear and missile programs in direct violation of the agreement signed in Singapore. This confirmed what many Koreans and skeptics had already feared. The summit created an atmosphere of loosening sanctions and an unhealthy North-South cooperation that threatens the ROK-U.S.-Japan alliance and its intention to curtail the North's nuclear ambition. Clearly, when one objectively assesses the events of 2018 and 2019, Kim Jong-un turned a potential disaster into a personal triumph.[384]

NEED FOR A NEW STRATEGIC FRAMEWORK

Due to these concerns, I urged the U.S. to adopt a new strategic framework for Korea with the clearly defined end goal of reunification based on the Korean Dream paradigm. That would entail building international cooperation in support of that goal and working closely with allies in the region, especially South Korea and Japan. Furthermore, I underscored the need for Korean civil society initiatives and international public support to complement any such governmental-level efforts.

My keynote address at the International Forum on One Korea in Washington, D.C. at the end of 2018 became the rallying call for the founding of Alliance for Korea United USA, a grassroots network of Korean-American organizations and individuals supporting the Korean Dream approach to unification on the peninsula.[385] The main thrust of the speech was well-received, and I wrote an editorial that was carried by *Newsweek Magazine* as a fresh new approach to the Korean issue.

Less than three months after the forum in Washington, President Trump and Kim Jong-un held their second summit in Hanoi, the capital of Vietnam. The Hanoi Summit sought to address the lack of substantial progress on denuclearization since their first meeting in Singapore. Yet, given the favorable view of the prior summit, many in the United States and the international community were anticipating that some kind of an agreement would materialize, talking of the possibility of a "big deal" or a "small deal."

Even before the talks began in Hanoi, I predicted in an interview with *Shindonga Magazine* that the summit would result in "no deal."[386] I knew that there would be no positive outcomes from the U.S. administration's blind attempts to negotiate with North Korea for full, verified nuclear disarmament, due to their naïve understanding of how the North views its nuclear program. More importantly, South Korea and the Korean people, who would be most affected by the outcomes of those discussions, were not at the table. As negotiations were underway in Hanoi, I delivered the keynote address at the 2019 Global Peace Convention in Seoul on February 28. Immediately after I delivered my speech, news reports confirmed my prediction. President Trump had abruptly walked away from the negotiation table in Hanoi, ending the summit early.

I once again emphasized that the U.S. should recalibrate its narrow bilateral approach to denuclearization. The U.S. needs to have a comprehensive strategic framework that has a clear vision of the outcome it is working toward, just as it did after World War II with the Marshall Plan in Europe and MacArthur's reconstruction of Japan. It should set aside the faulty assumption that narrowly defined CVID goals can somehow be accomplished and the delusion that North Korea is ready to negotiate in good faith. History has proven that this will never happen, and there are always unintended consequences that need to be considered.

If the United States were, in effect, to guarantee the survival of the Kim regime in exchange for denuclearization, it would set in motion a dangerous new foreign policy precedent that would undermine its moral authority as the champion of democratic self-government as well as fundamental human rights and freedoms. This legacy paid for in blood and treasure from the end of the Second World War to the conflicts in the Gulf would be overshadowed by American willingness to forsake its time-honored principles and values for short-sighted diplomatic gains. But, most importantly, it would also mean that the U.S. recognizes and endorses the permanent division of the peninsula, contravening the desire of the Korean people to eventually see the unity of their homeland. This would be another first, where the United States violates the will of a sovereign people to create a new unified nation in order to appease a dictator and his ruthless, corrupt regime.

It is obvious that the U.S., the ROK, and other nations must recalibrate their current approaches to the crisis on the peninsula. I believe that the

United States should widen its Korea focus, including denuclearization, in the larger context of unification since it is already the stated goal of both Koreas after the inter-Korean summits between Moon and Kim. American leadership would be essential to cement global support as well as provide regional strategic vision and cooperation. Korean unification will be a necessary strategic step in achieving the denuclearization of the peninsula, in addition to providing regional stability and economic prosperity.

With an impetus toward unification underway, the most important strategic question for the Korean people, the United States, the region, and the world will be: "What sort of unification will we have? What sort of country do we want the new Korea to be?" This is where the battle for the future of the peninsula will be fought.[387]

KOREAN DREAM APPROACH

I have actively pushed for a clear and broad strategic framework, as articulated throughout this book. First, the fundamental thesis of the Korean Dream paradigm is that unification should be understood as an opportunity to create an ideal nation in line with the founding ideals of Hongik Ingan that charged the Korean people to "live for the greater benefit of all mankind." By doing so, this vision challenges the existing Cold War paradigm of North and South on the peninsula, as well as the hyper-partisan divide of left and right in domestic South Korean politics, as foreign constructs imposed upon the Korean people after liberation.

It reminds all Koreans of our common heritage and shared historic cultural legacy that spans five millennia and has allowed us, as a people, to overcome untold difficulties throughout our turbulent past. In short, seventy-plus years of division cannot redefine 5,000 years of our common heritage. Thus, the inevitable destiny of the Korean people is to create a new model nation that contributes to global peace and prosperity out of the ashes of division and conflict.

These ideals and associated principles have shaped the Korean identity in the past and can provide meaning and purpose to the Korean people and Korean nation amid present turbulence and confusion. They motivated the drive throughout the twentieth century for a Korea that was "united, independent, and free" and will be central to achieving that goal in this century.

Significantly, the leaders of the Korean Independence Movement in 1919 understood the importance of this kind of vision. Hongik Ingan shaped the aspirations of the Independence movement to want more than just freedom from Japanese colonial occupation: the creation of an ideal nation, rooted in high principles, that would be an example to the world. This is evident in the Korean Declaration of Independence, which was produced by a diverse group of leaders of different religious and civic groups, including my own great grand uncle, Rev. Moon Yun-gook, one of the most influential Christian pastors of his day.

It is remarkable that the Declaration calls for both Koreans and Japanese alike to "correct past mistakes and open a new phase of friendship based upon genuine understanding and sympathy." Calling upon Koreans to move beyond hatred and resentment, it urged dignity and restraint toward their would-be enemies and simultaneously offered a hopeful vision to transform Japan-Korea relations from that of colonizer and colonized to mutual partners in promoting peace in Asia. Today, the example of the Korean Independence Movement can serve as a guide and inspiration for the Korean Dream movement toward a unified Korea of high ideals.[388]

Second, the Korean Dream approach is based on principles deeply rooted in Korean culture and history; they provide a philosophical and moral framework that can appeal to all Koreans and that far transcends the post-1945 ideological division. This is not a nostalgic appeal to a vanished past, far from it. The Hongik Ingan ideal and associated principles have not only shaped Korean identity in the past but also continue to provide meaning and purpose to the Korean people.

Among these principles is the understanding that the dignity and responsibility of the individual is linked to Heaven; in essence, our fundamental human rights and freedoms are endowed to us by the Creator. That this principle is expressed within Korea's founding ideals is highly significant. This basis for human rights and legitimate governance is not a Western construct but a universal ideal with traditional Korean roots. It guides our insistence that a new Korean nation must be founded on these ideals and that fundamental reforms in both North and South Korea are needed.

Third, the Korean Dream approach requires the engagement of Korean people from all walks of life, building broad public understanding of and consensus around the type of unification and new nation we want. The future of a new unified homeland should not be determined by political leaders alone; active participation from scholars and policy experts, religious representatives, lawyers and human rights experts, economists and businesspeople, and, of course, everyday citizens, is essential. Most importantly, people power coalesced in a civil society movement must drive the process.

Fourth, international support for the Korean-led process of unification is vital. One natural foundation for that support can be built in Korean diaspora communities around the world. Korean communities with deep roots in many key nations, such as the U.S., Japan, China, and the UK, are already actively participating in the AKU movement in support of the Korean Dream. In addition, international policy experts and think tanks provide important analysis and perspective in shaping policies in their respective nations. A growing global network of policymakers, scholars, and institutions is providing vital support and building consensus toward the end goal of a unified Korea.

Fifth, the Korean Dream approach taps the power of culture through music, the arts, entertainment, and sports to build awareness and support for a unified Korea. In Korea, K-pop artists have promoted the Korean Dream in their music and with their celebrity power, effectively reaching young Koreans in a demographic that previously had little or no interest in unification. Internationally, the power of music and the Korean Wave is expanding awareness and impact for the One Korea Global Campaign on every continent.

And finally, the journey of the Korean people speaks to the desires of people around the world. The formation of a new nation that all

Koreans, both North and South, can call their home and that upholds the fundamental values etched in the *Hongik Ingan* ideal can serve as a breakthrough model for addressing other identity-based, ideological conflicts in the world. Korea's experience of emerging from colonization and division, as well as its development out of deep poverty, resonates with most of the world's developing nations and offers them a model for their own futures. Essentially, the unification of Korea can inspire developing nations seeking new models of growth and prosperity, as well as contribute to global peace.

BUILDING THE MOVEMENT: A VISION FOR ALL PEOPLE

Today, the Korean Dream paradigm for unification is not merely a concept. It is the driving vision behind the largest citizen-based coalition for Korean unification in the history of both Koreas. Since its launch with 300 founding organizations in 2012, growing to nearly 1,000 member organizations in 2019, AKU has become the preeminent platform to actively engage and unite Koreans in pursuit of the Korean Dream. Now, with its expansion to diaspora communities, the Korean Dream approach is the foundation for the success of the AKU movement worldwide.

AKU has been making history as it has pioneered the way. Less than ten years ago, unification was an afterthought in South Korean public life. Yet, we began to turn the tide regarding the necessity and benefit of unification; we have moved the needle of public opinion from apathy to anticipation. Those who once believed that unification was impossible are now beginning to believe that it is closer than we ever imagined. Every person and every partnership that pursued the Korean Dream began to have an impact on those around them. Collectively, with time and consistent effort, this began to transform the attitudes of everyday citizens about unification.

Since 2014, the year *Korean Dream: Vision of a Unified Korea* was first published in Korea, every Korean presidential candidate has run on a pro-unification platform. While some may mistakenly assume that it was then-President Park Geun-hye who made unification a national priority, it was, in fact, "We the People" who had begun this process in the years ahead of her Dresden Declaration. Although there are many challenges and much work still ahead of us, the clarity of the Korean Dream vision and its call to average citizens to be engaged in the process continues to inspire more Koreans, as well as non-Koreans, to work for unification.

It is critical for us to understand that it was not government or higher-level initiatives that turned the tide for Korean unification in recent years. We must recognize the vital impact of our own initiative and efforts to "be the change we wish to see in the world." We must no longer be trapped in the thinking that outside forces control our destiny. We need to know that the power and responsibility lie with us, the citizens, to transform our current reality.

On August 15, 2019, the seventy-fourth anniversary of Korean Liberation at the end of World War II, 20,000 Korean Dream activists participated in the Action for Korea United Festival at the Ilsan Kintex Convention Center. Though I know the 20,000 who overflowed the Kintex Convention Hall represent a small percentage of AKU's activists, their enthusiastic participation signaled a dramatic shift in the national mood of South Korea. Addressing the rally participants, I emphasized that this anniversary should not focus solely on the past and Korea's painful history with Japan. Rather, we should learn from the past in order to build the future that so many Koreans before us aspired to but could not achieve in either 1919 or 1945. I stressed that the Korean Dream can empower us as Koreans to determine our own future together and not become, yet again, victims of circumstance.[389]

One of the host organizations was the Korean National Police Veterans Association, representing some 1.5 million veteran officers. In his welcoming remarks, the chairman of the association said, "The Korean policeman has pledged to keep our nation safe for 100 years since the founding of the Provisional Government. We are also ready to work together to prepare for a new era of unified Korea."

His statement expresses what I believe is true of each of us. We embody 100 years of investment in the Korean Dream. We carry the hopes and dreams of our ancestors in our blood. It is up to us to bring the work of 100 years to fruition through any and all means. Whether as a high school student or a leader of a million-strong organization, each of us can contribute to building a unified Korea.

If we look closer at the beginnings of the March First Movement, we can see clear parallels in our movement today. Individual owners of the Korean Dream—Methodist pastors, Buddhist monks, university students, and everyday citizens who were inspired by the spirit expressed in the Korean Declaration of Independence—shared the dream with their congregations, their students, their friends, and their families. One person at a time, Koreans across the world rose up for their long-held hope for a new republic that could fulfill their desire to be a light to the world, expressed in one word: "Mansei."

At the conclusion of the AKU Festival, 20,000 activists representing the depth and breadth of Korean society raised their hands and together sang out their hopes for unification.

Our hope is unification

The hope in my dream is unification

I will carry out unification with all my heart and soul

Let's achieve unification

Unification will revive our people

Unification will revive our nation

Unification, come quickly!

Unification, come!

These words express a desire that connects the past to the present in hopes of building a new tomorrow. I know the voices that joined together on August 15 are but the vanguard movement that continues to grow on a daily basis. The vision and spirit ignited among them will continue to spread and inspire those around them to join in this work. That day, I challenged each person to spread the Korean Dream to every Korean across the peninsula and around the world.

BUILDING INTERNATIONAL SUPPORT

The leaders of the March 1, 1919 movement, and those who sought to establish a united, independent, and free Korea at the end of World War II, knew the importance of international support. Koreans living in the diaspora actively established local associations to enlist the aid of international stakeholders, particularly the U.S., China, and Russia.

A representative was sent to Versailles at the end of World War I to meet with President Wilson and persuade him that his Fourteen Points should extend self-determination to the Korean nation. Yet, the established powers did not recognize any independent Korean representation at the time. In many ways, the lack of coordinated international support for the Korean efforts planted the seeds of the eventual division.

Presently, we can see how North Korea is playing off the uncoordinated efforts of the ROK, the U.S., China, Russia, and Japan. Without an overall guiding strategy that unites the regional allies, and without enabling the Korean people to lead in their self-determination, international involvement will only repeat the mistakes of history and perpetuate the Korean crisis.

As I strongly advocate for a Korean-led approach to unification, I am not discounting the importance of American leadership; in fact, it is essential to guide and incentivize the process of unification. We can learn from the example of President George H.W. Bush's approach to German unification. Bush offered quiet support to the democratic citizens' movements in East Germany and other Warsaw Pact states but made sure that the U.S. did not lead from the front. As a result, there was no open challenge to the Soviet Union, which would likely have produced a more aggressive response.

If the U.S. takes a similar approach today, pushing for a Korean-led agenda while refraining from direct intervention in inter-Korean developments, it would become a vital facilitator for peace and development in the region. Furthermore, the U.S. should leverage its global influence to encourage other nations to take a similar approach.

Moreover, if the U.S. backs this strategy with a contemporary equivalent of the Marshall Plan in Europe and Japan's reconstruction post-1945, U.S. aid and protection will continue to provide critical support for national and regional transformation to advance as the free expression of the people. America's post-war strategic investments in Europe and Japan have yielded significant returns to this day for the U.S. and the entire global economy. When we consider the potential of a future united Korean nation, and the extremely dynamic region it is at the heart of, I believe that any initial investments into the reunification of North and South Korea will pay dividends to match or even exceed the returns of the post-World War II era.

The One K Global Campaign has been an integral part of advocating such an approach for the international community. The campaign has collaborated and partnered with internationally renowned think tanks like the Heritage Foundation, the East-West Institute, and the Center for Strategic and International Studies to hold forums and conferences for experts, policy makers, and civil society leaders. It has explored the prospects of Korean reunification, the importance of civil society-driven efforts, and the role of the international community in supporting such Korean-led efforts.

These convenings have been instrumental in changing the discussion on Korean reunification, drawing attention to the importance of civil society and the contributions of non-Six-Party actors such as Mongolia and India. More importantly, they have been a valuable platform to address immediate crises with long-term, forward-looking, vision-focused perspectives that point to principled unification, national self-determination, and a potential model for international relations.

In the United States, United Kingdom, and Japan, Koreans living in the diaspora have joined the AKU cause in support of unification and the Korean Dream. Alliance for Korea United USA is drawing on the deep ties between the U.S. and ROK, as well as the significant historic ties of Korean Americans to the March First Independence Movement, to build strong support for a unified Korea, strengthen the U.S.-ROK partnership, and deepen the bonds of friendship between the Korean and American peoples.

AKU in Japan is engaging the Korean communities living there to address human rights issues and the complicated relationship between Japan and Korea, especially with a forward-looking approach that moves beyond resentments of the past. In the UK, the diverse Korean community in New Malden, which includes a high number of North Korean defectors, has been energized and activated by the Korean Dream to develop an effective model of bridging the North-South divide, starting within their own community.

We have found keen interest and support in unexpected places, such as Uganda, the Philippines, Tanzania, and Ireland, to name a few. The Korean story of seeking to establish a nation reflecting our founding ideals is not unique. It is the story of most peoples and nations. I have found in my travels around the world that most nations have a timeless dream that can unite its people and motivate them to work together to manifest that dream.

When I spoke at the Global Peace Leadership Conference in Uganda in 2018, President Museveni resonated with my message of opening a new era beyond colonialism and cultivating sustainable social and economic systems based on time-honored values. I delivered a similar message of vision and values-based national transformation the previous year at the Global Peace Economic Forum in the Philippines that garnered significant interest and coverage in the Philippine media. These forums have brought Korean unification to the forefront as a highly relevant issue, not only for policy makers and experts, but for local leaders and people around the world.

When Koreans can resolve the long-standing division of our people, cast off the vestiges of the Cold War, and stand together united by our desire to serve the world, we can be a beacon of hope for all. That beacon will shine with certainty that all other identity-based, ideological, and religious conflicts can be resolved, securing a peaceful and prosperous future for generations to come. Everything is possible; we just need owners of the Korean Dream.

THE POWER OF MUSIC AND CULTURE

Each new member of AKU has brought their unique contribution to the movement. This is a testament to the ownership of every AKU activist. This movement for Korean unification is truly propelled through the initiative of its members who are constantly birthing new and creative ways to make the Korean Dream a part of the everyday lives of Koreans around the world.

The One Korea Song Campaign has contributed significantly to the growing momentum of AKU. Elements of what would later become a global campaign began when we put together the popularity of our AKU cultural programs with the wider impact and reach that Korean pop music has not only in South Korea but in the wider global community.

In the United States, which had long been a difficult market for South Korean artists to access, K-pop stars had by 2012 developed loyal young fans. By 2019, all around the world K-pop stars had become household names, and in the United States, artists like BTS have earned the top spot on the Billboard 200. Youth enthusiasm for K-pop songs and stars reminded me of other times when American popular musicians used their talents for a particular cause. Whatever one might feel of its ultimate impact, American folk singers and songwriters had an enormous influence on how the Vietnam War eventually ended. By conveying anti-war sentiments through the power of music, they helped build strong popular support for their cause, thereby contributing to the war's eventual end.

Taking a note from that history, we launched the One Korea Song Campaign, drawing on the celebrity power of some of the most recognized pop stars, singers, songwriters, lyricists, and producers in the Korean entertainment industry. After sharing the Korean Dream vision with them, many were inspired to use their talents toward something so meaningful. This effort to promote the Korean Dream through music, arts, and culture has an ever-growing list of contributors that include well-known names like global K-pop sensations BTS and Psy; top boy bands EXO, SHINee, CNBlue, and Astro; girl bands Momoland, Red Velvet, and AOA; and soloists like Yangpa, Kim Johan, and Ha Sungwoon. Composer Kim Hyungsuk and lyricist Kim Eana have teamed up twice already to produce songs for Korean reunification.

The first Korean unification song began a process of remarkable creative collaboration. The song was performed by over thirty K-pop artists at the One K Concert in Seoul in October 2015 before an audience of 40,000 young people and broadcast nationwide by the SBS television network. Following this, "One Dream One Korea" inspired an entirely new genre of K-pop featuring unification-themed songs. Several years later, the song gained global recognition when it was played at the closing ceremony of the 2018 Inter-Koreas Summit between North and South Korea.

After launching with such a striking impact at home, the One K Campaign quickly spread beyond Korea, engaging award-winning singers, writers, and producers around the world like Korean-Australian sensation Dami Im and Filipina YouTube stars Sabrina and Zendee. One K Concerts have been held in the Philippines in 2017 and on the Korean National Assembly Mall in 2019 and broadcast around the world, touching the hearts of millions with the message of Korean reunification and global peace.

The concert in the Philippines had particular significance. It connected the Korean Wave and its young musicians with their youthful international fans in Asia and engaged those fans with the culture and cause of Korea. The One K songs have reached millions of K-pop fans as far as Brazil and Kenya, who have expressed their support for the peaceful reunification of the Korean peninsula. In the Philippines, the One K Global Peace Concert had 10,000 international K-pop fans shouting: "One Dream, One Korea, One World."

In many ways, the widespread support from the global community for Korean reunification further confirms Korea's pivotal role in contributing to a world of peace. As Grammy award-winning music producers Jimmy Jam and Terry Lewis said in their address at the International Young Leaders Assembly held at the United Nations Headquarters in New York, "The reunification of Korea shows that even with differences, our common humanity can come together, and that furthers the hope of world peace. And that is something that everybody can get behind."

Even beyond music, the movement has inspired the production of documentaries on the Korean Dream produced by both MBC and SBS, two of the biggest broadcasting networks in Korea. The Korean Artists Association used their annual art expo as a platform to spread awareness of the Korean Dream through a focus on the artwork of North and South Korean artists. And while there are too many projects and initiatives to mention all of them, the mediums of murals, artwork, songs, documentaries, service projects, educational initiatives, entrepreneurial programs, and cultural tours are examples of everyday Korean citizens building the Korean Dream.

A CALL TO ACTION

The year 2019 was pivotal for the Korean people. It marked 100 years since the March 1, 1919 Independence Movement and seventy-four years since the liberation of Korea from Japanese colonial rule. I believe we are standing on a threshold similar to those historic turning points, full of potential and hope. Today, the possibility of realizing the Korean Dream is so palpable we can almost touch it.

One hundred years ago, our forefathers put the Korean Dream into words when they wrote the Korean Declaration of Independence. Their articulation manifested in a mass movement, inciting protests and activism across the peninsula and in diaspora communities around the world. More than two decades passed before another such opportunity would come again. And when it did, we submitted to outside forces that determined our fate and enmeshed us in an ideological conflict for the next seven decades.

Although 100 years have passed, we have kept the dream alive, handing it down through generations in the virtues of the extended Korean family culture, instilling in each of us the ethic that we are beholden to each other and destined to benefit the greater whole. The spirit of Hongik Ingan has been kept alive in our families. Thus, we can readily envision a groundswell of owners of the Korean Dream; it is just a matter of awakening that fire in each of us.

The realization of that dream is within our reach, provided each of us becomes an owner of it. The opportunity before us is like that in 1919 and 1945, but now we have a movement, spearheaded by AKU, that is coalescing the determination of the Korean people, not just in the South, but also in the North and the diaspora. And the international community stands ready to support us in realizing the Korean Dream.

We as the Korean people must take the lead. We must cast aside divisive pretensions and foreign constructs that separate us and reconnect to our common identity. The past seventy-plus years of division cannot negate the fact that we Koreans are one family and one people. We share one identity and one aspiration that we have been pursuing since the birth of our nation.

As a student of history, I understand the transformative power of a people united in a noble cause. That is certainly true for the Korean people. Every major shift in Korean history was people-led. It was Korean "people power" that launched the first nonviolent civic protest in the twentieth century, that came together after devastating war to lift our nation out of poverty and create an economic miracle, and that pressed the government to transition from military dictatorship to a real modern republic. When Korean people are united in common purpose, we can digest any hardship and overcome any obstacle.

At the beginning of this book, I cited the profound words of Genghis Khan about the power of a dream. A dream that is shared, a vision that is embraced by many, can change the world. Though there are enormous challenges still to resolve on the Korean peninsula, some that seem insurmountable, I am certain that we are at a critical inflection point at which transformative change is possible. What is most essential to overcome obstacles and resolve seemingly intractable differences is an overarching vision. That guiding vision for a unified Korea as a nation of the highest ideals is the Korean Dream.

Unfettered by past tragedies, and undaunted by current realities, let us determine to take up the task to build a nation that reflects the aspiration and values of the Korean people. By doing so, we will create a new model of national transformation that ends the chapter of colonialism, breaks the last vestiges of the Cold War, and opens up a new era of self-determination and development for our nation, the region, and the world.

Inheriting the spirit of the March First Movement, the Korean Dream movement can become the new independence movement of our time. As the opening quote of this chapter by Nelson Mandela states, "it always seems impossible until it's done." I call upon all Koreans, in partnership with our friends and supporters across the world, to summon the same determination as our ancestors before us, to be owners of this noble cause. But, unlike the reality of their day, today we can realize our destiny to create a model nation aligned to the Hongik Ingan ideal. I invite you to become a part of this historic movement: to realize the Korean Dream of a unified Korea that will bring "benefit to all humanity."

2010-2011

"We need a clear vision of what kind of country a united Korea should be and have the commitment to build it together."

Global Peace Leadership Conference
October 2010 | Seoul, Korea

Held shortly before the G20 Summit, the conference looks beyond current challenges to highlight the global benefits of a reunified Korea.

Global Peace Leadership Conference
August 2011 | Ulaanbaatar, Mongolia

Experts explore new ways to secure Korean unification through new, innovative Track Two approaches. Dr. Moon encourages Mongolian leadership to be an important peace broker in the region.

Despite opposition, Dr. Moon makes Korean reunification the focus of global discussions. Laying out a comprehensive strategic framework, he encourages a Korean-led agenda driven by a grassroots movement complemented by coordinated support from international friends and neighbors. Kim Jong-il's death and his succession by Kim Jong-un destabilizes the region as many speculate the future of North Korea.

Global Peace Convention 2011
November 2011 | Seoul, Korea

Dr. Moon uses "Korean Dream" for the first time, calling on Koreans to dream big and lead in the next century through a new, unified nation that embodies moral and innovative leadership.

Kim Jong-il dies, Kim Jong-un succeeds
December 2011

DPRK leader Kim Jong-il dies from a heart attack. International interest rises as Kim Jung-un opens up new uncertainties for the future of the Korean peninsula.

2012

"A grassroots movement for Korean unification based on spiritual principles is urgently needed to resolve the challenges of this time."

Unification Pledge Campaign Launched
May 2012 | Korean National Assembly Hall Seoul, Korea

The online signature campaign asks Koreans:
"What can I do for a unified Korea?"

Action for Korea United Founded
July 2011 | Seoul, Korea

Leaders representing over 300 civil society organizations launch the first coalition to advance coordinated efforts towards Korean unification based on a shared vision for Korea.

Action for Korea United (AKU) is launched as a coalition of 300 non-governmental organizations to advance a shared vision for Korean reunification. AKU holds the Korea United Festival at Yeoido Plaza in Seoul with over 10,000 people. The "Everyday Unification" campaign begins and encourages all Koreans to take action every day for unification.

Korea United Festival
August 2012 | Yeoido Plaza, Seoul, Korea

Dr. Moon articulates the "Korean Dream," a guiding vision for Koreans and reunification, to a crowd of 10,000.

Global Peace Leadership Conference
August 2012 | Seoul, Korea

Experts and peacebuilders from Korea and around the world discuss the need for a vision-driven, people-powered movement for Korean unification.

2013

*"Every Korean can contribute to Unification
in small and large ways."*

Culture and History Tours

Tours connect Koreans at home and from the diaspora with the heritage, ethics and culture of Korea.

International Sports, Culture Festival

Community festivals connect international students with Korean culture and the issue of Korean reunification.

Miracle of 1,000 Won

A donation campaign supports a bread factory that feeds schoolchildren in North Korea.

Korean Dream Ping Pong Tournaments

Tourneys connect Korean defectors and international residents with their Korean community.

The Everyday Unification Campaign swings into full force, engaging Koreans young and old, with the topic of Korean reunification. Many creative grassroot activities connect ordinary citizens with the issue of Korean Reunification.

Economic Mentoring

Local business owners host workshops to help North Korean defectors gain jobs and life skills.

Talk U Concerts

A university program combines speeches, performances, and discussion to stimulate dialogue about reunification.

Overseas Service

Promoting the value of living for the world through overseas service initiatives like the All-Lights Village project.

Korean Dream Academy

Weekly classes teach students about the history of the Korean division and current prospects for reunification.

2014

"A textbook for all who long for unification."

International Forums on One Korea

October –December 2014 | Washington D.C., USA

A series of forums explores issues with Korean unification, such as the role of civil society, Six Party nations, and other nations like Mongolia.

Korean Dream: A Vision for a Unified Korea

published in Korean

Best NGO Award Conferred on GPF

December 2014 | Seoul, Korea

Global Peace Foundation is recognized by the Civil Society Organization of Korea for its work with Action for Korea United.

2014 Book of the Year

The Korean Culture and Arts Publication Award is given to Dr. Moon's book in the society category.

Dr. Moon defines a vision and framework for Korean unification in his book *Korean Dream: A Vision for a Unified Korea*. The book becomes Book of the Year. The Global Peace Foundation is recognized for its groundbreaking work with Action for Korea United and forums with partners like the Center for Strategic International Studies (CSIS) engage the international community to advance vision-driven efforts.

Global Peace Leadership Conference 2014
September 2014 | Seoul, Korea

International partnerships with renowned think-tanks and civil society organizations form at the conference in support of a vision-driven approach to Korean reunification.

Global Peace Convention 2014
December 2014 | Asunción, Paraguay

Dr. Moon highlights the importance of moral and innovative leadership in national transformation, drawing parallels between Paraguayan and Korean development.

2015

"If a thousand people dream a dream, it becomes reality."

Korean Dream:
A Vision for a Unified Korea
published in Japanese

Forums for One Korea
January – July 2015 | Washington D.C., USA

Forums continue looking at the roles of Japan, China, and Russia in Korean civil society.

70th Anniversary of
Korean Liberation
August 2015 | USA, ROK, China, Japan

Commemorations around the world feature the song
"One Dream, One Korea."

First Global Peace Economic Forum
and Unification and Civil Society Forum
October 2015 | Seoul, Korea

Dr. Moon addresses international public and private sector leaders, calling for economic reform and increased civil society engagement.

The One K Campaign is created as a platform to engage youth and spread awareness of Korean unification through music and pop-culture. To kick-off the campaign, K-pop song "One Dream, One Korea" is released on the 70th anniversary of Korean Liberation. The first One K Concert is held in Seoul with 40,000 fans. AKU membership expands to 930 civic organizations.

"One Dream One Korea" Music Video Released
August 2015

Featuring 30 top K-pop artists, leaders of opposing political parties, Kim Moo-sung and Moon Jae-In, and the Minister of Unification, the music video reaches millions of viewers in Korea and beyond.

First One K Concert, World Cup Stadium
October 2015 | Seoul, Korea

40,000 K-pop fans crowd the World Cup Stadium in Seoul for the One K Concert promoting a vision of a unified Korea. The grand finale features a full concert roster singing "One Dream One Korea."

2016

"Resolving the long-standing problems on the Korean Peninsula requires international cooperation and support."

One Korea Forums

July 2016 | John Hopkins University, US. Congressional Hall, Washington D.C.

Top international experts, U.S. Congressmen join civic leaders for the One Korea Forum in Washington DC. The forums are hosted in partnership with John Hopkins University's School of Advanced and International Studies.

One K Global Campaign
One K 글로벌캠페인

One Korea Global Campaign Launch

August 2016 | International Young Leaders Assembly, New York, USA

AKU co-president launches the global campaign with young leaders from around the world in New York. Jimmy Jam and Terry Lewis announce plans to produce "Korean Dream," with top singers from the USA, Korea, the Philippines, and Australia.

The One K Campaign expands to build international support for Korean-led efforts for unification through the One K Global Campaign launched at the International Young Leaders Assembly hosted by various UN Missions at the UN Headquarters in New York. Forums for One Korea continue.

Korean Dream:
A Vision for a Unified Korea
published in English.

Global Peace Leadership Conference
December 2016 | Seoul, Korea

The conference calls for moral, innovative leadership to navigate the challenges facing the ROK and DPRK.

2017

One Dream, One Korea, One World

Global Peace Convention 2017 and Global Peace Economic Forum 2017
February 2017 | Manila, Philippines

Dr. Moon calls for moral and innovative leadership to advance models of peace and development in Asia and the Korean peninsula.

One K Global Peace Concert 2017
March 2017 | Manila, Philippines

"Are you ready to dream big?"
Dr. Moon encourages concertgoers
to share the dream of a world of peace.
A-list stars like Psy and SHINee promote
One Dream, One Korea, One World.

The Korean Dream gains global attention with the Global Peace Convention 2017 and One K Global Peace Concert 2017 held in Manila, Philippines. The concert was attended by 10,000 concert-goers and broadcast to over 20 countries by KBS World. As the tensions rise over North Korea's nuclear weapons, Dr. Moon advocates for long-term solutions by first focusing on Korean reunification.

International Forums for One Korea
July, November, December | Washington D.C.,USA, Seoul, Korea

Forums address the precarious situation posed by a defiant nuclear North Korea. Dr. Moon encourages global cooperation to resolve the issue for good through pursuing the long-term goal of Korean reunification.

Release of Korean Dream Music Video
August 2017

The music video and track for the Korean Dream song features stars such as Korean-Australian singer Dami Im, Peabo Bryson, Filipina singer Sabrina, and Korean singer Jong Dongha.

Global Sanctions Regime
An unprecedented global sanctions regime is imposed on North Korea, including traditional allies, China and Russia, to push for denuclearization.

2018

"This is the time for a clear vision, wise leadership and bold action."

2018 DIA (Defense Intelligence Agency) Director's Reading List

March 2018 | United States

Dr. Moon's book is listed in the Global Analysis section of the reading list.

International Forums for One Korea

Mongolia | Japan | Uganda | India | Ireland | Washington D.C.

Action for Korea United and partners convene forums around the world to advance a forward-looking approach to the Korean issue.

100th Anniversary of the March 1 Movement Committee

August 2018 | Seoul, Korea

Partners of the One K Global Campaign form a commemoration committee for the centenary of the 1919 Korean Independence Movement.

In a dramatic shift, the DPRK comes to the negotiating table. Dr. Moon cautions South Korea and the international community to tread carefully and keep sight of the long-term goal of unification and the ultimate fulfillment of the Korean Dream. International forums are held throughout the world to garner global support for Korean-led efforts for a vision-driven movement for reunification.

Formation of Alliance for Korea United
December 2018 | Washington D.C., USA

Alliance for Korea United is established as a coalition of Korean-American organizations and individuals supporting the realization of the Korean Dream.

International Forum for One Korea
December 2018 | Carnegie Institute, Washington D.C., USA

Dr. Moon offers a straightforward analysis of the Korean peninsula and presses for international support for a Korean-led, strategic framework for reunification.

Winter Olympics
February 2018 | Pyeong Chang, Korea

North and South Korea march as one in the Winter Olympics as a symbol of good will and future cooperation.

Inter-Korea Summits
April, May, September 2018 DMZ | Pyeongyang

Summits reawaken hopes for unification; yet, concerns over the nature of a reunified country are raised.

First US-DPRK Summit
June 2018 | Singapore

The U.S. decision to directly engage with the DPRK invites other regional actors and weakens the global sanctions regime.

2019

"It is our calling and our destiny as Korean patriots, to be the change agents that can spark a new tomorrow by realizing the Korean Dream."

Global Peace Convention 2019
February-March 2019 | Seoul, Korea
International leaders address challenges and opportunities of reunification. Dr. Moon pushes for a clear vision and bold leadership.

One K Concert and Centennial of the March 1, 1919 Korean Independence Movement
March 2019 | National Assembly Plaza, Seoul, Korea

The concert, the first such event to be held on the National Assembly Plaza, is televised internationally through SBS. Dr. Moon calls on Koreans to realize the dream that inspired the March 1 Movement.

Campaigns and events commemorate the centenary of the March 1 Korean Independence Movement to build consensus around a vision for a unified Korea, drawing parallels to the Hongik Ingan-based dream that inspired the 1919 movement. One hundred years since the movement, Koreans are reminded of the opportunity to fulfill their destiny of building an "independent, free and united" Korea.

Action for Korea United Festival
August 2019 | Seoul, Korea

20,000 Korean Dream activists convened at the Ilsan Kintex Convention Center, committing to making the dream of 100 years earlier a reality.

International Forum for One Korea
August 2019 | Seoul, Korea

On the eve of the 74th anniversary of Korean Liberation Day, Dr.Moon calls on Koreans the world over to own the Korean Dream and urges the international community to support the efforts of the Korean people for reunification.

ABOUT THE AUTHOR

Dr. Hyun Jin Preston Moon is the driving force behind the Korean reunification movement centered on the *Hongik Ingan* ideal. Dr. Moon introduced the Korean Dream framework in 2010 when reunification was viewed to be an impossibility by both domestic and international experts. The framework has inspired a global movement spearheaded by Action for Korea United (AKU), the largest grassroots organization for Korean reunification in history. AKU engages thousands of Korean citizens in the reunification effort by empowering them to develop self-driven initiatives for peaceful reunification based on their shared history and aspirations. Today, AKU membership includes over 1,000 NGOs. Other chapters have been formed in Japan, the United States, and the United Kingdom to engage the Korean diaspora in the Korean Dream work.

Dr. Moon was born in Korea to a family that played a pivotal role in Korea's independence and its development across four generations. He has continued to build upon the family legacy of patriotism for the nation and service to the world for the past 32 years. At the age of 18, Dr. Moon represented South Korea as the youngest member of the Korean

303

Equestrian Team in the 1988 Summer Olympics in Seoul. Four years later, he once again represented South Korea in the 1992 Summer Olympics in Barcelona, Spain. He was recognized by the Blue House for his national service as an Olympian.

Following his athletic endeavors, Dr. Moon graduated *magna cum laude* from Columbia University where he studied history under famed historian Dr. Kenneth T. Jackson and wrote his senior thesis on the interwar years in Korea. He then went on to receive his Master of Business Administration from Harvard Business School. His other educational credentials include a Master of Religious Education from the Unification Theological Seminary, a professor *honoris causa* from the Uni-Anhanguera University Center of Goias in Brazil, and an honorary doctorate from Sun Moon University in Korea.

For most of his professional life, Dr. Moon worked closely with his father, the late Reverend Dr. Sun Myung Moon, to build an international foundation that has contributed significantly to South Korea's economic development and to humanitarian causes around the world. In 1991, Rev. Moon made a groundbreaking visit to North Korea, where he became the first South Korean public figure to meet with North Korean President Kim Il-sung. The historic meeting not only paved the way for separated families to finally meet but also led to the opening of manufacturing and tourism ventures, first by companies affiliated with Rev. Moon and later by other South Korean enterprises.

In 2001, ten years after his father opened North Korea to the international community, Dr. Moon established the global non-profit, Service For Peace, which engages volunteers in ongoing community development programs throughout the world. Service For Peace was the first volunteer organization allowed into North Korea to facilitate joint projects with South and North Koreans. Service For Peace currently holds special consultative status with the United Nations.

In addition to his record of service to Korea, Dr. Moon is best known for his leadership development and humanitarian work throughout the world. A man of deep faith and conviction, Dr. Moon recognizes that the most critical factor for building peace is moral and innovative leadership guided by spiritual principles and values. This conviction has guided his approach for over three decades to global peacebuilding efforts, nation-building roadmaps, family strengthening initiatives, and identity-based conflict resolution, including those fueled by religious extremism that he has been leading for over three decades. Starting at the turn of the millennium, Dr. Moon worked with his father on international and interreligious peacebuilding efforts through the Universal Peace Foundation, including building a global network of leaders committed to universal principles, shared values, and collaborative action as ambassadors for peace to address the critical challenges facing humanity.

In 2009, Dr. Moon founded the Global Peace Foundation (GPF) and currently serves as its chairman. Active in over 20 countries, GPF promotes and implements an innovative, values-based approach to peacebuilding, guided by the vision of One Family under God. With its ever-expanding network of vision-inspired partners, GPF has generated a growing record of effective community-driven peacebuilding models that tackle long-standing identity-based conflicts in regions around the world. In Africa, GPF has been recognized for its indispensable role in mitigating post-election violence in Kenya since 2008 and promoting the central importance of foundational ideals as the nation framed and ratified its new constitution. The One Family under God Peacebuilding Campaign, implemented in the most challenging conflict zone in Nigeria with remarkable positive impact, has gained international acclaim and is being successfully replicated in many other regions. In the United States, GPF has been actively engaged in urban peacebuilding efforts, working with federal, state and local agencies to prevent violent extremism and targeted violence. In Asia, GPF has cultivated a powerful multi-generational, multi-sectoral, interfaith leadership network united by a common vision and shared spiritual principles that has been generating innovative initiatives like the Millennial Peace Festivals, the Global Youth Summit and the All-Lights Village Initiative to secure peace and development. GPF has made Europe a peace-sharing hub where leaders from conflict regions can share challenges and successes as they seek fresh perspective and innovation. In Latin America, particularly Paraguay, GPF has been instrumental in demonstrating a process for national transformation undergirded by spiritual principles and values and driven by moral and innovative leadership. Dr. Moon has been a leading force in founding important organizations that promote good governance, social integration, and sustainable development such as the *Instituto de Desarrollo del Pensamiento Patria Soñada* (IDPPS), a prestigious think tank in Paraguay, and the Latin America Presidential Mission, an association of former heads of state from over a dozen countries throughout the region.

In 2017, Dr. Moon and his wife, Dr. Junsook Moon, co-founded the Family Peace Association (FPA). FPA engages individuals, families, and organizations in building God-centered families as the foundation of a peaceful world.

A loving husband and father, Dr. Moon lives in the United States with his wife of over 30 years, Dr. Junsook Moon, a Julliard-trained pianist who serves as the chairwoman of Global Peace Women, the women's division of Global Peace Foundation. They are the proud parents of nine children and currently have four grandchildren. Two of their children are graduates of and a third currently attends the United States Military Academy.

Learn more about Dr. Preston Moon's background, work, and current initiatives at: HyunJinMoon.com

 Twitter: @HyunJinPMoon

 Facebook: @hyunjinpmoon

 YouTube: Dr. Hyun Jin Preston Moon

 Instagram: @hyunjinpmoon

SEE WEBSITE
FOR ENDNOTES

KoreanDream.org